Screening
the Market

Founded in 1807, John Wiley & Sons is the oldest independent publishing company in the United States. With offices in North America, Europe, Australia, and Asia, Wiley is globally committed to developing and marketing print and electronic products and services for our customers' professional and personal knowledge and understanding.

The Wiley Trading series features books by traders who have survived the market's ever-changing temperament and have prospered—some by reinventing systems, others by getting back to basics. Whether for a novice trader, professional, or someone in-between, these books provide the advice and strategies needed to prosper today and well into the future.

For a list of available titles, visit our web site at www.WileyFinance.com.

Screening
the Market

*A Four-Step Method to Find,
Analyze, Buy, and Sell Stocks*

MARC H. GERSTEIN

John Wiley & Sons, Inc.

For general information on our other products and services, or technical support, please contact our Customer Care Department within the United States at 800-762-2974, outside the United States at 317-572-3993 or fax 317-572-4002.

Wiley also publishes its books in a variety of electronic formats. Some content that appears in print may not be available in electronic books.

Designations used by companies to distinguish their products are often claimed by trademarks. In all instances where the author or publisher is aware of a claim, the product names appear in Initial Capital letters. Readers, however, should contact the appropriate companies for more complete information regarding trademarks and registration.

ISBN 0-471-21559-7

10 9 8 7 6 5 4 3 2 1

acknowledgments

This book, a product of the information revolution, shows investors new ways to utilize some of the vast quantity of information now available to add reason to the investment process. At first glance, it seems obvious that rationality should play an important role. But achieving respect for relevant facts has been a long and ongoing struggle. We see that when we look at milestones of investment history such as the tulip craze and the South Sea bubble. We continue to see that when we look around in the modern era, as evidenced by the new economy surge in the late 1990s. Nevertheless, as we examine the big picture, we see that rational investing, although still not universally practiced, continues to gain ground. This book is dedicated to those who have been and still are helping to make this happen.

Some pioneers of fact-based investing are well known, such as Benjamin Graham and David Dodd, who taught the world how to extract valuable information from corporate financial statements. Others include Arnold Bernhard and Samuel Eisenstadt, who did much to bridge the gap between pure theory and the workaday investment decision process.

Spearheading the process today are Isaak Karaev and Christopher Feeney, CEO and president, respectively, of Multex, who drive the information and technology solutions that actually deliver vital content to investment community desktops with greater effectiveness than has ever before been seen. And I wish to give special acknowledgment to the Multex Content group, which collects and packages fundamental company data under the Market Guide brand name and for the Multex estimates database. Without their efforts, there is nothing to screen, nor any data to analyze. The Content group is led by Homi M. Byramji, who has been and still is ahead of many in seeing the role data could play in the investment process and who built and still guides the organization that makes it all happen. I am especially grateful for his continuing support and encouragement in the work that led to the development of the method presented in this book. It is also my pleasure to acknowledge the staff at the Content group for their great efforts in creating and maintaining a database that is the platinum standard in terms of accuracy and versatility. There are too many contributors to name all, but some key individuals include Domenic Graziosi,

Peter Sluka, David Coluccio, Mike Sferratore, Jerry Cazrzasty, Marivie Rances, Mukul Gulati, John Schirripa, Bryan Smith, Oguzhan Ege, Alex Klimenko, Elena Wakely, Konstantin Davydov, Konstantin Dolgitser, Patrick Ross, Bobby Peacock, and Alex Karavousanos, an early champion of Market Guide's old CD screening application.

I am grateful to the efforts of present and former colleagues for their help in allowing me to bring this method to the Internet: Richard Smith, Aziz Akin, Erik Dellith, James Waitword, and Vladimir Jornitski. I also thank Azhar Rafee and Samantha Topping for their aid and support in bringing my work to the rest of the world; Robin Spindel, who did more than she may realize to plant in my mind the idea of writing this book; and Lauren Keyson for her support and encouragement.

There's a long journey from having an idea for a book and the book itself. That path could not have been traversed with the support of my agents—Robert Diforio; Marilyn Allen, who was first to recognize a worthy project in little more than a hastily composed e-mail; and Coleen O'Shea, who pushed me to say it well in spite of myself. And at the crossroads stands Claudio Campuzano, who, as I was polishing up my book proposal, wandered over to the Multex booth at a Las Vegas trade show to ask if we knew anybody who was interested in stock screening. He subsequently played a key role in bringing this project to John Wiley & Sons, where Pamela van Giessen and her team drove the rest of the way to the final destination.

Finally, I wish to thank my parents, Bernard and Connie, and my sister Leah for their support all the way back before they fully recognized what this one-time struggling lawyer might do with an M.B.A. in finance, and Emma for being Emma. I also thank Heidi for helping to push me onto the Web, and Sheldon, who invested real money based on my screens even before I did.

M.H.G.

contents

introduction

Screening is absolutely, positively the best way to find stock investment ideas. We'll explore why this is so in Chapter 4, but for now, suffice it to say no other approach can match screening when it comes to calling stocks to your attention based on at least some objective showing of merit and without regard to what periodicals you read, what finance broadcasts you see or hear, what analysts you encounter, what tips your friends provide, or where you live, work, or shop. And having the right stocks come to your attention is a major determinant of investment performance. No matter how great you are at deciphering financial statements, understanding business dynamics, or reading stock price charts, you have no real chance to achieve investment success if you always wind up applying your skills to stocks that aren't really worthy of being looked at in the first place.

Stock screening is a natural for the computer era because at its heart it does something computers are especially good at doing: looking at two things and determining whether one thing is greater than, equal to, or less than the other thing. Under the hood, that's pretty much all there is to screening. Variations from one program to another relate to user interface and the kinds of things the computer can be asked to examine.

INTRODUCTION TO STOCK SCREENING

The way screens work is simple. We ask the computer to search through a database and identify situations that have certain characteristics. As just indicated, the core issues are quite straightforward: whether one thing is greater than, equal to, or less than another thing. In this book, I'll refer to each such question as a test. Usually we'll ask the computer to consider several tests at a time. A collection of tests is called a screen.

Let's suppose you like growth stocks. You might ask the computer to help by identifying a list of companies whose earnings per share (EPS) have grown at least 20 percent in each of four time spans: the latest quarter, the latest 12-month period, the latest three-year period, and the latest five-year period. Each screening program has its own way of phrasing such a screen, but generally speaking, it should look something like this. (*Note:* >= means "is greater than or equal to" and <= means "is less than or equal to.")

1. EPS Growth Latest Quarter >= 20
2. EPS Growth Trailing 12 Months >= 20
3. 3 Year EPS Growth >= 20
4. 5 Year EPS Growth >= 20

Let's see how this fits with the general framework given earlier. In the first line, one of the things the computer looks at is the latest quarter's EPS percentage growth rate. The other thing is the number 20. The nature of the comparison we seek is that the first thing, in this case the latest quarter's EPS growth rate, be greater than or equal to the second thing, in this case the number 20.

Notice that the line is not being phrased as a question. Computers work with statements. In screening, we want the computer to determine whether each statement is true or false. If for a particular company the statement is true, the name of the company will be added to a list. If not, it will be discarded. Then the computer will look at the next company in the database and evaluate its condition. Again, if true, the name of this company will be kept on the list; if false, it gets discarded. This process will be repeated until every company has been evaluated against the true-false test established on line 1.

As I wrote this, I actually created the screen and applied it to a database containing 9,450 companies. After evaluating each of them based on the first test, the computer wound up with a list of 1,254 passes. In other words, 1,254 companies out of a total of 9,450 experienced EPS growth of at least 20 percent in the latest quarter.

Then the computer moves to line 2. But it need not work as hard as it did the first time. The next test, a true-false assessment of whether the company's trailing 12-month EPS was at least 20 percent, is applied to only the 1,254 firms that made it over the first hurdle. It turns out that 610 companies out of 1,254 passed the second test.

The remaining 610 firms are now evaluated under the third true-false test. Only those whose three-year rates of EPS growth were at least 20 percent will survive. Out of 610 firms being evaluated this way, only 208 pass. This small list is then put through the fourth test. Only 135 of these firms also experienced five-year EPS growth rates of at least 20 percent. What we have done is reduce a 9,450-stock database to a mere 135 by eliminating all those companies that didn't meet the four growth tests we created.

Suppose ABC Company has a five-year average EPS growth rate of 35 percent, a three-year average growth rate of 38 percent, a trailing 12-month growth rate of 19 percent, and a latest quarter improvement of 26 percent. This company would not appear on our final list. It passed the first test. But it failed the second one. At that time, it would get dropped from the list. We see that it could easily have passed the third and fourth tests, had it been given an opportunity to do so. But because it failed to meet the trailing 12-month growth requirement, it never got a chance to be evaluated under the other two tests.

It could have stayed alive longer had the tests been presented to the computer in a different sequence (i.e., if the trailing 12-month test were placed third or last in the sequence). But at the end of the day, the result would have been the same. To make the final list, the company/stock must pass each test.

CREATING SCREENS

Suppose we use one of the top-of-the-line applications that allow us to create tests using an "OR" condition.

1. EPS Growth Latest Quarter >= 20 OR EPS Growth Trailing 12 Months >= 20
2. 3 Year EPS Growth >= 20
3. 5 Year EPS Growth >= 20

Now ABC Company makes the final list. But this is not an exception to the rule that every company must pass every test. We amended the screen to replace two tests with one test that is less stringent. ABC still has to pass all the tests. This time around, though, it benefits from a strategic decision we made to be less picky about more recent EPS performance.

This is one example of how our strategic screening decisions determine which stocks appear on our lists and which ones are omitted. ABC is not the only company to benefit from our shift toward leniency. The list will also include many other companies that meet the 20 percent growth hurdle for either the latest quarter or the trailing 12 months, but not necessarily for both periods. The revision boosts our list from 135 companies to 289.

That's way too many, a situation that introduces another decision point for our screening strategy. We could go back to the original pair of near-term tests (latest quarter and trailing 12 months), require again that each be separately satisfied, and bring the list back down to 135 names. We could cut further by raising some or all of the numeric targets to a level above 20. Or we can leave the latest set of EPS tests as they are and introduce some entirely new factors, such as price/earnings (P/E) ratio. Here's an example.

1. EPS Growth Latest Quarter >= 20 OR EPS Growth Trailing 12 Months >= 20
2. 3 Year EPS Growth >= 20
3. 5 Year EPS Growth >= 20
4. Projected Long-Term EPS Growth >= 20
5. 3 Year Sales Growth >= 20
6. 5 Year Sales Growth >= 20
7. P/E Based on Estimated Current Year EPS/Proj. LT EPS Growth <= 1
8. Mean Rating <= 1.5

Lines 4 through 6 are self-explanatory. Line 7 establishes a condition that the price/earnings to growth (PEG) ratio be no higher than 1.00. The eighth test may seem a bit obscure right now, but in Chapter 6 you will see that this is a measure of bullishness among Wall Street analysts, and that a score at or below 1.5 tells us analysts, as a group, view the stock very favorably.

These additional tests help cut the list to 18 stocks. That's a very manageable number, and our screen has accomplished its purpose. It started with a vast database and narrowed it down to an acceptable-sized list of opportunities that we have reason to believe are consistent with our investment goals. We started with a goal of growth (defined as 20 percent or more). We moved a bit beyond that, and even strayed into value (via the PEG ratio). But that doesn't alter the fact that we have a nice list of growth companies whose shares are also reasonably valued and well regarded by analysts.

By the way, I couldn't resist eyeballing the results of this screen after I created it. Even though this is not, by any stretch of the imagination, the best possible screen we can create (you'll agree by the time you finish Chapter 6), I recognized some legitimately attractive names on the real-life list, including three stocks that I actually own as of this writing and six more that I've been seriously considering. Hence you can create terrific stock lists even if you aren't using the top-of-the-line screening program and even before you master every technique that will be described in this book.

PERFECTION

One of the most annoying features I find in investment books is an unwritten assumption that you can achieve great success if you do exactly what the book tells you to do. But in real life, that's a big if. I suspect you agree that you can pick great stocks if you properly evaluate management talent, competitive edge, proprietary product features, the abilities of competitors, the quality of the workforce, and countless financial statement entries and stock price-volume chart characteristics. But can you actually do all that? I believe what you really need is a method that allows you to succeed even if you can't morph into a walking business library. This book meets that need. It does not presume you will be perfect. It assumes you will be diligent and competent, but it recognizes that you are human and that you will often operate under constraints that fall far shy of best-of-all-possible-worlds conditions.

We touched on one example in the previous section. There are a lot of screeners out there. Some are accessible on the Internet for free. Others are available for modest fees. And some are more costly. The sample screen we created does not come anywhere close to pushing the envelope in terms of sophistication. Yet it really worked! You can find more opportunities if you use the best programs. But the very nature of screening is such that even if you don't go top-of-the-line, you can still do well. Let me put it this way: One intelligently created screen, even if executed using a low-end application, can yield more good ideas than countless suggestions derived through other means. Not every free or low-priced screener is usable. But by the time you finish Chapter 7, you'll easily be able to determine whether a program is acceptable for your needs.

Here's more good news. You don't need a top-of-the-line computer. All but one of the screening programs discussed in this book are available on-line. That means you just need hardware capable of reasonably efficient Internet use, the kind of machine you can purchase at any ordinary consumer electronics retailer. The programs themselves tend to be extremely powerful (and the databases are tremendous memory hogs). But you need not worry about that. The heavy action takes place on the servers maintained by the companies that provide the screeners. From your perspective, where all you do is pose questions and deal with answers, an ordinary personal computer will do. You can even get by with a dial-up Internet connection (if you use broadband, so much the better). The one screener that still comes on CDs that have to be installed and run on your own computer is extremely manageable. You can do it with 16 megabytes (MB) of random-access memory (RAM), Windows 95 or better, a Pentium processor or better, and 240 MB of space available on your hard drive. Nowadays, low-end computers sold to casual retail users already exceed those thresholds.

You're also going to see that imperfection is acceptable even when you analyze the stocks you find through your screens. That's because, deep down, there really are no right or wrong answers. Every stock appeals to some investors and is hated by others (that's why every transaction has a buyer and a seller). We can't even say that down the road one of them will be proven wrong. For one thing, there are different time horizons. Expanding on that, we come to the key to the analytic process: Everyone has his/her own set of goals. Nobody can correctly tell you whether a particular set of financial fundamentals is good or bad. But you can determine whether a particular set of financial fundamentals is suitable for a particular investment goal.

An answer like that won't produce a winner every time. There is no such thing as a method that will yield 100 percent winners. (That's why we diversify our portfolios.) But assuming your goals are reasonable, you'll find this method superior to others in terms of its ability to effectively match individual stocks to those goals. That will enable you to prosper when your philosophy is in vogue. And when your chosen style hits a cold spell, you'll understand what is happening and why, thereby gaining the fortitude to either wait it out pending resumption of better (for you) times or make a thoughtful (as opposed to panicky) decision to alter your goals.

A METHOD

Take note of this book's subtitle: *A Four-Step Method to Find, Analyze, Buy, and Sell Stocks.* That's not just a cute marketing handle. I'm completely serious about presenting stock screening as a full-fledged method that covers the entire life cycle of an investment. What most observers think of as screening is really just Step 1, a way to find stocks that are worthy of closer scrutiny.

But if I were to stop there and just give you a tutorial on how to create great stock screens, you might become frustrated as you try to translate your screens into real-world investment success.

As we'll see later on, no matter how great a program you use and how thoroughly you master it, screening is still just as much an art as a science. That means any list can include some dogs. I believe screen-based lists will be less likely to be dog-intense than ideas that come to you in other ways. But that doesn't alter the fact that you need a method that extends beyond the screen itself and helps you identify exactly which stocks you should buy. And naturally you need a discipline that helps you address a question that can be even more challenging than the buying decision—when to sell.

Once you find a stock (i.e., it appears on your screen), there are many ways to go about analyzing it, deciding whether the things you learn mean you should buy the stock, and deciding when to sell. What's unique about the "analyze," "buy," and "sell" approaches presented here is that they are extensions of the screening process. The analytic techniques presented in

Chapters 10 and 11 are based on the same kinds of data assessment techniques that are used to create screens. (And you'll see later how these techniques allow you to function quite nicely even if you use a free or low-priced screening program.) Chapters 12, 13, and 14 will show you how to reach buy decisions by matching screening themes against what you learn during the course of your analysis. And Chapters 15 and 16 show you how all these techniques can be adapted to the issues that arise in connection with the selling decision.

There's a lot of material here. But don't worry about being overwhelmed by a massive number of recipes and procedures. Although you will probably want to return to this book in the future as a reference, you'll find that this four-step market screening method is not about cataloging and memorizing. It's about organizing what you already know or can discover with a few clicks of a mouse, and showing you how you can create your own recipes and procedures.

Getting Started

## CHAPTER 1

It Sounds Good, But . . .

With the personal computer era so well entrenched, especially among investors, you'd think everybody would now be expert at stock screening. Who could resist something as easy as telling a computer to list all stocks with P/E ratios below 15, EPS growth rates above 30 percent, debt-free balance sheets, and so on? In a matter of seconds, even bargain-priced hardware configured for first-time users can easily search massive haystacks and find the exact size and shape needle you seek. And in the Internet age, the haystacks, or databases, are more accessible than ever, even to investors who want to stick with free or very low-cost screening sites. What more could an investor want? It certainly sounds good.

DO SCREENERS DELIVER?

Indeed, most of today's best-known investment-oriented web sites do offer stock screeners. Some require subscription fees. Free programs are also readily available. But how often do you hear investors talking about the screens they create, their favorites among the prepackaged screens available on the World Wide Web, or the great stocks they found through screening? Not nearly as often as one would expect.

It's not that screening is overrated. In fact, it really can deliver everything investors might want from the process, and more. I sensed that screening was for real the first time I saw one of these programs back in the early 1980s. My initial optimism was confirmed in a big way in early 1999, after I joined Market Guide (which became a wholly owned subsidiary of Multex.com, Inc. later that year). Today, using the screens I created with Market Guide's old Market Guide for Windows screener (the predecessor to the current Multex premium screener), I can come up with more great investment ideas in less than an hour than I was able to find in my previous 18 years as a securities analyst. Really!

Note the nearly 20-year lag between my introduction to screening and my using it successfully day-to-day. Although I was quick to perceive what screening could accomplish, I endured years of frustration because the programs did not let me query the databases in ways I deemed useful. This may sound discomforting. You might get the idea that you won't be able to successfully screen the market unless you discover and gain access to the one-and-only truly good program. Don't worry. The relationship between computers and stock selection has evolved over the years. Today, it's easy to find quality screeners, even among those available on the Internet for free.

IT'S UP TO YOU

On balance, stock screeners have improved to the point where they definitely can deliver. But good results still won't come automatically. Some screeners are better than others, so you still have to pick and choose. The programs differ widely in the ways they allow you to state your preferences. And some available preference choices (known as tests) are more useful than others. For example, screeners often allow you to say you want a company's margin to be above a certain minimum and/or below a certain maximum. How useful is that? It's not always wise to automatically rule out low-margin companies. (Low margins are perfectly fine if turnover is high.) And off the top of my head, I cannot think of any reason why I'd want to set a maximum on something like margin. (I can't imagine myself saying a 20 percent margin is inferior to a 17 percent margin.)

Now, suppose you had a different type of screener that lets you ask for a list of companies whose margins are above their respective industry averages. This is more interesting. At first glance, Company A's 5 percent margin may not excite you. But if margins for other, similar, companies average 3.5 percent, your interest ought to be piqued. Suppose you were to also learn that the industry average margin over the past five years was 3.3 percent, but that Company A averaged only 2.9 percent over that span. In other words, you found a company whose margins used to lag but improved and now run ahead of the pack. This alone doesn't prove anything. Perhaps the latest margin is being impacted by some event that won't persist in the future. Then again, maybe the company really is coming on strong. Either way, the stock screen did its job. It helped you decide which among the thousands of companies out there are truly worthy of your attention.

Many similar examples can be constructed using a variety of screeners currently available on the Web. The key point is that not every variable presented is equally useful for stock selection. Just because a computer can whip through a database in a matter of nanoseconds and identify companies for which particular data items are above or below certain specified thresholds doesn't mean the information can enhance your stock selection efforts.

USEFUL TESTS

To screen successfully, you'll have to learn how to create tests that are truly useful, or learn to assess the usefulness of the tests contained in the many preset screens available on the Internet. A test requiring a margin above 5 percent and below 20 percent would not be useful. A test requiring a margin that's above the industry average would be useful. So, too, would a test requiring that the company's most recent margin be above its own five-year average margin.

There's nothing exotic about the process of assessing the worthiness of a particular screening test. Ultimately, you can evaluate any test by asking the following question: Does this characteristic enhance the probability that the stock will turn out to be a better investment? If the answer is yes, the characteristic would be a useful screening test.

GOOD HABITS

Sometimes the answer to the question is obvious. Few, if any, go out of their way to find companies whose margins are deteriorating and/or below industry averages. On other occasions, the answer isn't so clear. For example, you'll see on the Web prepackaged screens requiring that a company's market capitalization be equal to or greater than $1 billion. Whether or not that's useful depends on your individual preferences. If you have a special liking for smaller companies, you'd probably want to reverse the test and require capitalization to be less than $1 billion. In other words, the same test could be essential to one investor, but completely wrong for someone else.

Before you can evaluate the usefulness of a screener, you will need a solid understanding of your own investment goals and style. I feel no pressing need to limit myself to companies with market capitalizations of at least $1 billion. I could understand why professional money managers might disagree. They handle large amounts of money, so liquidity constraints often make it difficult for them to invest in very small companies. But when I screen, I generally don't use tests relating to market capitalization. (I do confess I'm a bit leery of exceptionally small firms, those with market capitalizations below $50 million, but I'm content to spot these as I sort or eyeball the results of my screens and decide case by case whether I want to accept a company that small.)

Nobody can tell me that my neutrality regarding company size is right or wrong. It's a matter of taste. What's important is that I considered the issue and made the decision I believe is right for me. Staying aware of one's goals and style is standard advice for all investors regardless of whether they use screens. But it's easy to lose sight of such basics when caught up in interesting news events, the novelty of a new investment idea, or the sense of panic that can grip the market when times turn bad.

This is an example of how screening forces you to be self-aware. Obviously, if you create your own screens you're constantly making decisions about which tests are consistent with your goals and risk tolerances. It's also so even if you stick with prepackaged screens. There are several I've seen on a variety of web sites that have tests requiring market capitalization to be at least $1 billion. If the site allows me to modify the prepackaged screen, I delete the size test. If I can't modify a test I dislike, I won't use that screen.

Multex's premium stock screener contains a market capitalization variable. So, too, does the slimmer version available for free on the individual investor–oriented MultexInvestor.com web site. My lack of interest in using such an item for screening does not diminish my devotion to both products. Any screener you encounter should contain more variables than you would be willing to use. These programs are designed to be useful to a wide variety of investors with their own sets of preferences. Look at it this way: In a good screener, nobody will use everything, but everybody will use something.

If you want to create your own screens, do not think less of a screener simply because it's loaded with variables that don't appeal to you. Instead see whether the screener offers enough variables you like, thereby enabling you to create tests that are compatible with your own preferences. Other investors will decide for themselves whether the other variables are suitable for them.

BEYOND THE SCREEN

The least appreciated aspect of screening is the fact that it need not be seen as only an exercise in database extraction. It can be a full-fledged method of investing that continually points you toward additional good habits beyond the self-awareness issues just discussed. This book presents what casual observers think of as screening as just the first part of a four-step investment method. In Step 1, you create your own screen or select prepackaged screens. This is the obvious part of the process. But there's a lot more.

Even under the best of conditions, a stock list obtained through a screen should never be considered a hard-and-fast buy list. Although computers have become extremely sophisticated, even the best of them are not yet able to completely supplant human discretion. Therefore, screens work best when used as idea generators. This is not a weakness in the process. If you start with a database containing 10,000 or so companies and quickly narrow it down to, say, 25 that presumably are consistent with your objectives and have a presumption of investment merit, you've accomplished something very valuable. Nobody can review 10,000 companies one at a time. It's much easier to give individual attention to 25. And it's much more satisfying when you know, even before you start, that you can approach each with a presumed-innocent-until-proven-guilty mind-set.

But you still need to get from 25 stocks (or 15 or 50) that appear on your screen at a particular point in time to however many stocks you're willing to buy. This brings us to Step 2, where you analyze each of the ideas that appear on your screen. What you look for depends on the kind of screens you are using. Whatever your approach, you can use Internet-based data presentations to examine data relationships that are often similar to the ones used in screening tests (but which cover more territory than is feasible in a screen) to learn far more about a company than many experienced investors thought possible. Qualitative considerations are always part of the picture. But you'll find them much easier to assess when placed in a solid data context.

If your company evaluations point you toward the one truly perfect stock from among all those produced by the screen, you're home free. But in the real world, that sort of thing rarely happens. Most likely, you'll find it necessary to balance a set of pros and cons. And when the dust settles, you may need to prioritize among several stocks all of which can be considered buyable. You cope with this in Step 3, where screening concepts are applied to help you decide which stocks, if any, should actually be purchased.

Finally, there's Step 4, where you review your portfolio to decide which stocks, if any, should be sold. All investors understand the importance of the sell decision. But many find this the hardest part of the process. In fact, however, screening can serve as an excellent foundation for a sound selling strategy. You can create screens specifically designed to identify sale candidates. Or you can use comparisons between your screen-based buy decision and the company's current status as a framework for evaluating potential sales.

SCREENING THE MARKET

This book treats screening in a new way, something that goes far beyond using software packages to generate lists. It's presented as a complete four-step method covering the entire investment process.

- Step 1: Find . . . a group of stocks worthy of further study.
- Step 2: Analyze . . . a specific company and its stock.
- Step 3: Buy . . . the best of the stocks that pass muster.
- Step 4: Sell . . . stocks that, after review, no longer seem suitable.

Chapter 3 will present a more comprehensive overview of each of the four steps. Then, Chapters 4 to 9 will comprehensively cover Step 1 (Find), focusing on the actual screening activities. Step 2 (Analyze) will be covered in detail in Chapters 10 and 11. Step 3 (Buy) will be presented in Chapters 12 to 14. And Step 4 (Sell) will be described in Chapters 15 and 16.

But even before we begin to explore the four steps, there are some preliminaries that need to be addressed. Screening is a highly systematic activity and as such differs considerably from many popular approaches to investing. So before you dive into this approach, it will be helpful if you can get comfortable with certain widely held attitudes about investing and how they relate to the screening method. We'll do that next, in Chapter 2.

A Winning Mind-Set

There are many correct ways to invest. Rather than trying to collect and follow as many good suggestions as you can, you'd be better off recognizing the kind of investor you are, and identifying those ideas that will help you execute your game plan. That's so whether you're a day trader or a buy-and-hold investor, a fundamental investor or a chartist, a growth investor or a value investor. Since screening is being presented here as a full-fledged investment method, it, too, will work best if you tune in to those beliefs that are most compatible with this style.

I've identified three broad concepts that will help you develop the mind-set you'll need to screen successfully. It's not that you can't screen successfully without accepting these beliefs. The purpose of this discussion, or pep talk, is to help you feel comfortable with what you're doing, and help you have the conviction to stick with it.

COMPANY KNOWLEDGE

I could not begin to count the number of times I've heard and read about how important it is for investors to know lots of things about the companies in which they invest. Traders and chartists would debate the point, but for fundamental investors, those who consider and invest based on earnings prospects or asset values, it seems like heresy to doubt that you should know all about any company whose shares you might buy. I agree, but suggest you reevaluate the way you apply this idea to your investment activities.

Let's examine one of the more widely held beliefs, the one that tells investors how important it is to focus on the quality of company management. Who could argue with that? But how do you plan to follow through? Traditionally, if you worked as an investment professional, you were able to attend meetings with chief executive officers, chief financial officers, investor relations executives, and sometimes a few other key operating managers. On some occasions, you'd visit the company individually. Often, you'd attend presentations (or participate in conference calls) for many members of the investment community. Between formal meetings, you'd stay in touch by phone.

But I don't believe such activities really teach you much about management. Phone calls are convenient for staying up-to-date, but it's hard to really take the measure of another person that way. At group meetings, you'll see well-rehearsed "road shows" that have been prepared in consultation with and sanitized by public relations experts. If you visit individually, the people you meet will step out of their normal behavior patters and go into presentation mode while you're there. If you really want to know what sort of people they are, you'd have to try to hide in a closet and, assuming security doesn't catch you and turn you over to the police, observe how they behave when they don't know you're watching. But even that may not be enough. Often, business success or failure depends on lower-level individuals whose names and titles you won't know. Imagine how much harder it got in late 2000, when Securities and Exchange Commission (SEC) Regulation FD limited the scope of one-on-one communication between corporate management and the investment community. Individual investors are especially bad off. Even before Regulation FD, they were lucky to get any responsible executive to take a phone call.

Recognizing these challenges, some suggest guerrilla-style alternatives, such as contacting customers, rank-and-file employees, competitors, and suppliers. Indeed, professional analysts whose traditional communications links are being obstructed by Regulation FD are being urged to do just that. So let's say you're considering General Electric (GE) shares. Where do you start? Do you know how to contact competitors, employees, and distributors for the gas turbines GE makes for power plants? How about the aircraft engine business? These operations are just the beginning for this massive conglomerate that makes a wide variety of industrial products, is a corporate media mogul thanks to its ownership of the NBC network and affiliated television stations, and is a major player in the financial services area. It's not clear that even professional analysts, much less individual investors, can truly learn about the people that make or break GE through grassroots digging.

Comparable challenges exist for other aspects of the know-the-company mandate. Investors are counseled to evaluate products, competition, technology, market stature, and so on. Professional analysts who have had prior experience in the industries they analyze are best able to cope successfully with such issues. Analysts without such experience and individual investors studying industries other than the ones with which they deal in day-to-day life find the task much more daunting.

So however sensible it may seem to know all about the companies in which you may invest, following such advice is easier said than done. But it's not impossible. The key is to understand what you really need to know to make your investment style succeed. If you screen the market, you'll notice that winning companies/stocks leave conspicuous footprints. Some of these will be picked up as the theme of your screens. Others will become visible as you review data presentations for the companies that appear in your screens.

Going back to quality of management, we just saw how hard it is to directly address such issues through interpersonal contact. But consider the data footprints left by talented management teams. On the Multex Investor.com web site, these are grouped together in a table called "Management Effectiveness." It presents three sets of ratios: return on assets (ROA), return on investment (ROI), and return on equity (ROE). Experienced investors are familiar with these phrases, but as they get caught up in the hype surrounding quarterly earnings trends, new product announcements, and so on, these ratios tend to get pushed to the back burner as topics that are interesting when you first study investing but not an integral part of the workaday process. The screening method takes the opposite approach and brings such core concepts to center stage.

Let's pause and think about what such ratios are really telling us. If I give you $100 million in capital and ask you to earn $1 million of profit next year, you'll have an embarrassingly easy time of it. I'd be asking for a return of only 1 percent. If you simply invested in risk-free one-year U.S. Treasury securities, you'd earn the $1 million and have plenty left over. But suppose I give you only $4 million to work with. Now your target return is 25 percent. That's still doable, but obviously it's going to require some talent and effort. (Investing in Treasuries won't do it.) Imagine what it will take to achieve a 25 percent return if I insist you stick to the office supplies business, where the average return on equity over the past five years was only 14 percent. Suppose you succeed and deliver a 25 percent return in office supplies. I can't be completely certain of your management talent. Perhaps you had a few lucky breaks. But unless and until I learn specific facts to the contrary, I'll feel a lot more comfortable with an assumption that you're a good manager than I would if I sat in a meeting for a couple of hours watching a PowerPoint presentation of your business plan.

Investors who screen need not, and in fact should not, turn blind eyes toward qualitative aspects of business performance. You will learn much from news stores, earnings releases, company descriptions, analyst research, and conference call webcasts (live and replay). You won't know as much as you would in an ideal world, where you'd be able to independently assess the quality of personnel, the sophistication of proprietary technologies, the efficiency of manufacturing, the capabilities of rivals, and so on. But if you follow the screening method, you'll see that data footprints interact powerfully with qualitative information (helping you assess the latter's reliability) in a way that gives you as much company information as you need to invest successfully.

PAST VERSUS FUTURE

We've all been cautioned, "Past performance is no guarantee of future success." Screening utilizes data that, by necessity, reflects the past. Investment success, however, depends on the future. Therefore screening is very limited. Right? A former professor of mine would respond to this by saying, "That sounds good if you say it fast enough." So let's slow down and take a fresh look at the issue.

Consider the process of forecasting. The past serves as an important starting point. For example, if we see that a company's sales have consistently outperformed annual gross domestic product (GDP) growth by 50 percent, an analyst might use that relationship to assume that if nominal GDP is expected to rise 5 percent annually over the next few years, the company's sales would be expected to grow at a 7.5 percent annual rate. If cost of goods sold is consistently coming in at 65 percent of sales, the analyst starts with an assumption that this relationship will persist into the future. Forecasts for other items would also use historical relationships as starting points (growth in capital spending and growth in sales, the relationship between capital spending and depreciation, etc.). Human judgment comes in as analysts search for instances where the future is likely to be better or worse than the past and then adjust the initial "naive" projections accordingly.

Expectations of bold change make for great headlines and sexy investment research reports. But as many investors learned in the 2000–2001 technology/new economy stock market bust, these visions don't always pan out. In fact, most companies are not able to change their characters or prospects overnight. It can happen. But the probabilities are such that the burden of proof lies with whoever is saying big change will occur. Your success with such investments will depend on your ability to recognize when that burden of proof has been met.

Given this context, let's see how screening addresses future expectations. First, good screening databases include analyst information such as earnings estimates, earnings surprises, estimate revisions, and stock recommendations. Such data shows what analysts are projecting and helps you see (and screen for) changes, for better or worse, in expectations. Second, you can commingle screening tests constructed using analyst data with others that use historic fundamental data to identify situations where the past is expected to differ from the future. You still have to use your judgment to decide, for each individual situation, if the burden of proof has been met. But at least you're aware of the need to do this. Many nonscreeners aren't in the habit of analyzing the past so closely, so they don't even bother to think about this issue. Finally, using historical data alone, you can look for situations where companies have already started to change their characters. An example would be a screen that searches for companies whose rates of EPS have been accelerating or slowing. The bottom line here is that while past performance is no guarantee of future success, screening can tune you in to future expectations at least as effectively as other approaches, and arguably better since the screening discipline focuses your attention on questions others don't even realize they should be asking.

INCLUSION AND EXCLUSION

There are many different kinds of companies out there, so you will always be able to point to instances where investment potential depends on factors other than historic data. In biotech, for example, crucial factors include new product pipeline, progress in moving new products through the regulatory approval process, or even financial strength (small firms often get sudden capital infusions form large companies as part of distribution deals, so you ought not necessarily avoid companies whose current balance sheets seem weak). Media investors look at program libraries (and current releases that will later enter the library) when considering television and movie companies. Cable TV stocks have long been valued with reference to subscriber base. Energy stocks are often evaluated based on the quantity and quality of oil, gas, and/or coal reserves. Other companies are analyzed based on the private market values of properties they own. When looking at financial companies, we consider loan quality and investment spreads.

Today's screeners can't directly address such issues. Although this sounds like a clear weakness in the screening process, screeners ought not rush to concede defeat. For example, energy reserves represent a status quo at one point in time. If the companies are to flourish, it's necessary that they continually discover new reserves to replace those they draw down. Few analysts or investors can make serious independent assessments of this kind of issue. Even an analyst who formerly worked as a geologist would be stymied by the fact that companies don't generally disclose enough information about their exploration programs to enable outsiders to evaluate them in detail. So ultimately, when we separate those questions that are answerable from those that really aren't, we see that investors depend on historic data more often than many like to admit. Screening databases don't generally track annual natural resource reserves data. But it's not such a big jump to assume energy companies that are good at managing reserves will eventually leave the same sort of footprints of success we see in other sectors: good returns, margins, turnover, growth, financial strength, and so on. And when energy companies succeed, that's also likely to be reflected in such data categories as analyst estimates and recommendations, insider buying, institutional activity, and (declines in) short interest, which can be screened.

To some degree, similar arguments can be made in connection with the other seemingly screening-challenged sectors. (For example, a perennially poor-quality bank loan portfolio will eventually impact earnings trends, analyst sentiment, etc.) Even so, if we investigate extensively enough, we will discover investment opportunities that are unlikely to be discovered through screening. When confronted with a situation that screening truly can't address, there's one simple answer. Accept it. There are lots of good stocks out there, and no investment method can be expected to find each and every one of them.

The mood of investors in midsummer 2001 was gloomy. Since mid-2000, the Standard & Poor's (S&P) 500 had fallen approximately 20 percent and the Nasdaq 100 had plunged approximately 50 percent. Yet in 2001, the Market Guide screening database contained about 9,500 stocks, 2,300 of which were up 20 percent or more over that same 52-week period. This was a time when smaller stocks were achieving recognition for generally strong performance. But the list of 2,300 20 percent plus gainers wasn't packed with penny stocks. There were 1,620 with market capitalizations above $50 million, and 780 with capitalizations above $500 million. Meanwhile, most individual investors own fewer than 50 different stocks at any particular time, and many own less than 20. So even during bear markets, there are plenty of attractive investment opportunities available to those who choose to screen the market, far more than any of them can plausibly own. The important question is whether the approach you choose will, after subtracting those the method typically misses, give you as much opportunity as you need to find attractive stocks. In the case of screening, the answer is a resounding yes.

SUMMARY

Screening isn't at present nearly as widespread as it deserves to be. To a large extent, that's because investors haven't yet had occasion to see it as a full-fledged investment discipline and discover what it can accomplish. These issues will be covered by the rest of this book. But before investors can appreciate screening, what some may see as inherent deficiencies in the process had to be addressed.

First was the topic of company knowledge. Screening can't teach us as much as we think we'd like to know about the companies. But if we separate that which we'd like to, but can't really, know from that which is truly knowable, we see that the screening method can give us the information we need to invest successfully. Second, we saw that in-depth data analysis does not trap us into erroneously acting as if past performance guarantees future success. Instead, an investment method that springs from the data gives us a solid foundation for making and assessing expectations about the future. Finally, we've seen that screening can embrace a wide variety of investment situations. Some opportunities may slip between the cracks. But the number and scope of ideas to which screeners are exposed provide ample opportunities for investment success.

3

A Four-Step Method
to Screen the Market

W e're now ready for an overview of the complete four-step market
screening investment method. What most observers think of as screening, the process of submitting queries to a computer database, represents
the core of the first step. The principles that help us formulate good database queries also set the framework we'll use to evaluate the companies
identified by the screen as being of interest; to decide which stocks, if any,
should be purchased; and to review existing holdings in order to identify
potential sale candidates.

This covers a lot of territory. Consider the four steps, which encompass the full range of investment-related activity, a road map to help you
keep your bearings. Step 1 is called Find. Here, you use screens to create a
list of stocks that are most worthy of consideration. Step 2 is called Analyze. This is where you study in depth the companies that came to your attention through your screens. Step 3 is called Buy. Now you balance each
stock's pros and cons and prioritize among those you are considering. The
end result is a set of decisions to buy or pass on specific stocks. Step 4 is
called Sell. This is an ongoing discipline that helps you recognize which, if
any, of your existing positions should be sold. Any situation, however
complex, can be made manageable if you identify which of the four steps is
relevant and apply the appropriate procedures.

The rest of this chapter includes a more comprehensive introduction
to each of the four steps. Then, Chapters 4 to 9 will cover Step 1 (Find)
in detail. Chapters 10 and 11 will then describe Step 2 (Analyze). Chapters 12 to 14 will explain Step 3 (Buy). Chapters 15 and 16 will cover
Step 4 (Sell).

STEP 1: FIND . . . A GROUP OF STOCKS
WORTHY OF FURTHER STUDY

Typically, investment books and courses jump right into discussion of how to evaluate a company and its stock. But that assumes you made good decisions about which stocks you're going to evaluate. This four-step market screening method takes a different approach. A major part of the method, the first of four steps, is devoted entirely to compiling a listing of stocks that are worthy of further study. The goal is to stack the deck in your favor even before you look at a single company.

For most readers, this step is the most novel. Consider your past practices. How is it that some stocks come to your attention while others don't? Typical answers include coverage in the financial media, recommendations by financial advisers, tips from friends, your coming into contact with the companies during the course of your day-to-day life, and so forth. Sometimes investors do well considering such stocks. Other times they don't. Either way, the outcome often contains a large element of chance. Investors are best positioned to succeed if they have smart friends, capable financial advisers, or the good fortune to live in one of the first areas served by the next great up-and-coming retailer. The screening method differs in that it allows you to be exposed to any stock at any time. Whether or not you see a particular stock will depend on your goals, the stock's investment merit, and the stock's compatibility with your goals. That's the approach that gives you the best probability of long-term success.

Chapters 4 to 9 will show you how to screen. The free program available on MultexInvestor.com and Multex's premium-priced application will be used as the primary examples. We will also cover other screeners. The main focus will be on elements common to all screening programs so you'll gain the wherewithal to easily figure out how to operate any other screening program in just a few minutes. And no matter what screens you use, your lists are still likely to include more stocks than you will have time to evaluate in detail. Chapter 8 includes techniques to help you decide which ones you should examine first.

But knowing how to use the software isn't enough. Chapters 6 and 7 will show you how to create or recognize tests that are truly useful for stock selection. This topic is really quite manageable. Chapter 6 will show you the kinds of data items, or variables, that are available and how to use them to build productive tests. And Chapter 7 will show you how to think strategically about the different ways you can select among the different tests and combine them into sensible screens.

STEP 2: ANALYZE . . . A SPECIFIC
COMPANY AND ITS STOCK

However successfully you implement Step 1, the output from your screens will still contain some names that are better than others. You address that in Step 2, where you will analyze individual companies and their stocks. This step is the one that will be most familiar to most readers. Potentially, it covers all possible approaches to security analysis or stock selection. You get acquainted with what the company does, review what it has accomplished in the past, develop expectations about what it will do in the future, and make judgments, based on your investment goals, about whether the stock has appeal at its current price.

What's unique, here, is the way you go about performing these tasks. As discussed in Chapter 2, this screening method is very sensitive to distinctions between that which investors can learn about a company and that which is not truly knowable. Accordingly, you are not going to be asked to evaluate the quality of wireless Internet patents, new semiconductor chip designs, and so on. You won't be asked to assess the soundness of arrangements companies make with their distributors. You will not be urged to evaluate the capabilities of companies that might someday decide to compete with the one whose stock you are considering. Nor will you be asked to assess the personalities of the top executives, the appropriateness of the organizational structure, or the soundness of employee incentives. If something in your individual background helps tune you in to such issues for a particular company, by all means use whatever edge you possess. But realistically, the typical investor will not be able to cope with such questions insofar as they apply to most companies.

The evaluation method presented focuses on the same sort of data relationships that were used in the screens. Indeed, the mere fact that a company appears on a particular screen immediately gives you some information. If, for example, you used a growth-oriented screen, you can expect the company to look good at least in data presentations geared toward the growth theme. But Step 2 goes further. You also examine data that does not relate to your screening theme. For example, a growth investor working with Step 2 will also consider financial strength, margins, stock valuation metrics, analyst/insider/institutional/short seller sentiment, and so on. And you'll want to enhance your understanding of the numbers with qualitative information such as company descriptions, news, and significant developments.

Focusing on MultexInvestor.com, you'll learn how to look at data reports in a way that helps you combat information overload and discover a unique story in each set of numbers. These reports will typify much of what you'll find on the Web, since many sites license data from Multex's Market Guide subsidiary, or at least use similar presentation formats. We'll also take a look at some unique presentations on other sites.

STEP 3: BUY . . . THE BEST OF
THE STOCKS THAT PASS MUSTER

It's easy to decide whether to buy a stock if everything you learn in the Analyze phase is either favorable or unfavorable. Often investors act as if that's exactly how it should be. But that rarely, if ever, happens. Usually you'll see both pros and cons. This should hardly be surprising, since every stock market transaction involves one party who wants to buy and another who wants to sell, both of whom have access to the same information and are making decisions with reference to the same stock price.

We address this in Step 3. It starts with three Analysis Keys that provide a systematic framework for balancing the pros and cons that surface during the evaluation phase. These are yes/no questions covering important aspects of the investment story. The first Analysis Key focuses on whether, in light of all you learned in your evaluation, you still believe the situation truly fits your original investment theme, as expressed in the screen(s) you used to uncover the stock. Remember, screening isn't a perfect science. For example, you might be a growth-oriented investor seeking companies that are growing because of attractive business prospects, such as expanding product demand or entry into new regions. A company whose earnings have been growing due to cost cutting would not fit your original theme. Going further, the Analyze step exposed you to data that stretched well beyond your initial screening theme. Users of growth screens will also have seen information about financial strength, stock valuation, and so on. Analysis Key 2 asks whether there are other factors (unrelated to the screen) you see as having a positive impact on the investment story. Analysis Key 3 covers the opposite situation. It asks whether the additional factors detract from the stock's appeal.

Now you have a set of three yes/no answers for each stock you evaluated. Each possible three-way combination of answers corresponds to one of eight Decision Paths. The best possible situation, the top path, is one where the situation is consistent with your original theme, additional factors add to the situation's appeal, and there are no other factors that detract from the story. These are your top-priority buys. The worst scenario, the bottom path, is where the stock is not really consistent with your original theme, there are no additional factors that give the stock appeal, and other considerations apart from the screen make the stock unappealing. These stocks should be avoided. The other six paths (yes/no combinations) constitute a gray middle zone. Chapter 14 ranks these paths in a best-to-worst hierarchy that helps you prioritize which stocks are most appealing (assuming you aren't willing or able, at this time, to purchase every potentially buyable stock).

STEP 4: SELL . . . STOCKS THAT, AFTER REVIEW, NO LONGER SEEM SUITABLE

Everyone acknowledges the need for a sound selling strategy, but so far, the quest for one has been largely elusive. Too often, investors continue to rely on folklore that sounds good in theory but doesn't necessarily work well in practice.

One of today's prime examples is advice to the effect that you should sell your losers and keep your winners. Another would have you lock in a predetermined level of profits. Chapter 15 will describe the flaws in such approaches. Meanwhile, Step 4 eschews folklore and offers a systematic way of monitoring your portfolio. It's based on the same Find, Analyze, and Buy steps you used to buy your stocks. But here they are adapted to accommodate the kinds of questions you face when you consider selling. This Sell discipline features three phases: Alert, Update, and Reconsider.

Nobody has the time to check up on every stock every day. So you can rely on Sell Phase A (Alert) to spotlight situations that warrant attention. Alerts can be triggered by events (such as earnings announcements or sharp and sudden movements in the stock price), screens (special screens designed specifically to identify sale candidates and/or the fact that a stock has fallen out of the screen that originally called it to your attention), or routine (a self-imposed policy calling for you to review any stock that hasn't been revisited in, say, the past three months). Next, in Sell Phase B (Update), you return to the same information (data reports, news items, etc.) you used in the original evaluation phase. But now you're seeing more up-to-date information so the conclusions you reach may change. Finally, in Sell Phase C (Reconsider), you decide to sell or to continue to hold. Similar to what you did with the original Analysis Keys, you'll now apply three Update Keys. The first asks whether your original reasons for buying remain valid. The second and third ask about additional positive or negative factors respectively. Finally, you'll use a series of Reconsideration Paths based on the various yes/no combinations you get through your answers to the Update Keys. The eight Reconsideration Paths range from best (stocks that should be held) to worst (stocks that definitely should be sold). The other paths are arranged according to priorities (that tell you which stocks should be sold first when you want to close only some of your positions).

one

Find . . . a Group of Stocks Worthy of Further Study

## CHAPTER 4

Dogs versus Gems

I t's tempting to assume that if you're reading this book you don't need to be sold on the value of stock screening. But there's a difference between being able to verbalize the benefits of screening and having the conviction to stick with it when you invest real money. The aim of this chapter is to help you develop that conviction by seeing screening not just as a useful time-saver, but as a powerful framework for the entire stock selection process.

Much has been written about different ways to analyze companies and evaluate stock prices. But to date, there's been little attention given to how one chooses which companies are going to be analyzed. This is an extremely important topic. Suppose you are the greatest analyst in the world, but are making choices from a list of 10 companies, all of which are dogs—mediocre at best. In this case, no matter how great your understanding of dogs and your ability to consistently identify the best in the kennel, you're still going to wind up buying dogs. Conversely, if your list is loaded with gems, there's a good chance your investments will shine even if you choose by pointing with your eyes closed.

Step 1 of the four-step market screening method is called Find. Your task, here, is to find stocks that are worthy of further consideration. You'll analyze each of the firms on your evaluation list in Step 2. Eventually, some will pass muster and you'll buy them. Others will fall by the wayside. But let's not run too far ahead. Right now, in Step 1, your goal is to put together an evaluation list that includes as many gems, and as few dogs, as possible. If you do this effectively, you enhance your chances of investment success even before you start to evaluate a single company.

YOUR EVALUATION LIST

An evaluation list is any group of stocks you consider. It might be something formal, like a recommended list issued by a broker, or a collection of names published on a web site or in a magazine. It can also be informal. Someone who simply likes tech stocks has an evaluation list. Because it includes so many more companies than the typical investor can really consider, it's not necessarily a good list. But it's still an evaluation list. These lists can be even more casual. Suppose you invest in stocks you read about in the newspaper, in magazines, or on web sites or hear about on television. Those companies, the ones that attract the attention of the financial media, constitute your list. Again, it may not be the best list you can find. But it's still an evaluation list.

It's important that you get in the habit of thinking about evaluation lists, even if yours amounts to little more than the names of stocks you remember having recently read about. The idea is that you be able to articulate why you are interested in some stocks as opposed to others. Once you're comfortable thinking about stocks that way, you'll find it easy to see how screening can help you compile the best collection of names you can find based on your investment goals.

IMPORTANCE OF A GOOD EVALUATION LIST

Suppose a magician came along and offered to help you invest in stocks. He refuses to do anything to improve your stock selection skills. So if you're a good stock picker in the real world, you'll stay good after he waves his magic wand. And if you're a mediocre analyst, you'll stay mediocre. But he does offer to let you choose whether the stock market goes up 20 percent or down 5 percent. I'll bet you'd accept the offer and would choose a +20 percent market. You might still pick some duds. But wouldn't you prefer to do your thing in a bull market that rises 20 percent?

Obviously, you can't single-handedly influence the real-world market. But you have considerable power to set the tone of your personal stock market, the tiny group from which you will make your choices. Let's pretend Jane Doe used a stock screen to create a list of 10 potentially interesting growth opportunities while the 10 stocks Bob Smith chose to evaluate were ones he heard about from his friends. Table 4.1 shows how the different "personal stock markets" impacted each investor.

Suppose Jane picked one stock from her list randomly. There's no guarantee she'd have done well. But 8 out of 10 stocks on her list performed better than the 8 percent overall average. So there's an 80 percent probability she could have beaten the market simply by drawing a ticker out of a hat. Meanwhile, Bob's list contained four stocks that beat the overall market average. So had he selected randomly, there was only a 4 out of 10 (40 percent) probability that he'd have outperformed the

TABLE 4.1 Two User-Designed Stock Markets

Bob Smith's Evaluation List		Jane Doe's Evaluation List	
Stock A	+6%	Stock K	+24%
Stock B	–10%	Stock L	+15%
Stock C	+5%	Stock M	–5%
Stock D	–5%	Stock N	+11%
Stock E	+14%	Stock O	–7%
Stock F	–12%	Stock P	+13%
Stock G	+17%	Stock Q	+17%
Stock H	+16%	Stock R	+9%
Stock I	+6%	Stock S	+14%
Stock J	+11%	Stock T	+21%
List average	+4.8%	List average	+11.2%

Note: Overall average return for all stocks is 8 percent.

market. Bob certainly could have helped himself through superior individual stock evaluation. Perhaps his skills might have helped him identify the top three stocks on his list. In that case, his average return would have jumped to an impressive 15.7 percent. But if he really was such a good analyst, it would have been a shame for him to waste his time looking at so many dogs. Suppose he devoted his talents to evaluating the stocks on Jane's list. If Bob could identify the top three stocks there, his average return would jump to 20.7 percent. But suppose Bob's evaluation skills were poor and he consistently gravitated toward the worst three stocks. Using his list, the average return would be –9 percent. If he were to work with Jane's list, though, the impact of his analytic errors would be mitigated. The worst three stocks there had an average return of –1 percent.

Every investor can benefit from using superior lists. Even though there are good stocks on Bob's list and bad stocks on Jane's list, it's probable that over time anyone would do better with a list such as the one created by Jane, whether one's stock evaluation skills are good, average, or weak.

CHOOSING STOCKS FOR YOUR EVALUATION LIST

There are countless ways one can go about choosing which stocks should go on an evaluation list. I've broken the methods down to three broad categories: popular, thematic, and screen-based.

Popular Evaluation Lists

Anyone who claims lists are too much trouble and says he/she doesn't use them is working with a popular evaluation list, even though he/she isn't openly acknowledging that this is what's being done. Popular lists are the names one remembers from reading financial newspapers or magazines, checking the Web, or listening to television or radio. Popular lists also include the stocks encountered on Internet message boards or chat areas, or discussed at real-world social gatherings. Popular evaluation lists have been used, in one form or another, since the beginning of investment history. And today it's easier than ever. No longer need an individual have the right broker or be part of an in crowd to collect the hottest names of the day. They are constantly plastered all over the online and off-line financial media.

Popular lists can lead to very profitable investing. The mere fact that the stocks are in the public limelight attracts share purchases and drives the stock prices higher. Many investors made huge amounts of money this way in the late 1990s, a sky-is-the-limit period for many widely discussed stocks, especially in technology and Internet. But starting in 2000 the bad aspects of popular lists came to the surface, and by mid-2001 stocks on these lists suffered massive losses. Valuation was one factor. Often popular companies are good companies. But a good company can be a bad investment if its stock price becomes overly inflated. The situation becomes much worse if the pace of business falters, leaving investors to wonder if the company is less good than was once believed. That's an important reason why Peter Lynch, in his classic, *One Up on Wall Street* (Simon & Schuster, 1989, p. 141), says: "If I could avoid a single stock, it would be the hottest stock in the hottest industry, the one that gets the most favorable publicity, the one that every investor hears about in the car pool or on the commuter train."

Thematic Evaluation Lists

While Peter Lynch made an eloquent case against what I refer to as a popular evaluation list, he is seen by many as the primary advocate for the next approach, thematic investing. Here, we don't look at stocks simply because they're in the spotlight. Instead, stocks are chosen for evaluation lists because they are consistent with some sort of story. Mr. Lynch is associated with the idea of investing based on what you know from your personal experience. He teaches that "the best place to begin looking for the tenbagger is close to home—if not in the backyard, then down at the shopping mall, and especially wherever you happen to work." (*One Up on Wall Street*, p. 83.) Put another way, you would put a stock on your thematic evaluation list if the company is one you encounter in your personal life and, for one reason or another, seems appealing to you.

But in the real world, this can be very hit-or-miss. For example, I like Coca-Cola. It was once a great company to discover through personal experience. But I fear those days are long gone. Its stock is priced at about 25 times the consensus estimate of next year's earnings per share (EPS), but the company is projected to grow at only a 10 to 13 percent annual rate. This is one example, among many, where thematic investors are late to the party. Krispy Kreme illustrates a different danger, the possibility that a thematic investor may get carried away with the story and lose track of the fundamentals. Mr. Lynch warned about this, but many fail to pay attention to that part of his thesis. Speaking for myself, I love Krispy Kreme doughnuts. But it seems too many are investing based on little more than a sweet tooth. The stock's price/earnings (P/E) ratio based on the estimate of EPS for the next fiscal year is now 50, while the company's projected EPS growth rate is only 20 to 25 percent. Then there's Amazon.com. I love the company from the customer's vantage point. But as an investor, I hate the losses it continues to incur. This is probably not an unfortunate coincidence. If Amazon's prices and selection were such as to rein in spending levels, would I be so happy to go on buying from Amazon?

I certainly don't mean to suggest you should ignore your life experiences. If some interesting idea comes to you based on where and how you or others you know live, work, play, and so on, there's no reason you should close your eyes to what you learn. Back in 1999, I noticed P. F. Chang's China Bistro on one of my stock screens. And my subsequent evaluation pointed me toward a buy decision. But as a native New Yorker, I couldn't help wondering how smart it would be to invest in Chinese restaurants, which in this region are a dime a dozen. But a couple of visits suggested the company really did have something interesting going for it. Its decor, service, and menu were distinct compared with the run-of-the-mill Chinese restaurant. That alone might not have excited me. After all, a good number of local Asian eateries can be considered upscale. But Chang's struck me as far superior to any Chinese restaurant I'd seen in most other parts of the United States.

So personal experience did play a role in my decision to recommend Chang's. But the extent to which you can count on this sort of thing to serve as the primary starting point for a major portion of your investment program will depend heavily on your lifestyle and your circle of experiences. It's very unlikely I would ever have discovered the local P. F.

Chang's restaurant during my day-to-day routine, since it's not near where I live or on my way to work. I found the company on a screen, and then used personal experience to enhance my basic data-oriented evaluation process.

Another approach to thematic evaluation lists is a top-down preference for a particular industry or sector. Many investors like technology. In other words, a stock is automatically included in the evaluation list if the company can be classified as technology. If not, the stock is excluded. Others use size as the main criterion for considering a stock. A stock might be included on an evaluation list if the market capitalization (the number of outstanding shares times the price per share) is above $1 billion. Other investors go the opposite way and favor small cap investing. Top-down approaches can lead to unworkably large lists. So thematic and popular approaches are often combined. In other words, a tech devotee might work with a list that includes every tech stock he/she hears or reads about. Those who like large caps would choose to evaluate all the large caps they know about.

But it need not always work this way. A tech investor may be very open toward a technology stock that is never covered by the financial media. Small cap investors have a special challenge here since the companies they favor are, generally, less likely to receive much attention. The question then becomes, if the company isn't featured in the press, how might an investor hear about it? This brings us to the third category of evaluation lists, the screening approach. In other words, an investor might use screens and focus only on the technology or small cap names that show in the list of results.

Screen-Based Evaluation Lists

Using stock screens to generate evaluation lists frees you from a variety of restraints on your selection efforts. It doesn't matter what magazines, newspapers, or Web commentators you read. It doesn't matter which financial television or radio broadcasts you see or hear. It doesn't matter where you live, what you do, or what companies you come into contact with in your day-to-day life. If you screen, there's only one thing that counts. A stock will get onto your evaluation list if it passes a series of objective tests that were established based on your investment preferences.

This sounds extremely sensible. But be warned that the habits eliminated by screening, however detrimental they may be, do have one thing going for them. They are comfortable. Once you start screening, you'll need to brace yourself for two changes: (1) Many names that are well known to you for a variety of reasons will be omitted from your screens. (2) Your screens will include many companies that are completely unfamiliar to you.

The upside is the number of true gems you can find. This can do wonders for your stock portfolio. When I look at my winning investments, I see such names as RehabCare, Mobile Mini, Chico's FAS, Graco, Hot Topic, and American Italian Pasta. These have two things in common. First, I never heard of any of them until they started appearing on my stock screens. Second, they flourished at a time while such high-profile stocks as Cisco Systems, JDS Uniphase, AOL Time Warner, and Nortel were collapsing.

5

Screening Applications

Each screener you encounter will have a unique look and feel. Fortunately, broad themes exist regarding user interface and the types of screens you can build. Hence you will not find it necessary to read a detailed how-to manual for each screener you encounter. In fact, such manuals hardly even exist anymore. This chapter will help you do what most screening sites hope you'll wind up doing: figuring out for yourself how to use the application.

Before looking at program features, let's start by discussing some of the screeners that exist at present. Over time, the list of available programs will change, so I cannot know precisely what's going to be available by the time you read these words. But the applications I'll mention here are leaders and will probably be around for a long time. Features may be revised, but with these programs change is most likely to be evolutionary, rather than revolutionary. If you gain comfort with the material here, you should be able to quickly adapt to just about any screener you might encounter.

One area that is likely to evolve is cost. As this is being written, some of these screeners are free. Some are available for modest fees ($100 to $250 per year). Others carry higher costs. Right now, user fees are the most fluid aspect of the Internet. Providers of free content may determine that it is impractical to build viable businesses based solely on revenue that can be gleaned from selling advertising. So fees may be imposed. But even the highest-priced among the screeners discussed here is affordable to anyone whose financial situation warrants investment in stocks. After all, the top cost is paltry compared to the potential gains from one good investment and the potential loss from one poor trade.

THE SCREENERS

This book emphasizes fundamental analysis. Accordingly, the material here draws heavily from Multex's two online screeners, both of which use company and analyst data produced by Multex's Market Guide subsidiary. Hence, these screeners are especially strong in fundamentals. The Multex premium product includes considerable flexibility in the kinds of comparative tests that can be created. We'll see in Chapter 6 that this is a very important method of screening. Meanwhile, Multex's free screener differs from the premium application only in terms of the number of data items made available. (As of this writing, the free screener features 80 data items while the premium product offers 640.) In other key respects (the ability to create user-defined tests, to import and export stock lists in text or Excel format, etc.), the programs are virtually identical. Note, too, that 19 prepackaged screens created with the premium application are available weekly on the MultexInvestor.com web site.

Stock Investor Pro is a CD-screener produced by the American Association of Individual Investors (AAII). At present it costs $247 per year for nonmembers. Since the company data is licensed from Market Guide, it should come as no surprise that this product, like the Multex offerings, is strong in the area of company fundamentals. In fact, it features more tests than the premium Multex screener. A new CD is sent to users once per month. But data updates are available once per week via downloads from the AAII.com web site. Broadband users can easily update the entire data set each week. But the full update could take three hours for users who have dial-up connections. To accommodate them, AAII offers another download option that allows them to update only part of the database, presumably the items most directly related to share prices. This is a smaller file that can be downloaded more quickly through a dial-up connection. Users who do this have to wait until the monthly CD arrives before updating the rest of the data. But neither option is perfect. Online screeners are usually updated daily. So those who are especially sensitive to data timeliness may be reluctant to go full-speed with Stock Investor Pro. But it is so strong in terms of its ability to accommodate very detailed historical comparisons and unusually flexible comparative tests, it's still worthy of attention.

SmartMoneySelect.com is a relatively new subscription offering from *SmartMoney* magazine. It includes a screening application that is quite robust, especially in light of its inclusion in the less expensive ($49.95 annual fee) price tier. Its strength is its ability to accommodate a very wide range of fundamental tests comparing companies to industry averages, sector averages, the S&P 500, the Dow Jones 30, the Nasdaq 100, the Russell 2000, or *SmartMoney*'s entire screening data universe.

MSN.Money (http://moneycentral.msn.com) offers a screener that's good in terms of proprietary ratings and takes a balanced generalist's approach to fundamental and technical analysis with an edge toward fundamental. A unique aspect of this program is its Advisor FYI data category that provides interesting ways for you to screen based on noteworthy trend changes.

Morningstar.com's Premium Stock Selector, part of that site's $109 per year (or $11.95 per month) Premium Membership, is also strong in terms of proprietary ratings and is outstanding in terms of the way it allows you to score your results (a topic that will be covered in Chapter 8).

Quicken.com's screener emphasizes ease of use. Yet this application offers more top-down flexibility and comparative screening opportunities than you'd expect given the simplicity of its interface.

ProSearch by INVESTools is available for a modest fee on WallStreetCity.com. A more advanced version of ProSearch, which includes a proprietary scoring system in the results, is available on InvestorToolbox.com. ProSearch is good in terms of fundamentals but rises to outstanding in terms of the technical analysis and proprietary ratings.

Ultimately, you'll want to do most of your screening with the application whose focus is closest to your own investment style. And if you prefer to use preset screens, you're likely to find the ones that most appeal to you among those created with applications whose areas of focus are closest to your investment style.

USER INTERFACE

If you take a quick glance at each of the screeners mentioned in the preceding section you might think each interface is completely unique. But in fact all of them follow a very consistent structure. Once you see that, you'll be able to master all of these screeners, and any others you might encounter, in a matter of minutes. In all cases, the structure is based on the idea that each screening test has four components: (1) category, (2) variable, (3) relationship, and (4) base.

Let's take a look at each component using, as an example, a hypothetical screening test that seeks companies with three-year EPS growth rates equal to or above 25 percent.

Category

If a screener offered 10 variables, it would be very easy to find the one you want. All you'd need to do is look at each variable one at a time. But as the number of variables climbs, so, too, does the burden of finding what you seek. Even more challenging is the initial task of getting acquainted with what's there, so you can make thoughtful decisions as to what you'll look for. The screening programs make life easier by classifying all variables into a reasonable number of categories.

The category lists vary from screener to screener. But the number of categories offered by even the most sophisticated applications is such that you can easily scan the list and figure out where to look for variables that might interest you. Chapter 6, which will go into detail about creating tests, will be organized on the basis of a typical category list.

In our hypothetical test, a three-year EPS growth rate would typically be included in a category called "Growth" or "Growth Rates."

Variable

Can I create a screen that seeks companies with share prices above $5? That depends on whether the screener includes stock price among the variables it offers. In virtually every application, the answer is yes. But it may be a lot harder to screen for stocks whose prices are, at worst, no less than 10 percent below the high achieved over the past five years. Most screens will provide as a variable each stock's 52-week high, but few offer the five-year high.

As you can see, variables are the facts upon which our screens are built. If someone tells you about a new store that opened up at the mall, you're likely to wonder what sort of goods it sells. If you see a new screener, you're likely to wonder how many variables and what kinds of variables it features.

Some variables are based on raw numbers, such as the stock price or the stock's 52-week high. Others are based on ratios or relationships calculated from the raw numbers. An example would be a price/earnings ratio. Here, the variable you work with is a precalculated relationship between the stock price and EPS. A growth rate is a variable calculated on the basis of past and present EPS numbers.

In our example involving a three-year EPS growth rate greater than or equal to 25 percent, the variable is "three-year EPS growth rate."

Relationship

To be useful in a screen, a data point has to be compared with something else. Relationship describes the nature of the comparison. If I want to screen for stock prices that are equal to 10, the relationship would be the condition of equality, the requirement that the data point be equal to the number 10. Equality is often not a good relationship to use when numbers are involved. Many stocks trade near 10, but few stock prices are exactly equal to that number. Recently, out of 9,497 stocks in the Multex screening database, only 15 were actually priced at 10. When I expanded the range from 9.5 to 10.5, the number of qualifying stocks jumped to 217. But even that improvement loses luster when viewed in light of the minimal investment significance of finding stocks priced at or very close to 10. In terms of mathematical logic, I could turn the relationship around and ask for stock prices not equal to 20. But that, too, would be unlikely to prove interesting from an investment standpoint. Equality and inequality relationships are best suited for qualitative tests, such as one requiring that companies be included in the technology sector (the screener would read this as "sector equals technology").

More worthwhile, to some investors, may be a requirement that stocks trade no lower than 10. This requires a different sort of relationship, one that sets a floor (or a ceiling). In this case, I'd ask that the stock price be greater than or equal to 10. There are four kinds of ceiling/floor relationships commonly used. They are (1) greater than, (2) greater than or equal to, (3) less than, and (4) less than or equal to.

> *In our example involving a three-year EPS growth rate greater than or equal to 25 percent, the* relationship *is "greater than or equal to."*

Base

This is the final part of the screening test. The base is the starting point against which all variables will be compared. If I seek a stock price greater than or equal to 5, then 5 is the base. All stock price variables will be compared with 5. If the price is greater, the stock will be accepted. If not, it will be rejected by the screen.

> *In our example involving a three-year EPS growth rate greater than or equal to 25 percent, the* base *value is "25 percent."*

On its face, this seems very simple. But in fact, the kinds of bases that can be accepted are a major factor in determining the quality and usefulness of a particular screening application. As we'll see in Chapter 6, you will more often than not prefer to have a base that's more complex than a simple number. Rather than requiring a three-year average EPS growth rate to be at least 25 percent, you may instead want it to be greater than the industry average three-year EPS growth rate, or the company's own five-year EPS growth rate.

Promotional literature for screeners tends to tout the number of variables offered. This is a worthy basis for evaluation. But there can be drastic differences between applications in terms of the sophistication of the bases they allow. In my opinion, flexibility in the sort of bases you can use may be more important than the number of variables.

Here are two special kinds of bases available in certain screeners.

Multiplication Factors   The Multex screeners and Stock Investor Pro allow you to create bases that include multiplication factors. To see the significance of this, consider the following progression.

A simple screener would restrict you to tests like this:

Three-year EPS growth rate is equal to or above 25 percent.

The better screeners allow you to go further and create tests like this:

Three-year EPS growth rate is equal to or above the industry average three-year EPS growth rate.

The top-of-the-line screeners allow you to go even further and create tests like this:

Three-year EPS growth rate is at least 25 percent better than the industry average three-year EPS growth rate.

The latter is created using a multiplication factor. Stated a bit more mathematically, the test might look something like this:

Three-year EPS growth rate >= (industry average three-year EPS growth rate) * 1.25

A multiplication factor doesn't just increase the base. It can also be used to reduce the base. The following test seeks a P/E that is no higher than 90 percent of the industry average P/E.

P/E <= (industry average P/E) * .9

When using multiplication factors, it's important to be careful about negative numbers that might find their way into the base. Suppose we create a test seeking EPS growth rates that are at least 25 percent better than the industry average. If a struggling industry has a –10 percent growth rate, multiplying by 1.25 results in a rate of –12.5 percent, which is worse than –10 percent.

There are two ways to address this: (1) When you use a multiplication factor, always add a test making the base—in this example, the industry average three-year EPS growth rate—greater than zero. (2) If you want to work with negative numbers (for example, to find companies whose declines are less severe than those of others in a struggling industry), add a new test to accomplish just that. Here's an example.

> Three-year EPS growth rate >= (industry average three-year EPS growth rate) * 1.25
> Three-year EPS growth rate >= (industry average three-year EPS growth rate) * .75

For positive base numbers, the second test will be redundant and have no impact on your screen. But if the base number is negative, the second test will filter out growth rates that are worse than the industry average. For example, if the industry average growth rate is –10 percent, a company having a –12.5 percent growth rate will pass the first test, but will fail the second test (since –12.5 percent is less than –7.5 percent) and be dropped from the list. Meanwhile, a company with a growth rate of –5 percent will pass the first test (–5 percent is greater than –12.5 percent) and the second test (–5 percent is greater than –7.5 percent) and stay on the list.

High/Low   Two screeners, ProSearch and MSN.Money, allow you to specify a preferred base as being "as high as possible" or "as low as possible." Strictly speaking, these aren't really screening tests at all, but are instead a jump start on a narrowing-down process we'll discuss in Chapter 8—specifically, sorting.

Here's a general idea of how it works. Consider the following three screening tests.

> Three-year EPS growth rate greater than 25 percent
> Three-year sales growth rate greater than 25 percent
> P/E ratio as low as possible

This screen would first collect all companies whose three-year EPS and sales growth rates are above 25 percent. These companies would then be sorted from lowest P/E to highest. Screens that allow you to utilize highest/lowest as a base also allow you to specify how many stocks you wish to see in the list of results. If you ask to see up to 20 stocks, your list will be confined to those companies passing the two growth rate tests and whose P/E ratios are among the lowest 20.

Recap

Here's a review of the four components of our sample test: three-year EPS growth rate greater than or equal to 25 percent.

Category:	Growth Rates
Variable:	Three-year EPS growth rate
Relationship:	Greater than or equal to
Base:	25 percent

You will find these four test components in all screeners. When you confront an interface that is new to you, look for each component.

Next, look for a way to add a newly constructed test to a screen (or delete or modify a test that's already there). Usually you'll see a tab or button labeled "OK," "Add Test," or "Delete Test."

Finally, look for a way to get the screen to sift through the database and collect stocks that meet your requirements. Some screens will perform this operation as soon as you input a test. Others will await a cue from you that involves something like clicking on a tab or button that says "Update," "Run Screen," or "Apply Tests."

Voilà! You are now ready to start building screens using any program you find.

ADDITIONAL FEATURES

The heart of any screening application is its ability to create worthwhile tests and produce lists of stocks that pass muster in all regards. There also are other kinds of features that can, if included in a program, make it much more usable.

Storing Your Screens

It seems logical that once you create a screen, you ought to be able to store it for future use. Some data items (such as share prices or analyst estimates) change daily, and the longest data shelf life you'll encounter (company financials) is only three months. So you can usually assume the same screen will produce different stocks when you rerun it later on.

Despite this, there are some applications that do not let you save your screens. So don't take the existence of this feature for granted. If you encounter a new screener, check to see if storage is available.

Displaying Results

One way or another, all screeners show you the companies that pass your screen in a format that looks like a spreadsheet. Each company has its own row. Each column shows a different data item.

The programs differ in terms of what data items you see. But most allow you to set your own preferences. In some cases, you'll be allowed to choose from among several prepackaged column sets. Other programs give you the freedom to select which data items (from among those included in the screening database) you'd like to include in the presentation. And often you'll be allowed to sort the results on the column(s) of your choice.

Export/Import

The Multex screeners, Stock Investor Pro, ProSearch, SmartMoneySelect .com, and MSN.Money allow you to export the spreadsheet-like display of the screen's results into a text and/or spreadsheet file. This is a very powerful feature. Once you convert your display into spreadsheet format, you have all the functionality of Microsoft Excel (and compatible spreadsheet programs) available to you for advanced analysis of your results. This will be covered in Chapter 8.

The Multex screeners and Stock Investor Pro also allow you to import data. This can be invaluable to power users. For example, you might like Stock Investor Pro's historical or relative variables but be reluctant to rely too heavily on the program because the data is updated no better than once per week. Export/import functionality provides a solution. You can use Stock Investor Pro to screen on the fanciest company-data variables (which are less likely to be stale, since companies report results only once every three months), and export large result sets (containing, perhaps, several hundred companies) into a spreadsheet file. Then you can import the tickers into a Multex screener (a procedure that requires no more than copying the ticker column from the spreadsheet into your clipboard and then pasting it into the Multex screener "user-portfolio" area). Then, using one of the latter programs, both of which are updated daily, you could create detailed screens based entirely on fast-changing data (price, valuation, analyst estimates, etc.). This latter screen would be run not against the complete group of 9,000 to 10,000 companies, but only against the smaller number of tickers (say, a few hundred) you imported from Stock Investor Pro.

In real life, the export/import procedure isn't nearly as cumbersome as it might sound. And it allows you to benefit from the best characteristics available in separate applications, each of which is powerful in its own right. Ultimately, you can wind up with breathtaking screening power for a surprisingly and pleasingly moderate price. Stay alert to future trends in screening software. If more programs add export/import capability, your opportunities to mix and match screeners will broaden.

Another way to use export/import is to combine tickers from several screens into one master list. That can be imported back into the program. Then, you can create broader screens to seek the best of the best. This process will be described more fully in Chapter 9.

6

The Building Blocks:
Creating Screening Tests

Each screener you encounter will be unique in terms of user interface and the tests you can use. Chapter 5 provided broad overviews of how to make sense of any program. This chapter will discuss the types of data categories and items that are generally available and provide suggestions as to the kinds of tests you can create. Then, Chapter 7 will show you how to organize this multitude of options and create screens with the right number and kinds of tests.

It's likely you will be very familiar with all the financial concepts covered here. But familiarity ought not cause you to take this material lightly. If you've ever returned to a place where you hadn't been in a long time (your old college, your childhood home), you've seen how the passage of time and a new perspective gained through experience can help you perceive old things in a completely new way. The same is true with ideas. You may have learned about such concepts as margin, current ratio, or asset turnover a long time ago. But they may not have stayed in the forefront of your investment process, given the extreme attention paid nowadays to near-term sales/EPS comparisons, surprises, and estimate revisions. What's more, you probably learned these concepts with the idea that you would use them to analyze situations that had, one way or another, already come to your attention (a Step 2 activity). But now we're doing something that, to many, is very novel. We're using these basic concepts to drive Step 1 (Find).

The Trojan Horse   Strictly speaking, this chapter is designed to help you create insightful screens. But effective screening goes hand in hand with a solid understanding of how to recognize data-oriented trends and relationships that signal attractive investment opportunities. When you screen, you work with a small number of trends or relationships. But all the concepts presented now, whether or not you actually use them in a screen, are relevant to, and serve as the meat of, what we'll do in Step 2 (Analyze). So this chapter really has a dual purpose: one, to stimulate screening ideas, and two, to describe what you'll consider in the Analyze phase as you review data presentations. Keep this in mind as you look at the sample screening tests. Even if you are working with a screener that can't accommodate a particular test (a common occurrence since no single application can handle everything), you can and still should consider these matters when you look at data presentations in Step 2.

Housekeeping   The sample tests will not be tied to the conventions of any specific screener. Instead, they'll be presented in a general plain-English adaptation of the Multex screening terminology. You will easily be able to adapt this terminology to any program you use. Comparative relationships are expressed using the following standard symbols:

=	Equal to
<>	Not equal to
>	Greater than
>=	Greater than or equal to
<	Less than
<=	Less than or equal to
/	Divided by
*	Multiplied by

As mentioned in Chapter 5, most screeners enhance user convenience by grouping similar tests under broad category headings. We'll do likewise here, and focus separately on each of the following categories:

Top-Down Themes
Growth Rates
Company Quality
Analyst Expectations
Sentiment
Valuation
Price/Volume/Technical Analysis
Proprietary Analytics

Different screeners have different category classifications. But these will provide a representative idea of what's out there and will help you navigate your way through your chosen screener.

Methodology   There's a lot of material in this chapter. You'll get the most from it if you approach it strategically.

- Read all the way through the material, focusing primarily on the general concepts and little, if at all, on the sample screening tests. Stick with this even if you quickly see that your screener(s) won't allow you to replicate the specific tests. Even in the latter case, these concepts will still help you see what to look for in Step 2 (Analyze).
- Look generally at all the screeners you have access to. Decide which one(s) you'll work mainly with, at least at first.
- Come back to this chapter and reread one category, this time in detail. Now, look closely at the sample tests and see which ones you can create with your chosen screener(s).
- Create some single-category screens and save them. In other words, you might create a Growth Rates category screen called Growth1 consisting of four growth tests. You may then create another one called Growth2 consisting of different combinations of growth tests. Perhaps there will even be a Growth3 screen, and more.
- Repeat the preceding step for each of the other categories.

You won't actually use these practice screens to pick stocks. At this point, your goal is to become comfortable with the screening application(s) you plan to use. And you're developing a good understanding of how to translate your personal investment ideas into screening tests. Once you've gone through this process, you'll be ready to move to Chapter 7, where you'll learn how to combine tests from different categories to create the kinds of screens you will use to compile evaluation lists, or how to evaluate preset screens to determine whether they are right for you.

TOP-DOWN THEMES

This group of tests lets you combine thematic and screen-based approaches to compiling your evaluation lists. Most programs allow you to impose minimum and/or maximum thresholds for market capitalization. You can also narrow your results to companies that are in sectors and/or industries of your choice. Some screens let you selectively eliminate certain sectors and industries. For example, one who is averse to technology might include the following test in a screen.

Sector <> Technology

Be careful about using industry or sector classification. Often, you'll not want to confine yourself to a single industry or sector but would prefer to mix and match. For example, if you are interested in retailing, you might want to eliminate department and mass discount stores and focus on various specialty retail chains such as those in apparel or consumer technology. Or you might want to focus on a broad mix of new-economy categories that include the technology sector and some industries drawn from elsewhere, such as biotech (health care sector) and communication services (services sector). Most screeners will not allow you to mix and match, but will instead force you to choose between taking one specific industry or all industries.

If you want to refine sector/industry themes this way, you have two choices. One is to limit yourself to applications that permit you to mix and match, such as Multex or Quicken screeners. You can also do this with Stock Investor Pro if you feel comfortable using that application's features relating to parenthetical statements and its "OR" capabilities. As an alternative, you can create general screens, include the industry as a display-only item, and visually scan for stocks in industries or sectors that appeal to you, or you can download your results to a spreadsheet and sort based on industry.

GROWTH RATES

Growth, a key reason why one would choose stocks over bonds, is a conspicuous category in just about any screener. Even though we know the past isn't necessarily predictive of what's likely to occur in the future, it is acceptable to use historical data as a starting point. Note that most of the discussion and examples in this section focus on EPS growth. You can create similar tests using sales growth and, if permitted by your screener, net income growth, cash flow growth, and so on.

Life Cycle Considerations

There appears to be infinite variation among all the living human bodies that at present exist on earth. Nevertheless, each is programmed, so to speak, to exhibit various growth and decline characteristics based on the life-cycle progression from birth to maturity to death. The same is true of business entities. Generally, the early part of the business life cycle features small size and very robust rates of growth (similar to humans). As the company progresses toward maturity and gets bigger, growth rates decelerate toward some sort of normal level. There are three classes of normalcy: (1) a growth rate that is more or less stable (neither accelerating nor decelerating to any marked degree) at a pace above the peer company (i.e., industry) average; (2) a growth rate that is generally stable near the peer average; and (3) a growth rate that stabilizes at a point below the peer average. Some companies pass step-by-step through all stages. Others show just one or two kinds of stability before moving on to the final phase, decelerating growth caused by the declining phase of the life cycle (e.g., the one-time market-leading buggy whip manufacturer).

Investors tend to favor companies experiencing acceleration or the top class of normalcy. The other phases of normalcy are acceptable to conservative investors who are willing to forfeit potential growth in exchange for reduced stock valuation risk and/or dividend income. If a company in decline is favored, it's usually seen as a "special situation" (e.g., the potential value of assets that could be sold, or the possibility the company may reorient its business and shift back to a more favorable life cycle phase).

Always be aware of life cycle considerations when screening based on growth. If you are an aggressive investor seeking rapidly growing companies, a simple number-based test (e.g., an EPS growth rate equal to or above 30 percent) might not work as you expect. Many who use such tests don't realize that for many companies, 30 percent growth could represent a point on a path of deceleration that, for example, was at 50 percent in the recent past and is in the process of slowing to 15 to 20 percent. The latter range could still be considered pretty good, but not if you assumed 30 percent and bought based on stock valuation metrics reflecting that assumption.

Here are four approaches to creating growth tests based on proper consideration of the business life cycle.

Thoughtful Aggression　　If you seek young companies that are likely to still be in acceleration mode (and you accept the risks inherent in so doing), ask your screen to search for exactly that kind of company. The following trio of numerical tests combines to do just that.

5 Year EPS Growth >= 20
3 Year EPS Growth >= 25
Trailing 12 Month EPS Growth >= 30

This is a good example of why numeric tests are of limited value. When seen as "floor" values, the acceleration theme is correctly expressed. But this screen would accept a company whose growth rate is decelerating from 60 percent to 50 percent to 35 percent, a pattern that is the opposite of what we really want. So I prefer to use the comparative approach:

Trailing 12 Month EPS Growth > 3 Year Annual EPS Growth
3 Year EPS Growth > 5 Year EPS Growth

Then, if you wish, you can establish a minimum threshold by adding a numerical test.

Trailing 12 Month EPS Growth > 3 Year EPS Growth
3 Year EPS Growth > 5 Year EPS Growth
5 Year EPS Growth >= 20

Finally, you can really swing for the fences with screeners such as the Multex applications or Stock Investor Pro that allow you to add multiplication factors:

Trailing 12 Month EPS Growth > (3 Year EPS Growth) * 1.3
3 Year EPS Growth > (5 Year EPS Growth) * 1.3

This means that the trailing 12-month growth rate must be at least 30 percent greater than the three-year growth rate and that the three-year growth rate must be at least 30 percent greater than the five-year rate. If you used a 15 percent five-year rate as a floor, the three-year rate would have to be at least 19.5 percent and the trailing 12-month rate would have to be at least 25.4 percent.

Note: Negative growth rates occur frequently. Be sure to take the appropriate safeguard, as described in Chapter 5, to protect your screen from accidentally collecting companies with growth rates that are worse than the negative historical base.

Measured Deceleration This theme doesn't sound sexy at first glance, but it can produce a large number of companies that combine still-attractive growth rates with risk levels that are reasonable by growth-investor standards. Do this by combining a high floor with a pattern of deceleration. Here's an example.

3 Year EPS Growth <= (5 Year EPS Growth) * .85
3 Year EPS Growth >= 25
Trailing 12 Month EPS Growth >= 20

The second and third tests are self-evident. The first is a requirement that the three-year growth rate be no higher than 85 percent of the five-year rate. If the five-year rate was 35 percent, the three-year rate cannot exceed 29.8 percent.

The benefit of this theme is that when deceleration is conspicuous, there's a good chance the market has noticed and that the stock's valuation metrics are realistically related to the company's proper life cycle status. You'll want to verify this with one or more tests from the Valuation category and/or by extra attentiveness to valuation when you reach Step 2 (Analyze). Ultimately, most growth investors would be quite happy to find realistically valued shares of companies growing above 20 percent (or even 30 percent; remember that the 20 percent and 25 percent numbers in the preceding example are floors, and there's no limit as to how high the five-year growth ceiling can go).

Basic Stability　　The easiest way to screen for companies in the stable portion of their life cycles is to use one or more numeric tests and establish thresholds at moderate levels you believe can be sustained for prolonged periods. Here's an example:

3 Year EPS Growth >= 8
Trailing 12 Month EPS Growth >= 8

Again, it's important to remember that the numbers represent floors. You can add ceilings if you wish. But I don't recommend doing that. I'd rather filter out the risky highfliers with other tests relating to valuation, company quality, or financial strength. And if, after doing that, some high-growth companies still appear on the screen, that's okay. One of the beauties of the screening process is that it allows you to establish basic thresholds of acceptability while still allowing for the possibility of finding stocks that offer much more than you originally sought.

Rational Expectations　　Nowadays, many investors are hyperattentive to analyst expectations. Unfortunately, too many are too quick to forget that expectations are just that—expectations. You will not be happy to wind up buying shares of a company based on a consensus 20 percent growth forecast if it turns out that the company delivers only 6 percent. Attention to the business life cycle can go a long way toward helping you assess the credibility of growth forecasts.

Learn to envision a red flag whenever analysts predict the company will achieve a rate of growth that seems inconsistent with what you might expect based on life cycle considerations alone. An example would be a forecast of 20 percent annual EPS growth over the next three to five years for a mature company that has grown at single-digit rates for the past five years. Such rejuvenation does happen from time to time. It can come from the invention of new product categories, from acquisitions, and so on that give the firm another run at the upward portion of the life cycle. But this is not an everyday occurrence. Impose a burden of proof on whoever is advocating such a scenario. Beyond that, you can screen based on the match between projections and life cycles. Here is a basic example that filters out analyst projections calling for more growth than the company, over the past five years, has demonstrated it can achieve.

Forecasted Long-Term EPS Growth <= 5 Year EPS Growth

If you are inclined to give analysts some latitude in the screening process and defer close attention to the issue to Step 2 (Analyze), you might want to add a forecast cushion.

Forecasted Long-Term EPS Growth <= (3 Year EPS Growth) * 1.25

For a company that has achieved a five-year annual average EPS growth rate of 12 percent, the screen would accept without question a projected three- to five-year growth rate as high as 15 percent.

The negative-number multiplication-factor distortion is not likely to be troublesome here, since as a matter of professional custom analysts generally don't forecast negative growth rates for the long term.

Comparative Growth

If you use a screener like the Multex premium application, Stock Investor Pro, or SmartMoneySelect.com, you will have considerable opportunity to create tests based on benchmark comparisons. Most of Multex's comparisons are to industry averages. Stock Investor Pro offers comparisons to industry and sector means as well as universal medians. (Universal refers to all companies in the screening database. The median is the number in the middle of a highest-to-lowest sort.) The SmartMoneySelect.com screener uses a relative strength approach. It allows you to specify a growth rate in the top 50 percent (or any other percentage) when compared to other companies in the same industry or sector, the data universe, or one of three major market indexes. (The screener also allows you to seek companies in the bottom 50 percent or any other percentage of a specified peer group.)

If you have an opportunity to use comparative tests, I expect you'll come to prefer this approach as I do. Comparing growth rates to benchmark averages spares you the burden of trying to come up with a numeric threshold that's high enough to weed out unappealing companies, yet not so high as to eliminate reasonably valued strong outfits that are no longer in the first, highest-growth stage of their respective life cycles. My favorite benchmark is the industry average. Any above-industry-average comparison justifies a favorable presumption, since you know the company has been accomplishing something many similar firms could not achieve. Comparative growth tests can be adjusted to accommodate whatever life cycle preferences you might have.

The following test calling for a growth rate that's double the industry average is for the high-growth phase of the life cycle:

3 Year EPS Growth > (3 Year Industry Average EPS Growth) * 2

If your screener uses a relative strength approach, you could phrase the test as follows:

3 Year EPS Growth in Top 20% within Industry

The following tests are alternative ways to accommodate better companies within the normal phase of the life cycle.

3 Year EPS Growth > 3 Year Industry Average EPS Growth

3 Year EPS Growth in Top 50% within Industry

The following pair of tests combines to establish a 15 percent zone of acceptability above and below the industry average. They might be of interest to a more conservative investor who wishes to avoid the hottest growth companies (whose shares presumably command the hottest valuation metrics) and who intends to combine growth with other kinds of tests to identify quality companies in all classes within the stable zone.

3 Year EPS Growth >= (3 Year Industry Average EPS Growth) * .85
3 Year EPS Growth <= (3 Year Industry Average EPS Growth) * 1.15

Remember when using multiplication factors to add the negative number safeguards described in Chapter 5.

Using the SmartMoneySelect.com relative strength approach, the tests could look like this:

3 Year EPS Growth in Top 65% within Industry
3 Year EPS Growth in Bottom 65% within Industry

Here, one test starts measuring downward from the top and the other starts measuring upward from the bottom. Each one overshoots the 50 percent midpoint by 15 percentage points. The only companies that pass will be those whose relative strength is within 15 percentage points, either way, of the midpoint.

Line-Item Comparisons

Most investors focus on EPS growth, since that's the measure most directly linked to share price performance. But there are periods when EPS growth outpaces sales growth. You can screen for them numerically:

3 Year Sales Growth >= 15
3 Year EPS Growth >= 20

I prefer to screen this relationship comparatively:

3 Year EPS Growth > 3 Year Sales Growth

At first glance, tests such as these seem very desirable. If earnings are growing more quickly than sales, that means margins are expanding, a state of affairs investors like to see. That is, indeed, a good thing if a growing sales base is allowing fixed costs to be spread over a greater number of products, thereby lessening the per-unit cost of each individual item.

But sometimes margins go up even though sales growth is stagnant because the company finds ways to cut costs. We all like the idea of companies becoming more efficient (producing more goods than in the past using the same amount of resources). But there's a limit to how long efficiency gains can persist. The following sample test calls for the sales growth rate to be at least 90 percent of the EPS growth rate:

3 Year Sales Growth >= (3 Year EPS Growth) * .9

If you seek income, you can screen for similar line-item comparisons involving dividends per share and EPS (the former cannot continue indefinitely to outpace the latter). And if your screener allows you to compare sales growth to growth in capital spending, think about adding it to a screen that has sales growth as an important theme. There's usually a relationship between the value of a company's assets and the amount of sales that those assets can generate. A rate of sales growth that exceeds the rate of capital spending growth might indicate that a company is finding new ways to generate more sales from the existing plant. But it could also mean that capacity is getting tight and that big capital spending increases are around the corner. When you create a screening test, look for a long-term capital spending growth rate that's at least close to the comparable-period rate of sales growth.

It's tempting to assume you can do the same thing using the relative strength approach by creating a pair of tests that looks like this:

3 Year EPS Growth in Top 50% within Industry
3 Year Sales Growth in Top 25% within Industry

But bear in mind these tests establish floors, not ceilings. You could wind up with a company whose sales relative strength position is in the top 20 percent but whose EPS growth is superior and in the top 10 percent. Even so, if your screener offers only the relative strength approach, it may be worthwhile to use this pair of tests and rely on Step 2 (Analyze) to finalize the list of firms with superior sales growth trends.

COMPANY QUALITY

The ultimate measure of company quality is return on invested capital, which shows how much profit a company can generate from a given amount of resources. Financial theorists cherish this concept because it facilitates comparison between risky businesses and risk-free investment alternatives (government securities). Academicians have built quantitative models that allow them to specify how risky a particular business is and calculate whether the return generated by the business is enough to compensate the shareholders for the amount of risk they assume when they bypass Treasury securities.

There's another angle that may appeal to the growth orientation most investors have. Simply put, companies that have strong returns have more capacity, so to speak, to generate future EPS growth. Suppose Company A and Company B each started year 1 with $100 million in capital, and during the year each had net profit of $10 million, or a 10 percent return on equity (ROE). Assuming there are no dividends, each enters year 2 with a capital base of $110 million. Suppose Company A's

ROE is trending upward; in year 0 its ROE was 8 percent, and in year 2 it is likely to have a 12 percent ROE. If that's the case, we can assume year 2 net income will be $13.2 million (12 percent of $110 million), representing a one-year growth rate equal to 32 percent. Now, assume Company B's ROE is trending lower. In year 0 it was 12 percent, and in year 2 it is likely to be 8 percent. In that case, we'll project year 2 profits at $8.8 million (8 percent of the new $110 million capital base), a 12 percent year-to-year decline.

You might argue that it's just as hard to forecast next year's ROE as it would be to forecast EPS. But here's the catch: ROE measures asset utilization talents of a management team. To gauge the impact, suppose analysts forecast 15 percent annual long-term EPS growth for Company X and Company Y, each of which has $100 million in equity capital. If the long-term average ROE for Company X is 15 percent, while Company Y has a 6 percent long-term ROE, you'd have every right to be skeptical about the credibility of the projection for Y. The latter may need a large capital infusion. At the very least, you'd want to see some evidence that its management is about to allocate resources far more efficiently than they've done to date.

So in a practical real-world sense, ROE, especially long-term average ROE figures, can help you assess the credibility of specific growth forecasts. Or it can support a more open-ended assumption to the effect that Company X has a better chance of generating superior earnings growth in the future than does Company Y.

Actually, ROE is only one of three ways to measure corporate return on capital. Investors can screen on any or all of them. Moreover, investors can screen on margin and turnover, the key fundamentals that combine to determine overall return, as well as financial strength. There are various kinds of data items within each of these categories.

In the Company Quality category, defining attractive relationships and building them into the screens is relatively easy. The challenge is to decide which of the numerous data items you should emphasize. It's important that you prioritize, since it's rare that you'll find a company that looks good in every category. That is generally the reverse of the situation we had when dealing with the Growth Rates category. There, it was generally easy to decide which data items to consider (primarily EPS growth, secondarily sales growth, and beyond that cash flow growth and so on if available in the screener you're using). The challenge was to decide what sort of growth trends are most compatible with your investment style and, hence, which ones belong in your screen.

Building Company-Quality Screening Tests

We'll start with a discussion of the basic screening tests you can apply to whichever data item(s) you select. The examples presented here will use a generic return test. The principles presented will be applicable to all varieties of return on capital as well as the other company quality data items. The examples will use the return for the trailing 12-month (TTM) period. If your screener allows, you can also create similar tests covering historical periods (such as five-year averages).

Basic Numeric Test The following test is a simple requirement that the trailing 12-month (TTM) return meet or exceed a particular numeric threshold:

TTM Return >= 15

The advantage of such a test is that the test is easy to use and can be applied in most screeners. The disadvantage lies in the fact that it's hard to pick a numeric threshold that works for a large cross section of companies in different kinds of businesses in different market environments. You can get some guidance regarding numeric thresholds by retrieving comparison data for a particular company (such as can be found on the MultexInvestor.com ratio comparison reports). Check to see the average for the S&P 500. If you know you are interested in certain kinds of stocks (such as energy or technology), retrieve ratio comparison reports for companies in those groups and check the industry or sector average return.

Cross-Sectional Comparison Use tests such as the following, which finds companies whose TTM returns are above the average relative to their respective industries.

TTM Return > TTM Industry Average Return

If you want to be aggressive, you might consider adding a multiplication factor. The following test seeks companies whose returns exceed their respective industry averages by more than 15 percent.

TTM Return > (TTM Industry Average Return) * 1.15

While it's standard for screening databases to show negative growth rates just as easily as positive ones, the various categories of company return are tricky. Some applications eliminate below-zero return numbers and simply label them NM (not meaningful). But others do pick up negative numbers. If your application does that, you should add to the preceding test another one requiring the base return to be above zero.

You can also go the other way and add a conservative multiplication factor. The following test accepts any company whose TTM return is at least 90 percent as high as its industry average:

TTM Return >= (TTM Industry Average Return) * .9

The rationale for this approach is flexibility. If you refrain from demanding that the company excel in every area, you open your screen to inclusion of a bigger variety of company quality indicators. You may find that you prefer companies that are more or less okay, even if not spectacular, in a large number of items to those that may be outstanding in one or two but weak in the rest.

If your screener uses a relative strength approach, you can accomplish the comparison through a test that looks like this:

TTM Return in Top 50% within Industry

Adjust the percentage higher or lower depending on how aggressive or conservative you want to be.

Time Series Comparison   Here you compare recent data to historic information. You are seeking companies that demonstrate improvement. A basic example would look like this:

TTM Return > 5 Year Average Return

As was the case with the preceding cross-sectional comparison, you can add a multiplication factor above 1.00 if you wish to take an aggressive stance or a factor below 1.00 if you prefer flexibility.

Double Comparison   This is a sophisticated test that will be available only on high-priced screeners such as the Multex premium application. It combines historic and cross-sectional comparisons to ask the following question: Is the company's time series comparison (recent data versus its own history) better or worse than that of the comparative benchmarks? Here's an example of what such a test would look like:

(TTM Return/5 Year Average Return) > (TTM Industry Average Re-
turn/5 Year Industry Average Return)

Companies will pass this test if one of the following is true:

- The company is improving over time while the industry average is deteriorating.
- The company is improving over time to a greater extent than the industry average.
- The company is deteriorating to a lesser extent than the industry average.

As noted, free or low-priced screeners cannot accommodate such a test.
But remember the Trojan horse. All the concepts in this chapter are crucial
to Step 2 (Analyze). Whether or not you can screen based on a double
comparison, you should certainly examine a relationship like this while
you are analyzing a company (on MultexInvestor.com, all the information
you'll need is on the ratio comparison report).

SmartMoneySelect.com offers an interesting variation on this theme
for its margin variables.

% Change Margin in Top 50% within Industry

First the program computes the percentage change in the margin from the
five-year average to the TTM period. Then the test selects companies
whose percentages rank in the top half relative to industry peers.

Once you're comfortable with the differences between basic numeric,
cross-sectional, and time series testing, you can apply them to whichever
company quality indicators you prefer. Ideally, you'd like to use all the data
items. But as a matter of practical reality, if you want to have a reasonable
number of stocks pass your screen you'll have to limit yourself to just a
few. And during Step 2 (Analyze), you'll have to decide which core fundamentals are most important, lest you wind up rejecting every company you
see. (Chapter 10 will introduce concepts that will help you prioritize.) Let's
turn now to the individual data items.

Returns on Capital

The definitions used here are those of MultexInvestor.com. There's likely to
be some variation from site to site, so check the glossaries. But all the defi-

nitions will be sufficiently close to allow you to assume the same sort of investment significance.

Return on equity (ROE) is the most widely known measure of corporate return. The formula is net income divided by shareholder equity. If you put $100 million into a business that generates $10 million in net profit, ROE is 10 percent.

Return on investment (ROI) is net income divided by total investment (defined as long-term debt, other long-term liabilities, plus equity). This shows how much return the business earns on all capital—that which is owned by the shareholders and that which is contributed by long-term creditors. Assume you put $100 million of your own money into a business and decide to supplement your funds with $50 million in long-term debt. Net profit is $15 million. As in the preceding example, the business earns a 10 percent return on the capital at its disposal—in this case $150 million.

Notice the difference in the two examples. The first time, all the capital consisted of equity, so ROE and ROI would both equal 10 percent. In the second example, some capital is equity and some is long-term debt. The 10 percent return applies to this entire capital base and is the ROI. Look what's happened, however, to ROE. Dividing a $15 million net profit by $100 million in equity gives us a leveraged-up ROE of 15 percent.

This creates an interesting screening choice. ROE and ROI sound similar, but they tell us very different things. ROI measures the performance of the bread-and-butter business and allows you to make direct comparisons between two companies that are in similar businesses but have very different balance sheets. With ROE, you are comparing the effectiveness of complete corporate entities, each of which combines the bread-and-butter business and management's financing strategies.

When I screen, I prefer to use ROI whenever the screener gives me that option. I know that a test calling for ROI to be above the industry average will filter out companies I really don't want to see—companies that are lackluster in the day-to-day operation of the business. I can't say the same about a cross-sectional ROE comparison. The latter would block companies that are superior in terms of the business but have more conservative balance sheets—companies that combine above-average return with below-average risk. It's possible that a company may be too conservative. For example, an excessive aversion to debt may prevent the firm from pursuing attractive growth opportunities. But when I'm prospecting for ideas in Step 1 (Find), I try to aim for maximum return and minimal risk. I prefer to tackle subtle issues such as excess conservatism as part of Step 2 (Analyze).

There is a third category, return on assets (ROA), which is net income divided by total assets. Assume a business uses $100 million of owners' capital and $50 million of long-term debt. Also, the company, in the course of its day-to-day operations, usually has about $20 million of funds that it needs to pay to trade vendors within 60 days. By the time that money is paid, the company will have accumulated another $20 million, more or less, in accounts payable that will be paid 60 days further into the future. On a full-year basis, the company has, on average, $20 million of this short-term money available to it. Assuming profit is $15 million, we know ROI is 10 percent. ROA is 8.8 percent ($15 million in net income divided by $170 million in total assets). ROA comparisons tend to more or less track ROI. I use ROA mainly as a backup in the event a particular screener doesn't feature ROI.

Margins

The basic definition of margin is easy: the amount of each sales dollar that is left over after subtracting costs. The challenge is to decide which categories of cost, and which type of margin, are most relevant to you. Net margin, the percent of each sales dollar that has been brought to the bottom line after subtracting all costs, is the one that would be used if you wish to replicate standard calculations of EPS or return on capital. But for screening, the agenda isn't necessarily the same, so you can't automatically assume net margin is the most useful.

When you screen, you are searching a database for clues that lead to attractive investment opportunities, footprints of company quality. For this purpose, it is often more productive to identify smaller components of corporate performance, noting distinctions between operation of the day-to-day business and other noncore corporate strategies and agendas. Key noncore considerations that impact certain kinds of margin include financing strategies (interest expense), investment activity (such as gains/losses from asset transactions or nonoperating investment income), unusual situations (plant closing costs, litigation expenses, and awards), and strategies that impact the tax rate.

I prefer to screen the business-oriented components. If a company fares well here, I'll assess noncore issues case by case in Step 2 (Analyze). If a company is weak in its core day-to-day business and my goal is to screen based on fundamental excellence, there's little chance I'll be willing to add the company to my evaluation list based on noncore factors.

Gross margin (sales minus direct costs, often referred to as cost of goods sold), operating margin (sales minus direct costs and overhead), and EBITD (earnings before interest, taxes, and depreciation) margin are the main business-oriented margins. (Check web site glossaries since different sites have different specific definitions.) Generally speaking, I'd be willing to screen using any of these that are offered by the screener with which I work.

If my screener allows me to choose among them, EBITD margin is my lowest preference. That's because I'm not completely comfortable eliminating depreciation from my assessment of business performance. True depreciation is a noncash charge against income. But it is often a useful proxy for routine plant-related expenditures that are classified as capital spending and therefore aren't recognized on the income statement.

Between gross margin and operating margin, I prefer using the latter because it allows me to be more confident in comparing one company to another. That's because there is room for discretion when companies decide whether certain types of costs should be considered direct costs or overhead. An example is a recent controversy involving strong gross margins reported by Amazon.com. Critics of the company objected to its having classified shipping costs as overhead and argued that gross margin would look much worse if these costs were acknowledged as direct costs and accounted for in the gross margin calculation. Focusing on operating margin spared me from dealing with this controversy. Whether shipping costs are considered direct costs or overhead, they are accounted for in the operating margin, and Amazon.com showed extremely poor results here. My aversion to dealing with such controversies isn't based on lack of confidence in my ability to properly assess the issues. The real problem is visibility. You're often likely to be unaware of such issues when you screen large numbers of companies, most of which don't attract nearly as much media attention as Amazon.com.

Pretax and net margins are often seen as interchangeable if you seek to analyze the entire company (core plus noncore factors). But one way or another, you should stay sensitive to unusually low tax rates caused by issues that aren't likely to persist over time, such as carryforwards from prior years' losses that will eventually be exhausted. When the tax rate moves toward a more normal level, EPS may decline even if the business fundamentals are improving. You can address this by screening based on pretax margin. And some screeners allow you to create a test based on the tax rate, in which case you might consider including a requirement that the tax rate be in line with the industry average or above a basic threshold such as 25 percent or 30 percent. Alternatively, you can omit tax rate from your screens and make a habit of checking for oddities when you reach Step 2 (Analyze).

Turnover

Asset turnover (defined as revenues for the railing 12-month period divided by average assets for that interval) tells you how quickly the company is converting its physical asset base into sales. This concept is important from a theoretical standpoint (it's used in standard calculations of return on capital). But many find it hard to visualize in the real world.

Still, its importance goes way beyond theory. Turnover is the antithesis of margin. Hence it's possible for a company with very low margins to have high returns on capital (and be considered excellent from a standpoint of company quality) if asset turnover is high. Since many investors and much of the financial media are more attuned to margin than to turnover, powerful turnover-oriented companies are less likely to be appreciated, and their stocks may be more modestly valued. Don't assume you'd have to hold indefinitely until the world comes to appreciate turnover. Strong turnover leads to strong returns on capital, which in turn indicates a capacity to generate good EPS growth in the future, and that's what the market will notice.

Be willing to screen based on asset turnover, if your screener incorporates it, even though it's a bottom-line item that, like the net margin and return on equity concepts, reflects a mixture of core day-to-day business with noncore corporate agendas. The opportunistic benefits of asset turnover can make it worth your while to tolerate this sort of mixture.

If you would like to focus more sharply on day-to-day business, some screeners allow you to focus on the specialized kinds of turnover: receivables turnover (trailing 12-month revenues divided by average annual accounts receivable) and inventory turnover (trailing 12-month cost of goods sold divided by average annual inventory).

Occasionally you'll find a screener that lets you create tests based on revenue or net income per employee. Such ratios are not really components of standard corporate quality calculations, but they are conceptually compatible with turnover in that they do provide some indication of efficiency. But be careful about how you use such data. Industries differ in terms of labor intensity versus capital intensity, and neither is inherently good or bad. Don't create numeric tests based on employee ratios. If your screener won't let you create cross-sectional or time series comparisons, you're better off bypassing these variables.

Financial Strength

This is an area that requires particular sensitivity to the need for comparative analysis. The amount of debt a company can comfortably carry and the amount of working capital it needs depend on the level and stability of cash flows, something that can vary widely from one industry to another. Investors who impose numerical limits on such ratios (avoiding companies with debt ratios above or liquidity ratios below a certain target) wind up limiting the range of opportunities they consider without gaining nearly as much, in terms of risk protection, as they believe they are getting. If your screener does not permit you to create cross-sectional (or at least time series) comparisons, keep financial strength ratios off your screen and limit your consideration of them to Step 2 (Analyze).

Debt Many investors regard debt ratios as key indicators of corporate risk. Most screeners have variables based on debt-to-equity ratios. If the ratio is 1.00, that means the company's debt and equity are equal. Sometimes, though, you might see a debt-to-capital ratio. If debt and equity are equal, the debt-to-capital ratio is .50 since debt comprises 50 percent of total capital. Before you screen, double-check to make sure which ratio your program is using.

Some screeners allow you to consider ratios based on long-term debt (due more than a year hence) or total debt. Typically screeners opt for long-term debt, since this is usually considered a permanent part of the company's capital structure. But don't underestimate the valuable insights you can gain from looking at total debt, if not during Step 1 (Find), at least during Step 2 (Analyze). Total debt ratios that are unusually large (based on cross-sectional or time series comparisons) can signal trouble. Inventories may be piling up (meaning the company isn't getting cash fast enough to maintain its usual schedule for pay-down of temporary trade borrowings). Or a struggling company may be using preexisting lines of credit to offset an operating cash drain or because it is having trouble raising new permanent capital that it really needs.

Here's a test similar to the double-comparison format you can create in the Multex premium screener that lets you screen out companies that may be overly aggressive in their use of short-term debt. If you use a different screener, you can look at this data relationship when you go through Step 2 (Analyze).

(Total Debt Ratio/Long-Term Debt Ratio)/(Industry Average Total Debt Ratio/Industry Average Long-Term Debt Ratio) <= 1.00

This compares a company's total debt ratio to its long-term debt ratio, and then does likewise for industry averages. You can screen out results above 1.00, or you can create a cushion like this:

(Total Debt Ratio/Long-Term Debt Ratio)/(Industry Average Total
Debt Ratio/Industry Average Long-Term Debt Ratio) <= 1.25

Needless to say, if you're especially conservative you could use a smaller
cushion (perhaps setting the base at .75) to identify firms that are significantly less aggressive in their use of short-term debt.

Some screeners let you analyze debt by looking directly at how much
borrowing the company can handle given the cash it generates. You can do
that by examining interest coverage ratios (trailing 12-month pretax income divided by interest expense incurred over that same period). If your
screener doesn't allow this, you can still examine it in Step 2 (Analyze). A
ratio of 1.25 means the company generated 25 percent more pretax income
than it needed to cover its annual interest expense obligation. During the
mid-1980s junk bond heyday, that sort of ratio was considered adequate.
A ratio of 2.00 was deemed excellent. But in the next few years, as businesses faltered (including a period of recession), the investment community
learned that 1.25 was not sufficient. Use cross-sectional comparison to determine what's acceptable for an individual company.

Liquidity   Many believe a heavy debt burden is the main sign of financial
danger. That's not necessarily so. As long as a company has or can quickly
obtain cash, it can continue to survive. But once liquidity drains, its ability
to survive depends entirely on accommodation from the outside world (an
infusion of new capital or creditors' willingness to relax or renegotiate debt
service obligations). So if safety is your concern, give liquidity at least as
much attention as you give to debt, if not more.

Current ratio (current assets divided by current liabilities) is the primary screening item dealing with liquidity and the one that is most likely
to be present in any screener you use. Some screeners also include the more
stringent quick ratio (cash and short-term investments divided by current
liabilities). Note that each kind of business is different in terms of what
sort of liquidity ratios are appropriate. Several industries, such as lodging,
utilities, restaurants, and airlines, have cash flow patterns that permit average current ratios below 1.00. So it is advisable to avoid using a numerical
test to screen for liquidity. Use screeners that permit cross-sectional and/or
time series comparisons, or confine your liquidity analysis to the company-
by-company examination you'll do in Step 2 (Analyze).

ANALYST EXPECTATIONS

In theory, stock prices are based on expectations about the future. And the
consensus expectations of professional securities analysts have come to

represent investment community expectations. Hence data summarizing analyst expectations (as reflected in earnings estimates and stock recommendations) is an important category in most screeners.

Analyst Coverage

The number of analysts covering a stock is an instance where numerical tests are reasonable. At the time of this writing, the average number of analysts covering a stock is five. But if we confine our inquiry to those stocks that are included in the S&P 500, the average number of analysts jumps to 15. You can use those as general benchmarks for tests requiring analyst coverage to be larger or smaller. Skimpy coverage can be good in the sense that it opens you to the possibility of finding stocks that are little-known gems. Conversely, a small number of analysts (one or two), especially for the smallest companies, spotlights the continuing controversy over the extent to which analyst opinion is impacted by investment banking relationships between the company and the analysts' firms (the firms' desire to get or retain this lucrative business). It's hard for very small companies to get coverage by analysts whose firms don't have such relationships.

Range of Estimates

Company investor relations executives work hard to keep the range of estimates as narrow as possible. So screening tests designed to identify narrow ranges may not be especially productive. However, a wide gap between high and low estimates can be noteworthy in a contrarian-style screen or a screen designed to alert you to potential sell opportunities. This is another place where it's reasonable to construct screens using numerical benchmarks. The following test, which measures the range between high and low estimates and seeks bigger than average spreads, is based on the average spread that existed at the time of this writing.

Current Year High Estimate/Current Year Low Estimate > 1.35

Standard deviation is another way to screen based on the range of estimates. To understand how standard deviation works, consider that the numbers 6.5, 8, and 9.5 average out to 8; so, too, do the numbers –7, 8, and 23. Note, though, that the ranges are very different. It's not necessary to go into the calculation details here (these are built-in functions in spreadsheet programs). Just note that the standard deviation of the first set of numbers is 1.5. The standard deviation of the second, more dispersed set, at 15, is much larger. In a big sample, about two-thirds of all observations will fall within one standard deviation above or below the average. The ratio between the standard deviation and the average is another way to quantify the extent of a distribution of numbers. Hence you can screen for a wide range of analyst estimates with a test like this:

> Current Year Standard Deviation/Current Year Consensus Estimate
> > 1.2

At the time of this writing, the average ratio was about 1.2.

Earnings Surprises

Traditionally, an earnings surprise (the gap between estimated EPS and the number that is ultimately reported by the company) was seen as indicative of the analyst's forecasting skill or lack thereof. But nowadays, with companies giving so much guidance to analysts, an earnings surprise is seen as a measurement of management's candor and/or forecasting skill. That's why stocks react so vigorously to surprises, especially on the down side.

Typically, one might create tests requiring any earnings surprise for the most recent quarter, and perhaps also for a few prior quarters, to be above zero. Contrarian screens might require a recent negative surprise (a requirement that surprise be less than zero).

But be careful about using earnings surprise data when business cycles are abruptly changing for better or worse and forecasts are subject to greater-than-usual revision. Under such circumstances, a database might show a 2 percent positive surprise for a company that reported $1.02 a share when analysts were expecting $1.00. But you won't want to draw favorable conclusions from this if, three weeks earlier, management issued a preannouncement urging analysts to lower a $1.50 consensus estimate to a range of $1.00 to $1.10.

Estimate Revision

Estimates are made to be changed. It's one thing to know that a present-day consensus estimate of next year's EPS is $1.75 and that analysts have been using this same $1.75 forecast as far back as four weeks ago. But if we were to learn that three months ago analysts thought the company would earn $2.35 next year, and that as recently as one month ago they were expecting results to come in at $2.00 a share, today's $1.75 estimate is seen in an entirely different light. Rather than focusing on the $1.75 estimate, it's more important to note the pattern of deteriorating expectations and wonder when it will stabilize and improve. Conversely, you'd feel very good about a $1.75 estimate if, four weeks ago, analysts were predicting $1.60.

The power of screening tests based on estimate revision is matched only by the ease with which they can be created. In bad times, you have to raise an eyebrow anytime a company can pass a test like this:

> Current Year Consensus Estimate >= Current Year Consensus Estimate 4 Weeks Ago

Here's an alternative:

> Upward Estimate Revisions Past 4 Weeks >= 0
> Downward Estimate Revisions Past 4 Weeks = 0

During normal or good portions of the business cycle, you can be more aggressive in your expectations. The following series of tests seeks a sustained pattern of rising estimates:

> Current Year Consensus Estimate > Current Year Consensus Estimate 4 Weeks Ago
> Current Year Consensus Estimate 4 Weeks Ago > Current Year Consensus Estimate 8 Weeks Ago
> Current Year Consensus Estimate 8 Weeks Ago > Current Year Consensus Estimate 13 Weeks Ago

Recommendations

As this is being written, there's considerable agitation over the scarcity of sell recommendations issued by analysts. Do yourself a favor and ignore it. Most Wall Street analysts serve institutional clients that, because of liquidity issues, simply cannot eliminate many large-capitalization stocks from their portfolios. For example, it's probably impractical for the manager of a large mutual fund to sell IBM shares even if he/she is bearish on the company. More likely, the position will be underweighted (the percent of the portfolio invested in IBM will be less than IBM's percentage weighting in the S&P 500). Members of the media contend that analysts avoid sell recommendations for fear of offending management. There's probably something to that. But they fail to mention that institutional clients get especially angry when analysts issue sell recommendations on shares they can't really eliminate.

If you want to make constructive use of analyst recommendations, learn to interpret them as you would if you were one of their institutional customers. Forget terminology such as strong buy, market performer, accumulate, neutral, and so on. Focus instead on the fact that there's a best-to-worst scale. For the sake of convenience, data providers supply their own labels for each of five levels. Multex uses the following best-to-worst terminology: Strong Buy, Buy, Hold, Underperform, and Sell. Learn the terminology of your screener, not for purposes of searching for your e-broker's strong buy (as opposed to regular buy) menu option, but to enable you to construct good tests based on recommendations.

Before you construct your tests, understand that, as a matter of industry ritual, analysts rarely use the bottom two rating categories. But they aren't the least bit shy about shifting their ratings up and down within the top three. When you screen, search for top-heavy ratings profiles. In an extreme sense, this could entail a series of tests requiring at least one strong buy rating and no ratings in any category below that. But a quest for best-case unanimity may cause you to lose out on interesting investment opportunities. Get used to the fact that there's going to be diversity of opinion, and be willing to accept a rating profile that generally shows more ratings as you move up the scale.

Here's an example from a screen I created using analyst bullishness as a primary theme.

> \# Sell Recommendations = 0
> \# Underperform Recommendations = 0
> \# Hold Recommendations = 0
> \# Buy Recommendations <= 3
> \# Strong Buy Recommendations >= 5
> \# Strong Buy Recommendations >= (# Buy Recommendations) + 5

Notice how I eliminate any possibility of seeing stocks with any ratings at all in the seldom-used bottom-two doomsday categories as well as in the third category, the one that's as bearish as analysts usually get. I'll take as many as three ratings in the second (Buy) category but want at least five in the top (Strong Buy) group. But I won't allow the top two to be as close as three Buys and five Strong Buys. The last line requires at least a five-rating gap between Buy and Strong Buy. So if there are three Buys, I need at least eight Strong Buys. If I have five Strong Buys, the minimum acceptable number, I leave no room for any Buy ratings.

SmartMoneySelect.com offers an interesting variation. That screener lets you create tests based on the percent of Strong Buy ratings (the number of Strong Buys as a percent of the total number of all ratings), the percent of Buy ratings, and so on. Such tests can be phrased in terms of Smart-MoneySelect.com's relative strength comparisons. The following group of tests can help you identify stocks that are strongly favored relative to others in their own industries.

% Strong Buy in Top 25% within Industry
% Buy in Top 25% within Industry
% Hold in Bottom 25% within Industry
% Sell = 0
% Strong Sell = 0

As this book was going to press, some brokerage firms have indicated a desire to simplify their ratings by moving to a three-part scale, generally labeled Buy, Hold, and Sell. Data aggregation services such as Multex will, of course, have to map these new ratings into appropriate places on the existing five-part scales. At present, it's hard to say how many firms will change their rating systems. But whatever happens, we're still likely to see some companies with more top-heavy ratings distributions than others and you'll continue to be able to screen for them in a manner similar to what is presented here.

Mean Rating

Often it's hard to decide whether one rating profile is more bullish than another. Are analysts more bullish on Stock A, with three Strong Buys and four Buys, than on Stock B, which has five Strong Buys, two Buys, and one Hold?

The mean rating reduces each profile to a specific numeric score that can easily be compared to others. This is a weighted average of all the individual ratings. The best possible score would be 1.00 (to achieve that, every analyst would have to rate the stock Strong Buy) and the worst possible score would be 5.00. Realistically, most mean ratings would fall between 1.00 and 3.00. Mean ratings for Stock A and Stock B are computed in Tables 6.1 and 6.2, and help us see that on the whole analysts are more bullish on Stock B.

There are two ways this can add value to your screens. First, it's easier to create a test requiring the mean rating score to be less than, say, 1.50, than it is to design appealing five-part rating profiles as illustrated in the

TABLE 6.1 Sample Mean Rating Calculation, Stock A

Category Name	Category Score	×	Number of Ratings	=	Category Total
Top (e.g., Strong Buy)	1	×	3	=	3
Second (e.g., Buy)	2	×	4	=	8
Middle (e.g., Hold)	3	×	0	=	0
Fourth (e.g., Underperform)	4	×	0	=	0
Worst (e.g., Sell)	5	×	0	=	0
Total			7		11

Mean rating = 11 divided by 7 = 1.57

TABLE 6.2 Sample Mean Rating Calculation, Stock B

Category Name	Category Score	×	Number of Ratings	=	Category Total
Top (e.g., Strong Buy)	1	×	5	=	5
Second (e.g., Buy)	2	×	2	=	4
Middle (e.g., Hold)	3	×	1	=	3
Fourth (e.g., Underperform)	4	×	0	=	0
Worst (e.g., Sell)	5	×	0	=	0
Total			8		12

Mean rating = 12 divided by 8 = 1.50

preceding section. SmartMoneySelect.com lets you test for the best ratings within a particular peer group such as an industry. Second, it's easy to measure changes in analyst sentiment. Here's an example.

Mean Rating Current < Mean Rating 4 Weeks Ago

Look closely at the relationship symbol. Remember, when dealing with mean ratings, lower numbers signify greater bullishness.

If you want to be more aggressive, consider something like the following requirement that the mean rating improve by more than 10 percent.

Mean Rating Current < (Mean Rating 4 Weeks Ago) * .9

SENTIMENT

Analysts are important, but they are not the only investment community constituency worthy of attention. There are various ways you can create screening tests based on the behavior of the analysts' main client group, institutional investors, as well as corporate insiders and short sellers.

Institutions

Many view institutions with respect, given that the portfolio managers who trade these accounts and the in-house analysts they work with are intelligent, well-trained, and wholly immersed in the investment process, as other kinds of professionals are in their respective fields of expertise. If you feel this way, you'll want to search for stocks that are favored by institutional investors.

Others view institutions with skepticism, citing a short-term focus (to be fair, this often occurs in response to clients' demands) and charter-type constraints limiting how they can invest (the manager of a large-cap fund must stay in large caps even if he/she personally believes prospects look better for small caps).

But whatever your attitude, everyone should at least be aware of institutional behavior simply because those funds are so large. If institutions decide en masse to buy, the stocks will rise, whether or not the buying decisions are sound. The reverse is true if they decide to sell. The impact of such movements tends to be short-term, but the magnitude is sufficient to force you to make thoughtful decisions whether you wish to follow their leads (as you would do if momentum is important to you) or you would rather pursue a contrarian approach.

Following the Trend   If you wish to follow the institutions' leads, you will want to construct screening tests that identify institutional tendencies to buy. Here is one potential format for such a test.

Net Institutional Share Purchases Latest Quarter > 0

Make sure you screen based on *net* purchases, which is shares purchased minus shares sold. You don't want to accidentally wind up screening only for increased share purchases, and not addressing the possibility that such purchases may be more than offset by an increase in the number of shares sold.

Another test tracking purchases that might be possible with some screeners is as follows.

> % Institutional Ownership Latest Quarter > % Institutional Ownership Prior Quarter

Besides tracking trading activity, some screeners allow you to take a head count. Consider this:

> # Institutional Shareholders Latest Quarter > # Institutional Shareholders Prior Quarter

This is interesting because it focuses on the number of institutional decision makers that have decided they want to be in the stock, irrespective of how many shares they can or wish to buy. This may not be helpful with large stocks, since changes may tell you more about the formations or elimination of funds that are required to be in a particular type of stock. But it can be invaluable for small-cap investing, where no institutions need own any shares unless the portfolio manager truly likes the stock.

Contrarian   If you wish to pursue this strategy, obviously you can reverse the tests just presented that tracked institutional trading. Now you will require net purchases to be less than zero or shares owned to be less than shares owned in the prior period.

But there's something more interesting you can do if you want the long-term benefits of a well-conceived contrarian strategy but want to avoid the short-term impact of trying to stand firm when faced with a speeding freight train. Few screeners can handle this (it can be done using Multex's premium screener). But even if yours can't, at least make a point of examining such data in Step 2 (Analyze).

> % Institutional Ownership Latest Quarter < Industry Average % Institutional Ownership Latest Quarter

You might even want to stretch the point, like this:

> % Institutional Ownership Latest Quarter < (Industry Average % Institutional Ownership Latest Quarter) * .5

In SmartMoneySelect.com, you can phrase it this way:

% Institutional Ownership in Bottom 50% within Industry

If you wish, you can supplement such a test with a numerical one that seeks a small number of institutional shareholders. To help you set an appropriate benchmark, consider that as of this writing, the average number of institutional shareholders for all companies is about 150. Note, though, that this tally is influenced by the fact that there are many very small companies. If we look at the market capitalization–weighted average, which gives greater emphasis to bigger firms, the typical number of institutional shareholders comes in at about 1,200.

Such tests can help you establish a very appealing backdrop for investing: modest institutional ownership, which, of course, implies future buying as the company becomes more discovered. Combine this backdrop with growth, quality, valuation, and other tests designed to identify companies that deserve to be discovered and/or activity-based tests (institutional buying, increased analyst coverage and bullishness, etc.) that suggest the discovery process has commenced.

Insiders

Many investors see significant stock ownership by insiders as a plus. They believe this will cause management's objectives to be closely aligned with those of shareholders. And they see inside ownership as an expression of confidence on the part of a group that, presumably, is in the know. Those considerations do justify favoring stocks with high insider ownership and/or insider buying.

The reverse is not necessarily so. Insider selling may, indeed, reflect worries about the future. But investors have no way of knowing whether this is so. Insider selling often reflects little more than a desire on the part of key employees to convert part of their compensation (stock options) to cash for other uses as well as a desire to diversify their stock holdings (this being a generally prudent approach to personal financial planning). And even if an insider really does think the stock will drop, there's no assurance he/she is correct. Share price valuation, especially during momentum-driven markets, often perplexes even the most experienced professional investors. A non–investment professional who knows his/her company may still have a poor sense of stock valuation.

Therefore, I recommend using insider data only to seek buy signals. If you want to create a numeric test of insider ownership, note that it is normal for the percent to be higher for smaller companies. As of this writing, the average percent of stock ownership by insiders is about 45 percent. But typically the percent of insider share ownership is usually greater in smaller companies. If we use the market capitalization–weighted average, which gives greater emphasis to larger firms, we find that the insider percent share ownership averages closer to 20 percent.

If you create tests based on insider buying activity, try to use a screener, such as the premium Multex application or Stock Investor Pro, that allows you to work in terms of the number of transactions, rather than the number of shares. Here's an example.

Net Insider Buys Latest Month > 0

"Net insider buys" means insider buy transactions minus insider sell transactions. Each transaction represents a decision, which is the most effective gauge of sentiment. The number of shares traded is less direct in that it also incorporates information about the rank and personal wealth of the decision maker.

Short Interest

The Multex screeners and, to a much more limited degree, SmartMoney Select.com and Stock Investor Pro allow you to screen based on short interest. If you use a screener that doesn't offer such tests, at least examine short interest data as part of Step 2 (Analyze).

It is generally assumed that short sellers, those who sell now and buy later, act because they expect prices to fall. But don't assume every short seller is really bearish. Many such sales are made as part of broader hedging strategies. Focus mainly on big numbers or number changes, which are more likely to truly indicate bearish sentiment. On average, short interest (stocks sold short as a percent of the total common stock outstanding) is a little below 2 percent. If you use a short interest test equal to or greater than 3 percent, you'll be seeing stocks with enough short interest to warrant close attention. You don't necessarily have to agree with the short sellers. But you should at least approach such data as if it were a signal of a need for further investigation. Be especially alert to negative factors.

Assuming you have a basic short interest test setting a floor at, say, 3 percent, you might want to create Step 1 (Find) tests based on declining short interest (suggesting something happened to cause the bears to rethink their views). Here are two alternatives.

Short Interest Current Month < Short Interest Prior Month

Change in Short Interest Past Month < 0

If you seek sale candidates with a screen created in Step 4 (Sell), you would reverse the relationship test to find stocks with rising short interest.

VALUATION

Many investors like to include one or more tests relating to stock valuation, even if this isn't a primary focus of the screen. This doesn't mean they are all value investors per se. Whether you pursue value or not, it's always a good idea to be at least aware of such issues, if for no other reason than investment discipline, something that will prove very helpful when we reach Step 4 (Sell). There's nothing inherently wrong with a stock that sells for 50 times earnings, even if the growth rate is well below 50 percent, if you understand the true nature of your investment—that in all likelihood you are betting the farm on pure momentum. An investor who considers such metrics and makes a thoughtful decision to go entirely with momentum is better prepared to assess subsequent events, pro or con, than someone who liked the chart and never bothered to look at the valuation ratios. So even if you don't use value tests in your screens, at least consider them as part of your Step 2 (Analyze) endeavors.

The Ratios

There's no mystery about the key valuation ratios. Price/earnings (P/E), price/sales, price/book value, and price/cash flow are all featured on most screeners. Many investors use price/earnings-to-growth (PEG) ratios in their screens. Some screeners include PEG ratio variables. In other cases, you can construct these by creating tests such as those illustrated (which seek PEG ratios equal to or less than 1.25).

P/E/Growth <= 1.25

P/E <= (Growth) * 1.25

The Multex screeners let you get fancy by adding price/tangible book value and price/free cash flow ratios. But be careful about using these.

- Tangible book value (standard book value minus the value of intangibles such as goodwill) can be a tenuous measure, since important assets such as brand identity are often intangible. This exacerbates the main disadvantage of considering book value: the fact that the accounting conventions on which it is based may produce numbers that bear little relationship to real-world asset values.
- Free cash flow, calculated based on cash generated by the company's operations minus important nonoperating cash outlays such as capital spending and dividend payments, can be volatile as capital programs ramp up and wind down. So this is an imperfect antidote to the problem with valuing stocks based on regular cash flow concepts.

When all is said and done, there is much to be said for the often-maligned P/E ratio. Depreciation expense is determined by accounting formulas rather than by cash outlays. Nevertheless it arguably comes closer to matching annual sales with the capital costs incurred to produce the sales than does the volatile free cash flow figure.

Note that P/E works best when EPS is on or near some kind of long-term sustainable trend. So it's normal to expect higher-than-usual price/earnings or PEG ratios when EPS is depressed—by a weak business cycle, for example. Conversely, when business conditions are hot, price/earnings and PEG ratios should be relatively low. If you believe EPS ratios are far above or below normal levels, it may be a good idea to focus on price/sales. The latter also is subject to ups and downs, but the swings generally aren't as volatile as in the case of EPS.

If you're interested in seeking potential asset plays or buyout candidates, you may want to check SmartMoneySelect.com's enterprise value/EBITDA (earnings before interest, taxes, depreciation, and amortization) ratio. It defines enterprise value—the minimum (absent a control premium) a would-be acquirer would have to pay to purchase the company—as the market capitalization of equity (stock price times number of shares) plus long-term debt plus preferred stock minus cash. Over time, EBITDA tends to shift back and forth into and out of favor as a tool for valuation. The argument against it is that we ought not eliminate interest and taxes, legitimate corporate outflows, or depreciation, a general proxy for another outflow, capital spending. But whether theorists like it or not, EBITDA does figure prominently in private market asset valuation.

Benchmarks

I strongly urge you to avoid using numerical tests for value-oriented screens. A P/E of 15 means absolutely nothing to me. I can only make sense of it when I compare it to something else: the company growth rate, the industry average P/E, or even the S&P 500 average P/E. Fortunately, modern screeners are generally well able to accommodate such preferences.

When using PEG ratios, it's tempting to impose the classic requirement that the P/E not exceed the growth rate (i.e., that the PEG ratio be less than or equal to 1). While this is a perfectly appropriate test, it can also be useful to stay aware of differences between theoretical ideas about how things should be versus real-world observations regarding how things are. If you are a growth-oriented investor, you may find it worthwhile to relax your adherence to theory and allow PEG ratios to climb above 1 (even during times when earnings are at normal levels). In such cases, you'd use the PEG ratio to filter out more extreme situations (such as ratios above 2). If your screener allows you to compare PEG ratios to industry averages, this can be a very useful thing to do.

Backward and Forward

When you create tests based on P/E or PEG, make sure you understand the exact definition of the ratios used in your screener. Some programs calculate P/E based on trailing 12-month (TTM) numbers. Others use estimates for the current and/or next fiscal year. Some screeners accommodate several alternatives. A similar situation exists with the growth rates used to calculate PEG ratios. Some screeners use consensus analyst projections of three- to five-year EPS growth. Others use historical growth rates. And others give you a choice.

At present, price/sales ratios are based on TTM sales. But in the next few years, consensus sales estimates may become more widely available and included in screeners.

As to which approach is better, arguments can be made both ways. I tend to prefer using forward-looking numbers where available. That's because strictly speaking, stock valuation is based on expectations for the future. But if the screener affords more opportunity to create tests comparing TTM company ratios to industry averages (as is the case when I screen based on price/sales), I'm comfortable accepting the historical figures.

High and Low

Most of the time, valuation-oriented tests are designed to accept stocks with ratios at or below certain thresholds (e.g., P/E below the growth rate or P/E below the industry average). Make sure you don't get so carried away with this that you wind up creating an evaluation list filled with dogs that are modestly valued because that's all they deserve (usually because of poor prospects). Add other kinds of tests to the screen to identify companies that deserve better treatment than they are getting in the market. Here's a simple two-test example:

> TTM P/E < Industry Average TTM P/E
> 3 Year Average Annual EPS Growth > 3 Year Industry Average EPS Growth

If you don't add such tests of deservingness to your screens, at least make sure you examine the issue in Step 2 (Analyze).

Speaking of deservingness, use of such tests can help you turn value screening upside down. Years ago, one might have assumed a stock with an extremely high P/E was valued that way simply because many investors didn't have enough timely information to realize the stock was overvalued. Now, in the information era, such an assumption would be naive. It's okay to assume consensus opinion is wrong, but don't assume it's ill-informed. Tests based on high valuation ratios combined with tests of deservingness can produce some interesting investment ideas.

PRICE/VOLUME/TECHNICAL ANALYSIS

For the most part, screening programs attempt to accommodate both fundamental analysis (evaluating investment opportunities based on company attributes) and technical analysis (which focuses on share price and trading volume trends). But as it turns out, most applications wind up being better at one style. If you are a dedicated technical analyst, you'll find ProSearch to be the best among the applications discussed here. The others stress fundamentals.

But even the most committed fundamental investors should still pay close attention to this section. If you can get comfortable seeing share price and volume trends as windows into the analytic conclusions reached by others who have studied company fundamentals, you'll find that just one or two price/volume/technical tests can add tremendous power to an otherwise fundamental screen. And even if you don't use the most exotic variables, knowing the concepts will enhance the visual chart study you'll do in Step 2 (Analyze).

Numerical Tests

Be careful about using numerical tests in connection with stock prices. Much of a stock's price performance depends on general market activity, as opposed to company-specific factors. For example, a 15 percent price gain would be considered lackluster over a period where the market rises 25 percent. But even in a bull market, you might draw favorable conclusions from a 2 percent gain that marks a turnaround from a prolonged downtrend for this particular stock. A 2 percent gain would also be considered great if it occurred at a time when the market fell 10 percent. So you will almost always be better off creating price-related tests based on relative or time series comparisons.

One occasion where you might want to use a numeric test is if you prefer to avoid stocks below certain numeric price levels (such as $1). You could accomplish the same thing with a test requiring that market capitalization be above a stated threshold.

Sometimes you may want to impose certain share price boundaries on your screen regardless of what's going on in the market. For example, those who pursue a contrarian or distressed-company theme might want to establish performance ceilings, such as a requirement that the latest month's price change must be no better than –25 percent. On the other side of the fence, you might want to establish an absolute floor, such as a test limiting consideration to stocks whose prior four-week performance is greater than zero. But even in these instances, it can be helpful to add relative comparison testing, as discussed in the next section.

Relative Comparison

Here is a very effective price-related test that can be created with Multex's premium screener.

> Share Price % Change Last 4 Weeks > Industry Average Share Price % Change Last 4 Weeks

If you use Morningstar's Premium Stock Selector, you would express the same idea this way:

> 1 Month % Rank Industry < 50

Morningstar's "% Rank Industry" variable measures a stock's total return (share price performance plus dividends, if any) against its industry average. A percentile score of 1 means the stock is in the top 1 percent of its industry (i.e., it outperformed 99 percent of its industry peers). The preceding example seeks stocks in the upper half of their industry comparisons.

Strictly speaking, the Morningstar variable is measuring something other applications refer to as relative strength. This situation illustrates the importance of checking glossaries. With Morningstar, low numbers signify strength. But more typically relative strength is defined the other way, such that a score of 99 means the stock outperformed 99 percent of all others. So if you use Stock Investor Pro, your test would look more like this:

Relative Strength 4 Weeks > Industry Relative Strength 4 Weeks

If your screener doesn't offer industry-oriented price variables, you may be able to compare stock prices to a broader universe. Here are two examples.

Price % Change Last 4 Weeks > S&P 500 % Change Last 4 weeks

Relative Strength Past 4 Weeks > 50

Tests like these are important because stock price movements are determined by two sets of factors, company-specific and general market. Relative comparisons allow us to filter out stocks that are strong solely because of good market conditions and zero in instead on shares that do well because of good things that are happening to the individual companies.

Time Series Comparison

Many investors like stocks that are going up. Sometimes this preference is naive (they assume stocks that went up in the past will continue to rise in the future). But positive price trends can serve as windows into the thoughts of other investors who studied the stock and weighed the pros and cons. Hence time-series share-price comparisons can be useful in your screens.

At first glance, the number of ways you can screen based on time series can seem overwhelming, especially if you use an application that is especially strong in this area, such as ProSearch. It's easy to go overboard and wind up with screens that have no passing stocks. The task becomes much more manageable once you realize that many different kinds of variables measure similar things, most of which fall into one of the following classifications: range, trend, breakout, and volume.

Before choosing specific variables, decide which kinds you want to work with and decide how heavily you want to emphasize each. If you are extremely aggressive in one area, you'll probably find that you'll have to be very restrained regarding the others. Or you might opt for balance, seeking stocks with generally acceptable readings in all areas. You could also take any sort of in-between approach. Once you pick your categories and make your emphasis/balance choices, you'll be able to more easily make sense of the variables available in the screener(s) you are using.

Range This refers to where the stock stands in relation to a recent pattern of trading activity. The easiest kind of range test seeks stocks trading near a 52-week high or low. The Advisor FYI category in MSN.Money's screener includes a general variable that lets you search for stocks that hit a new 52-week high (or low) within a time period that you specify. A more typical approach to boundary testing involves stating how close you want the stock to be to its 52-week high or low. The following test seeks stocks whose current prices are equal to or greater than 90 percent of the 52-week high.

Price/52-Week High >= 0.9

The example assumes you want stocks that are in favor among investors. Note, though, that this is a market-sensitive test. During bull markets, many will pass muster. But in bad times, few will make the grade. You can assume those that do have something special going on.

You can also search for stocks trading near the low end of their respective ranges. This can appeal to those who pursue contrarian or distressed-company themes. Here's an example.

Price/52-Week Low <= 1.2
Price/52-Week High <= 0.5

The first test is obvious. It seeks stocks whose prices are no higher than 20 percent above the 52-week low. So if the low is 20, the current price can be no higher than 24. But this isn't enough to allow us to conclude the current stock price is really depressed. Suppose the 52-week high is 30. A price of 24 isn't great, but it cannot be seen as deeply depressed. To nail that down, we need the second line. A stock currently trading at 24 can't pass unless the 52-week high was at least 48.

Those proficient in technical analysis can use ProSearch to create tests based on the stochastic oscillator, an indicator used to measure the stock's position within its trading range. The formula used in ProSearch is as follows:

(Current Price – Low Price for Period)/(High Price for Period – Low Price for Period)

In the example, for a stock with a range of 20 to 30 and a current price of 24, the math comes to 0.40, which would be equivalent to a ProSearch stochastic value of 40. A price of 24 within a 20 to 48 range yields a stochastic value of 14. Scores below 25 suggest oversold stocks, while scores above 75 suggest the shares may be overbought.

ProSearch also offers an interesting variable that lets you measure stocks based on how near or far they are from a more or less central area within the high-low range.

Figure 6.1 shows plots of stock prices over a particular period of time. The sloped line represents a trend that best summarizes the individual

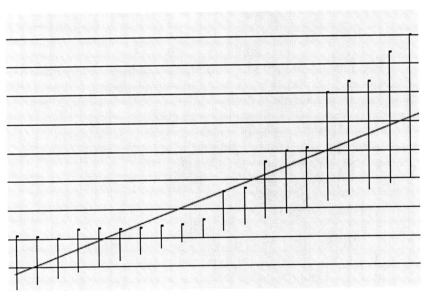

FIGURE 6.1   Plots of Stock Prices over a Time Period, with Least Squares Line

prices. It is referred to as the "least squares" line (named after the mathematical techniques used to calculate its exact position on the graph). The ProSearch "Least Squares Deviation" variable allows you to seek stocks whose prices are above or below the line (positive or negative deviations, respectively). This is best used in relative mode (e.g., a test requiring that least squares deviation be as high or low as possible) in connection with other tests.

Trend Saying a stock is near the upper end of a trading range is broadly interesting. But it doesn't give you all the information you need. Sometimes a stock will hit a 52-week high after a sharp upturn; other times it will get there very gradually. And sometimes a stock will hit a 52-week high but, although still close to the peak, be in the early stages of a downward correcting trend. Traditionally, trend analysis is seen as a visual discipline. You can approach it that way by studying price charts as part of Step 2 (Analyze). But you can also create screening tests that will help steer you toward the kinds of charts you'll most want to see.

We already touched on one of these, the least squares line calculated by ProSearch. You can screen for stocks whose lines are most heavily sloped by using that application's "Price Growth Rate" variables. If you like, you can set the variable as being equal to or greater than a particular numeric (growth rate) threshold. But once you start using numeric bases, your results become vulnerable to shifting market conditions. A screen for all seasons would use the price growth variable in relative mode (by setting the base "as high as possible").

Another way to identify trend strength is to use a moving average. This is the average stock price computed over a particular period of time. Suppose today is Monday and it's the 10th of the month. A five-day moving average would be the average closing price from last Monday (the 3rd of the month) through the most recent Friday (the 7th of the month). Tomorrow, on Tuesday the 11th, we would redo the calculation based on a new five-day sample starting on Tuesday the 4th and continuing through Monday the 10th. We call it a "moving" average because the time period used in the calculation shifts every day. The most useful approach is to create a test that identifies a stock whose moving average for a short period is higher than or recently broke above a moving average for a longer period. You can do this with the ProSearch or MSN.Money screeners.

ProSearch also includes variables based on the moving average convergence/divergence (MACD) line. This is a very well regarded trend measurement technique. Most other screeners don't include it, but it's standard fare on financial web sites. These have interactive price charts that let you plot and visually examine the MACD. So even if MACD isn't part of your screen, you can examine it when you go to Step 2 (Analyze).

INVESTools, the proprietor of ProSearch, recommends using what it refers to as an 8-17-9 MACD to search for possible buying opportunities. To calculate this MACD line, ProSearch starts by computing the daily differences between the stock's 17- and 8-day moving averages. It then calculates a 9-day moving average of these differences using a slight variation of the basic moving average calculation known as the exponential method, which guards against distortions caused by unusually high or low prices by weighting the most recent price most heavily. The difference between this line, known as the signal line, and the basic moving averages (8- and 17-day moving averages in this case) is known as the histogram. Movements of the histogram from minus to positive territory are seen as bullish. The distance between the histogram and zero measures the strength of the trend.

Another alternative to MACD or moving average that can be done with most screeners is to simply compare price performances over differing time periods. Here's an example of something you can do with several screeners.

Price % Change Last 4 Weeks > Price % Change Last 13 Weeks

This test seeks stocks that have gained more ground in the past four weeks than they did in the past 13. Stocks that declined in both time periods also can pass. If you seek positive trends, you may want to accompany such a test with another that requires a percent change to be greater than zero or that there be strong relative strength over the 13-week interval.

There are numerous ways you can adapt this theme. One approach will require a bit more price acceleration:

Price % Change Last 26 Weeks > 0
Price % Change Last 13 Weeks > 0
Price % Change Last 4 Weeks > Price % Change Last 26 Weeks
Price % Change Last 4 Weeks > Price % Change Last 13 Weeks

On some applications, you can create the same sort of tests using relative strength.

Breakout   This refers to stocks experiencing a noteworthy change in trading pattern. Most screeners offer little opportunity to create tests like this.

But many web sites have interactive price charts that let you add indicators that will help you visually identify breakouts. So even if you can't screen for breakout, understanding the nature of these tests shows you what to look for when you review the charts in Step 2 (Analyze).

The MSN.Money screener addresses this directly with a variable in its Advisor FYI category called "Near Low with Positive Momentum." This is a yes/no type of test seeking stocks trading within 10 percent of their 52-week lows that seem to be turning upward.

ProSearch offers some interesting breakout variables. One, called "Basing Pattern Breakouts," allows you to define a trading range (the high and low over the stated time period could be 5 percent, 10 percent, 20 percent, or 30 percent apart) and then seek stocks that broke out of the range one, two, or three days ago. Another variable, "High/Low Breakout," allows you to screen for stocks that broke above or below a 4-, 6-, 13-, 26-, or 52-week high or low.

Volume   Don't fall into the trap of assuming that heavy or rising volume is a positive sign. It does mean investors are more definitive in whatever opinion they hold, but that opinion could just as easily be negative. So if you create screening tests based on volume, be sure to accompany them with other tests seeking positive price performance.

ProSearch lets you measure volume directly through its "Volume Ratio" variables. You can specify that volume over a recent period, say five days, be at least a certain percentage above a longer-term (usually 30-day) average. The Multex applications and Stock Investor Pro allow you to create a similar test by combining variables relating to different periods. Here's an example from Multex.

10 Day Average Volume >= (3 Month Average Volume/20) * 1.5

This example serves as another reminder of how important it is to check glossaries to make sure you know exactly how your application defines its variables. In Multex, the 10-day variable is a per-day average, while its three-month variable is a monthly average. Before you can use them together, you'll have to convert to three-month variable to a per-day average. To do that, divide by 20 (a ballpark estimate of the number of trading days in a month). Once you grasp that adjustment, you can see that the test seeks stocks whose average daily volume is up at least 50 percent over the past 10 days compared with the past three months.

Some screeners offer variables that combine price and volume.

MSN.Money allows you to create tests seeking stocks whose prices rose or fell on heavy volume. It also lets you screen using an indicator known as on balance volume (OBV), as does ProSearch. To illustrate how this is computed, assume a stock rises by two points on 500,000 shares of volume. Multiply 2 (the price change) by 500,000. This is the starting OBV. Suppose the next day the stock falls half a point on volume of 300,000. Multiply the –0.5 dollar change on day two by 300,000. Add that to the starting OBV to get the cumulative OBV for that two-day period. In this example, the tally is 850,000, based on 1,000,000 for day one minus 150,000 for day two. Continue to do that in succeeding days. Technical analysts suggest that trends in cumulative OBV moving in the opposite direction of the price trend signal a change in the latter. ProSearch also includes a set of variables relating to accumulation/distribution (which is similar to on balance volume but limited to a 50-day period).

PROPRIETARY ANALYTICS

Thus far, all the screening variables and tests we have examined presented basic facts about the company or its stock and left it entirely up to you to determine which facts are positive from an investment standpoint. But increasingly, modern screeners are adding categories that embody opinions as to what makes for an attractive investment opportunity.

Morningstar's Premium Stock Selector lets you use three proprietary Morningstar Stock Grades (Growth, Profitability, and Financial Health) as screening variables. Each is based on a variety of factors. For example, the Growth Grade is based on the magnitude of five-year sales growth, acceleration/deceleration in growth, and consistency of growth. The data for each company is compared with others in its own sector. The Profitability Grade reflects a similar analysis of return on assets. And the Financial Health Grade assesses trends in cash, cash flow, and debt.

Another analytic tool provided by Morningstar is its five-star stock rating system. At present, it applies to only 500 (well-known, mostly larger) companies. But it can serve as an effective way to apply Step 1 (Find) to the kinds of stocks often present on what Chapter 4 described as popular evaluation lists. The best rating, five stars, is given to stocks for which a Morningstar analyst's estimate of fair value is 30 percent or more above the current market price. If estimated fair value is 10 percent to 30 percent above the market price, the stock gets four stars.

Stocks priced within 10 percent of estimated fair value get three stars, and so on down to one star for stocks that are deemed overvalued by 30 percent or more. The Morningstar web site provides a very detailed explanation of how it calculates fair value using a discounted cash flow model based on projected five-year revenue growth, profitability, and asset efficiency.

MSN.Money offers a similar set of variables based on its Stock Scouter ratings. These are overall ratings based on four factors: fundamentals, ownership, valuation, and technical. Companies that rate high in terms of fundamentals have achieved strong growth in the past, and are expected by analysts to grow quickly in the future. Helping, too, are positive earnings surprises and/or upward estimate revisions. High scores in ownership go to companies whose shares are being purchased by insiders. Valuation scores are based on relationships between stock prices and earnings, sales, and so on. The technical factor measures stock price movement and acceleration. You can create screening variables based on any of the individual factors as well as on the overall StockScouter rating.

ProSearch also offers a collection of proprietary ratings. It rates stocks based on the following: analyst ratings, fundamentals, insider activity, long- and short-term growth, technical, value, momentum, volume, EPS, and industry group.

The biggest advantage to screening based on proprietary ratings is that you can get a lot of mileage from one test. The MSN.Money StockScouter rating, for instance, is a single number that combines four factors, each of which in turn combines several more data items. Another advantage relates to expertise. We can assume these ratings were created by professionals based on their opinions regarding the kinds of data relationships that are associated with superior share price performance and that these opinions are supported by real-world testing.

The disadvantage is that these variables require a leap of faith on your part. In the preceding paragraph, I stated certain assumptions about the creation and testing of the ratings. But they are just assumptions. I cannot verify the extent to which they are accurate. Different organizations have different policies regarding the extent to which they disclose how the ratings were created and the results of any testing they performed. It's up to you to read whatever explanations are available and assess your own degree of comfort.

Also, even under the best conditions, you cannot expect every stock to perform in accordance with its rating. For example, you may find that over a specified time period, stocks in the best group rose 10 percent on average, while the worst group posted average appreciation of only 2 percent. But even here, you cannot assume every stock in the 10 percent group is better than every stock in the 2 percent group. There will be wide ranges of results in each category. The best way to use ratings is as a second opinion. If you screen based on ratings, do a thorough review of the other data relationships in Step 2 (Analyze). Or you can omit ratings from your screens and look closely at them as part of your Step 2 activities.

## CHAPTER 7

Screening Your
Personal Stock Market

As we saw in Chapter 6, there are a lot of different tests you can create. The good news is that these constitute all the tools you need to screen for the kinds of stocks you seek. In other words, you really can design your own personal stock market. The bad news is that one can easily get buried under too much of a good thing. If you put a lot of tests into your screen, no companies will pass. My screens usually contain 5 to 10 tests, with many screens being near the lower end of that range. (The most I ever had was 11, which I reached just once.)

At first the selection burden may seem daunting, especially if you use a top-of-the-line application that gives you the widest range of choices. But it becomes considerably easier once you adopt a screening strategy. Even if you don't create your own screens, you'll still find that a strategic approach will help you choose among the many available preset screens. There are two components to a screening strategy. The first deals with the kinds of tests you will use. The other consists of functional themes that help you decide which combination of tests will go into your screener.

SELECTING TESTS

Chapter 6 provided many sample tests across a variety of data categories. All of them can be described as being either direct or behavioral. The direct group consists of two subcategories: basic or comparative.

At the outset, the kinds of tests you want to use will help you determine the screening application(s) appropriate for you. Given our druthers, we'd all pick the application that offers the most flexibility. But not everybody is willing to pay top dollar for the absolute top-of-the-line program. Each investor decides for himself/herself what sort of cost/benefit trade-offs will be made. Once you select your application(s), the kinds of tests you want to use will help you identify which variables you'll go back to again and again, and which ones you'll ignore.

Direct Testing

A direct test is one that looks at a specific aspect of the company or its stock that is presumed to have a direct bearing on investment merit. Growth rate tests are a good example. We assume stronger growth rates indicate superior investment merit. Financial strength ratios are direct tests. So, too, are tests involving return on capital and stock valuation ratios. Direct tests are easily understood and widely used. The more challenging decision involves the kinds of direct tests you'll use.

- **Basic Tests:** These are the numeric tests. A requirement that the EPS growth rate be greater than 20 percent is basic. So, too, are tests available on many simple, free, Web-based screeners that allow you to specify a minimum and maximum range of acceptability. But as we saw in Chapter 6, these are the least sophisticated tests. Cost considerations will be most crucial in establishing your level of tolerance for them.
- **Comparative Tests:** These tests are based on cross-sectional comparison (where you compare a company or its stock to a benchmark such as an industry or market average) or time series comparison (where present-day company or stock traits are compared to what has been the case for the same company/stock in prior periods). These are the staple of good screening, so you should seek access to as many kinds of comparative tests as possible in light of how much you're willing to pay for access to more sophisticated programs. Fortunately, applications have evolved to such a degree that nobody needs to completely forgo comparative screening. The free Web-based Quicken.com and MSN.Money applications contain some comparative capabilities.

Direct tests are the ones novice screeners usually expect to use, right from day one. In fact, their role in screening is so obvious that many investors aren't even aware of the other category, behavioral screening, which we'll now examine.

Behavioral Testing

Behavioral tests gauge the attitudes of other investors based on objective evidence showing what they are actually doing. The reason many screeners don't think of tests as being behavioral is because on the surface they look just like direct tests.

Consider, for example, a test involving upward earnings estimate revision. Suppose the consensus estimate for current-year EPS rises from $2.45 eight weeks ago to $2.50 four weeks ago to $2.85 at present. We aren't really going to bet the farm on the company actually earning $2.85 a share this year. (Had we made such a bet eight weeks ago, when the consensus stood at $2.50, we'd have lost the homestead.) What's valuable here is the fact that analysts who follow the company closely are seeing that things are better than they previously believed. We can translate this to a pair of screening tests looking like this:

Consensus EPS Estimate Now > Consensus EPS Estimate 4 Weeks Ago
Consensus EPS Estimate 4 Weeks Ago > Consensus EPS Estimate 8 Weeks Ago

These aren't direct tests because we don't care whether the estimate is $2.85, $3.50, or $.10. We don't even care if the estimate represents a one-year growth rate of 3 percent, –15 percent, or 25 percent. The tests are behavioral because they show us what analysts are doing (raising estimates); from this we can make reasonable assumptions about what they are thinking (that prospects are better than previously assumed).

We can treat analyst stock recommendations the same way. Consider a simple test that seeks a lower (i.e., more bullish) mean rating than that which prevailed four and eight weeks ago. It isn't direct because we don't care what the mean rating is. The screen will catch ratings that improve from 2.75 to 2.50 to 2.25 (very, very weak to very weak to just plain weak) just as easily as stock for which ratings are jumping from 2.00 to 1.75 to 1.25 (neutral to somewhat bullish to more bullish). What we do care about is that analysts think the stock is more attractive (or less unattractive) than they believed in the recent past, as evidenced by their behavior (raising their ratings).

It's not much of a stretch to see that tests involving institutional activity, short interest, and insider buying can be used the same way. But sometimes behavioral tests look so much like direct tests that we can argue to a stalemate about how to classify a particular test.

Consider a simple test requiring that the current stock price be no more than 5 percent below the 52-week high. If we're in a bull market, it would be easy to characterize that test as a direct one that would be of interest to momentum investors. But suppose we've been in a bear market for a while. By definition, most stocks will be well below their 52-week highs. If we can find one that has held its ground, we can legitimately expect that something is happening that is making investors sit up, take notice, and act (by purchasing enough stock to keep the price high despite a bear market). So now the test is taking on a behavioral role.

Here's my single favorite behavioral test:

Share Price % Change Last 4 Weeks > Industry Average Share Price % Change Last 4 Weeks

In Chapter 6, I said this test was effective because it helps us identify situations that are attractive because of company-specific, as opposed to general market, factors. Let's now look more closely at how this works.

In the realm of investor behavior, nothing is more informative than share price movement. Stocks perform well because on balance, the investors who considered the company drew favorable conclusions and want to own it (i.e., prices rise for as long as demand for shares exceeds supply).

But we aren't just looking for stocks that go up. A stock could rise because investors drew favorable conclusions about the market in general. I want stocks that are behaving well because investors drew favorable conclusions based on something they see in this specific company. In fact, this test doesn't even require that the stock be going up. It will accept a stock that has been falling if its decline is less severe than that of the comparative benchmark. That would tell me investors are bearish on the overall market, but still see worthwhile qualities in this specific company.

There's one more important wrinkle. It's reasonable to define relative performance by comparing the stock to the market as a whole, especially if that's the only kind of price comparison your screener supports. But when I have a choice, I'd rather compare an individual stock to its industry average. This is the best way to determine the extent to which share price signals are based on company-specific factors.

Suppose the S&P 500 rallied by 7 percent over the past four weeks. But semiconductor stocks may have fallen, on average, 6 percent due to reports of a slowdown in the pace of incoming orders. Assume shares of ABC Semiconductors Inc. fell only 1 percent. ABC would fail a test that compares its share price performance to that of the S&P 500. But it will pass my industry comparison test. That's exactly the sort of result I want my screens to deliver.

I don't know from this alone why ABC has been singled out from the semiconductor group as a whole. To make the screen, ABC may also have had to pass tests calling for above industry average returns on capital and financial strength. But for now, suffice it to say there will always be important qualitative issues that don't easily lend themselves to the sort of number crunching we do when we screen. Behavioral tests are powerful because they provide an important window into the thoughts and judgments of those who have encountered and studied all the issues, quantitative and qualitative. As noted, I don't yet know the whole story behind ABC Semiconductors. But its having passed behavioral tests increases the probability I'll learn something interesting in Step 2 (Analyze). That's the best possible outcome from my efforts here, in Step 1 (Find).

Don't worry too much about which tests are direct and which tests are behavioral. The important thing is for you to be aware of the fact that many innocuous screening tests can provide valuable insight into the qualitative judgments of investors who are looking at the stock based on factors other than numbers. If the test result can be cited as evidence that they are voting thumbs-up or thumbs-down, then it is serving as a behavioral test. (This is so regardless of whether it could also be used as a direct test.) Being aware of the behavioral qualities of various kinds of tests will enable you to create far more interesting screens than would otherwise be the case.

FUNCTIONAL THEMES

Once you're comfortable with your repertoire of variables and the kinds of tests you will create, you need to put them together in a useful way. That will be easy if you think in terms of four themes based on which function a test fulfills in the context of a particular screen: primary, secondary, alternative, and layered. You should be able to look at any screen and state which theme is served by each test.

You don't need to use all four themes at once. But I suggest that each screen always have a clearly identifiable primary theme and at least one additional selection.

Primary

Your primary theme is based on your investment goal. If you are screening for growth stocks, then growth is your primary theme and you'll implement it through the growth-oriented tests you put into the screen.

This is an easy concept to accept. I wouldn't go quite so far as to say it's intuitive. (Often, novice screeners mix and match tests with little rhyme or reason.) But once we articulate the idea of identifying a primary theme, it becomes an easy sell. The challenge is to avoid acting as if this is all there is. As noted, a good screen should always have at least one additional theme beyond the primary one. So let's go on to look at the others.

Secondary

A secondary theme embodies an important investment goal that differs from, but is still compatible with, the one that forms the basis of your primary theme. The primary theme is like a movie star who aspires to an Academy Award for Best Actor, while the secondary theme is analogous to the costar who hopes to be named Best Supporting Actor. When I first began using secondary themes, I described them as "the sidekick" and used the old *Honeymooners* TV show as an example. Jackie Gleason played the primary role of Ralph Kramden. Art Carney played the secondary role of Ed Norton. When I conducted a seminar in Chicago in the 1990s, I switched the analogy to Michael Jordan (primary) and Scottie Pippin (secondary).

But you can't just pull any different theme out of a hat and say it is playing the secondary role. To be a true secondary theme, it's important that the tests (which could be direct and/or behavioral) be consistent with, or truly supportive of, your primary theme.

Here's an example using a value screen. (*Note:* TTM means trailing 12 months, and Indy. Avg. means industry average.)

1. PEG Ratio <= 1.00
2. TTM P/E <= Indy. Avg. TTM P/E
3. TTM Price/Sales <= Indy. Avg. TTM Price/Sales
4. TTM ROE > Indy. TTM ROE
5. 5 Year Avg. ROE > 5 Year Indy. Avg. ROE
6. TTM ROI > Indy. Avg. TTM ROI
7. 5 Year Avg. ROI > 5 Year Indy. Avg. ROI
8. Company Long-Term Debt Ratio < Indy. Avg. Long-Term Debt Ratio

The first three lines implement the primary theme, which is value. I could stop there. But as of the day this is being written, the first three lines left me with 485 stocks, far too many to analyze individually. What's more, many of those companies are dogs whose stocks trade cheap because of poor company quality. The next five lines, which constitute my secondary quality theme, solve the problem. These bring the result set down to 55 stocks. The size of the list is now more manageable, and there's a high probability it contains few, if any, serious dogs.

Don't get hung up on the fact that the number of secondary tests exceeds the number of primary tests. The important thing is to articulate the main goal (the primary value theme) and a strategy for enhancing the odds that stocks in the list will not be dogs (the secondary quality theme). The themes are simply there to help us organize our thoughts and quickly narrow our focus down to the variables that will most likely help us. (That's no small task. I use Multex's premium screener, which has over 600 variables. But because of the strategic decisions I make, it rarely takes me more than a minute or two to zero in on the ones I need.) Articulating functional themes also makes it easy to modify a screen if the first try doesn't look quite right. Suppose I decide a 55-stock list is too big and that I prefer more oomph in the primary theme. Here's a quick modification.

1. PEG Ratio <= 0.75
2. TTM P/E <= (Indy. Avg. TTM P/E) * .75
3. TTM Price/Sales <= (Indy. Avg. TTM Price/Sales) * .75
4. TTM Price/Cash Flow <= (Indy. Avg. TTM Price/Cash Flow) * .75
5. TTM ROI > Indy. Avg. TTM ROI
6. 5 Year Avg. ROI > 5 Year Indy. Avg. ROI
7. Company Long-Term Debt Ratio < Indy. Avg. Long-Term Debt Ratio

I'm now down to 27 stocks.

Now let's try a growth screen that uses price-related tests for secondary support based on the notion that favorable share price trends serve as a behavioral confirmation that the strong growth record compiled through your primary theme is widely expected to continue in the future.

1. EPS Growth Latest Quarter > 0
2. EPS Growth Latest Quarter > Indy. Avg. EPS Growth Latest Quarter
3. 3 Year EPS Growth > Indy. Avg. 3 Year EPS Growth
4. Sales Growth Latest Quarter > Indy. Avg. Sales Growth Latest Quarter
5. 3 Year Sales Growth > Indy. Avg. 3 Year Sales Growth
6. Share Price % Change Last 4 Weeks > Industry Average Price % Change Last 4 Weeks
7. Current Price > (52 Week High) * .9

The primary growth theme is expressed in the first five lines. At that point, there were 165 passing companies. The secondary price performance theme is set forth in the last two lines. The final list has been narrowed to 28 companies.

Analyst-related data is another category that can effectively play the secondary role in a screen that is primarily geared toward growth. Upward estimate revision and/or positive trends in the ratings profile can provide behavioral support for the growth theme. Let's change the secondary theme in the screen.

1. EPS Growth Latest Quarter > 0
2. EPS Growth Latest Quarter > Indy. Avg. EPS Growth Latest Quarter
3. 3 Year EPS Growth > Indy. Avg. 3 Year EPS Growth
4. Sales Growth Latest Quarter > Indy. Avg. Sales Growth Latest Quarter
5. 3 Year Sales Growth > Indy. Avg. 3 Year Sales Growth
6. Mean Rating Now < 1.5
7. Mean Rating Now <= Mean Rating 4 Weeks Ago

This screen returns 25 names, again a very manageable number.

Analyst data can also be secondary in a value screen. Favorable rating or estimate revision data would support an inference that the company isn't a dog. Or at the very least, if the company is a dog, analysts see reason to believe it is starting to mend its ways or is starting to move out of what was just a temporary-canine period. Both of the latter scenarios are generally acceptable to value investors.

Here is the first (less stringent) primary value theme demonstrated earlier, combined with the latter analyst-oriented secondary theme.

1. PEG Ratio <= 1.00
2. TTM P/E <= Indy. Avg. TTM P/E
3. TTM Price/Sales <= Indy. Avg. TTM Price/Sales
4. Mean Rating Now < 1.5
5. Mean Rating Now <= Mean Rating 4 Weeks Ago

This screen produces 71 stocks. Many would regard such a list as being a bit too big. But since I'm articulating primary and secondary themes, it's easy for me to adopt a strategy for narrowing down. I could tighten up the primary theme, as per the second value example. Alternatively, I might tighten the analyst-oriented secondary theme, say, by requiring that the current rating be less than (not merely less than or equal to) where it stood four weeks ago. (Remember, with mean ratings, lower numbers indicate greater bullishness.) Or I could introduce another secondary theme, for example, by adding a company quality test. As you can see, there are many ways to solve a screen-design problem. You can comfortably get a handle on and think intelligently about an otherwise unwieldy process simply by articulating functional themes.

Alternative

As in the preceding section, we add a new theme to accompany the primary tests. But now we're not seeking a supporting player. We're looking, ideally, for an adversary. But I hesitate to leave it at that lest you bog down in trying to decide whether theme A is really incompatible with theme B. (Other than growth and value, how many themes are really considered opposites? And many argue that growth and value ought not to always be seen as enemies.) So let's also say an alternative theme is like a dance partner who moves to a different tune. Other phrases I use for this kind of screening are "second opinion," "two heads are better than one," and "best of both worlds." That probably helps you get the idea of why alternative themes would be used.

It's easy to accept the idea of a secondary theme that is compatible with the primary one. And it probably wouldn't be hard to convince investors that it can be good for screens to combine such alternative themes as value and growth/momentum. But it may seem odd to go so far as to introduce another theme that is not at all relevant to your investment goal. To illustrate the benefits of dancing to different tunes, let's look at the "Fastest Turnover" screen I currently use on MultexInvestor.com. Here are the tests.

1. TTM Asset Turnover > (Indy. Avg. TTM Asset Turnover) * 1.25
2. TTM Inventory Turnover > (Indy. Avg. TTM Inventory Turnover) * 1.25
3. TTM Receivables Turnover > (Indy. Avg. TTM Receivables Turnover) * 1.25
4. 5 Year Average Return on Investment > Indy. Avg. 5 Year Average Return on Investment
5. This Year's Consensus EPS Estimate Now >= This Year's Consensus EPS Estimate as of 8 Weeks Ago

The first three tests are easily recognizable as constituting my primary turnover-based theme. As of this writing, these three tests narrowed the choices from 9,459 (the number of stocks in the full database) to 251. That's way too big a list. I could have easily narrowed it further by raising the multiplication factor. If I used 2 instead of 1.25 (meaning I seek company turnover ratios that are twice the industry averages, instead of only 25 percent better), the list would shrink to 44 stocks. That's a workable list that I could bring to Step 2 (Analyze).

But is it really as good a list as I can get? As discussed in Chapter 6, turnover is a valuable and often underappreciated concept. At some point, however, enough is enough. The 251 stocks I got using the 1.25 multiplication factor represent a very impressive narrowing of the database. I eliminated 97.4 percent of the stocks I started with. Raising the multiplication factor to 2 would drop another 207 stocks off the list. That's just 2.2 percent of the original database.

Do I really help myself by tightening the turnover tests to squeeze out another 2.2 percent of my original universe? Personally, I think I got more than enough benefit out of the turnover theme the first time around; pushing it further produces only marginal benefit. So I switch gears. The fourth test represents a compatible secondary theme. It eliminates another 167 stocks, thereby bringing the list down to 84.

That's still too big. So I finish with an alternative theme, a sidekick that dances to a completely unrelated tune. That's the fifth test. It seeks situations where there have been no downward estimate revisions in the past eight weeks. That brings the list down to a beautifully manageable 20 stocks.

Suppose you don't really trust or respect analyst estimates. I could suggest that you pick another alternative theme; perhaps you could use growth, or price momentum, or insider transactions, or a decrease in short selling. Suppose you're really adamant. You read every book you can find on Warren Buffett or Graham and Dodd and you are absolutely committed to sticking with company quality. Now I'd have two answers. One would be to pick another quality test for number five (perhaps something to do with margin or financial strength). You need not force yourself to use all four themes in each screen you create. But let's pause before doing that. The first four tests (three primary and one secondary) all dealt with company quality. They served to narrow a 9,459-stock database down to 84. In other words, the quality variables swept away 99.1 percent of the original haystack.

Personally, I think these four quality tests have done a magnificent job. We've put an extremely powerful company-quality stamp on an evaluation list that now represents a mere 0.9 percent of the original group. If ever there's a good time to consult with another point of view, this is it. No matter what stocks make it through the next alternative test, we know that they ranked among to top 0.9 percent in terms of our company quality preferences. So I'll accept input from my screening sidekick. After all, kings consult with ministers, presidents consult advisers, and in the Chicago Bulls' glory days Michael Jordan passed the ball to Scottie Pippin.

Think of it this way. Even if you don't really like to rely on analyst estimates, what's the downside? We're only looking at estimates in connection with a tiny, elite, quality-oriented 0.9 percent of the database. The benefit we can enjoy if the alternative theory has merit far outweighs the so-called damage we might sustain if the alternative is a dud. The key is that we're applying it to a very small group that's already been selected through our own (primary and possibly also secondary) theories. We take a chance by letting the proverbial other guys have a say in our screens. But this risk is infinitesimal compared to the usual kinds of risks and uncertainties stock market investors bear every day.

There's no science to determining when it is a good idea to use an alternative theme. To get a sense of when it's right, think of the phrase "enough is enough." Note the number of stocks that are in the screening database. Then note how many (in percentage terms) are left over after applying your primary and secondary (if any) themes. Ask yourself if it's really necessary to force your primary/secondary themes to work harder. If you answer "enough is enough," even though your list still needs further narrowing, you're ready to introduce an alternative theme.

Using Proprietary Analytics as Alternative Themes   The preceding paragraphs have illustrated one way to create an alternative theme: pick one or more tests relating to a goal that's unrelated to your primary theme. In some screeners, the proprietary analytics category serves as a great source of alternative themes. Here's an example of how I consult the MSN.Money StockScouter Value Grade for a second opinion.

1. 5 Year Earnings Growth, High as Possible
2. EPS Growth Year to Date versus Prior Year to Date Period, High as Possible
3. 3 Month Relative Strength >= 20 Percentage Points above 12 Month Relative Strength
4. Valuation Grade >= B

The first two tests establish my primary growth theme. The third test, based on price momentum rather than growth, is a secondary theme. It differs from but is generally compatible with growth. The fourth test is an alternate theme because it is, as said earlier, dancing to a different tune. I could have ignored the StockScouter Value Grade and created value-oriented tests on my own. But StockScouter gives me more mileage than I could have gotten with tests I can create directly from the screener. The grade starts with the basic P/E, price/sales, and PEG ratios we are accustomed to using. It compares those ratios to industry averages. And it goes a step further by deciding how important these relative ratios should be in light of this company's size.

I can also make use of the stock grades available in the Morningstar.com Premium Stock Selector. Here's an example.

1. 1 Year EPS Growth >= 1 Year Sector Average EPS Growth
2. Latest Quarter Year-to-Year Net Income Growth >= S&P 500 Average
3. 1 Month Stock Total Return >= Sector Average
4. Profitability Grade >= A

As in the screen I created using MSN.Money, the first two lines of the Morningstar screen reflect a primary theme of growth, and the third line brings in the secondary theme of price momentum. With Morningstar, I used profitability as my alternative theme. Morningstar does not claim its profitability grades will predict future share price performance, but its web site provides good information about what goes into the grade. The verbal explanation lists the following as factors that contribute to high profitability grades: higher average levels of return on capital over the past five years, returns that trend upward over the five-year period, and more stability (than other companies) in the year-to-year pattern. That packs a lot of information into a single test.

Here's a screen that lets you use the Morningstar Premium Stock Selector to apply the Step 1 (Find) screening discipline to a group of stocks that would otherwise represent the antitheses of this approach—hot well-known growth stocks.

1. 3 Month Total Return >= Sector Average
2. 1 Week Total Return >= Sector Average
3. Growth Rating >= A
4. Star Rating >= 4

The first two lines articulate a primary momentum-oriented theme. The third line provides a secondary theme based on growth. The fourth line is an alternative theme, because Morningstar's ratings are based on value, specifically its analysts' estimates of fair values. I describe this screen as one that finds well-known stocks because if a stock isn't well-known, it probably won't have a star rating. (Note that Morningstar's grades and ratings differ in that the former are objectively calculated based on historic financial data, while the latter involve forecast judgment on the part of Morningstar analysts.)

Interestingly, as of this writing, there's little overlap between the Morningstar stock grades and the MSN.Money StockScouter ratings. Mindful of the risk of overgeneralizing, I'll suggest that the Morningstar grades are based on factors that are usually associated with traditional fundamental investing, while the StockScouter ratings are more sensitive to here-and-now market preferences.

Meanwhile, Pro Search offers an interesting collection of proprietary analytics of its own, both technical and fundamental. The latter are especially interesting considering the application's special strength in technical variables. Consider the following simple example.

1. Positive Breakout in 14/5 Day Stochastic Oscillator within Last 3 Days
2. Analyst Rank above 80

Investors inclined toward technical analysis know that the first line, my primary theme, seeks good news from an oscillator designed to give short-term overbought/oversold signals. Critics of technical analysis point out the hazards of assuming the future will resemble the past. The second test is an alternative theme that addresses this. It's a behavioral test that combines a lot of analyst information into a single percentile ranking. The rating is based on the number of analysts covering a stock, the tendency of the company to beat analyst estimates, the mean rating, and the trend of upward revision. Even those who are reluctant to project past price patterns into the future might take comfort in a "sidekick" test that incorporates so much information about what analysts are thinking.

Remember, as Chapter 6 pointed out, use of proprietary analytics requires some leap of faith since you don't know exactly what went into the ratings. But MSN.Money, Morningstar, and Pro Search disclose enough to enable you to determine whether the ratings and grades are generally consistent with your investment philosophy. Those explanations may not be sufficient to induce you to buy stocks solely because they appear in a screen. But here, screening is only the first of a four-step procedure, one that helps you find stocks that seem worthy of further examination. Since you'll look at the details and make up your own mind in Step 2 (Analyze), there's little, if any, chance you can get burned by a rating or grade whose under-the-hood specifications don't exactly match your stock selection preferences. In the context of this four-step market screening method, the benefits of using the ratings far exceed the risks.

Layered

This is a complete change of pace. In fact, strictly speaking, we are no longer thinking in terms of a single screen. Simply put, it's a process wherein we run a screen and then create a second screen to pick the best among those stocks that made the first cut. In theory, you could run the second set of winners through a third screen, and so forth for as many layers of screening as you wish to implement. But in practice, we approach layering more systematically than that (lest the number of passing companies quickly fall to zero).

Layering is most appropriate for those whose investment goals are more general than specific. Let's look at the general versus specific distinction by considering the following sample sets of growth tests, each of which could serve as the primary screening theme.

Growth Tests—Package A
1. Latest Quarter EPS Growth > 0
2. Latest Quarter EPS Growth > Indy. Avg. Latest Quarter EPS Growth
3. TTM EPS Growth > Indy. Avg. TTM EPS Growth
4. 3 Year EPS Growth > Indy. Avg. 3 Year EPS Growth

Growth Tests—Package B
1. Latest Quarter EPS Growth > 0
2. Latest Quarter EPS Growth > Indy. Avg. Latest Quarter EPS Growth
3. Latest Quarter Sales Growth > 0
4. Latest Quarter Sales Growth > Indy. Avg. Latest Quarter Sales Growth

Growth Tests—Package C
1. TTM EPS Growth > Indy. Avg. TTM EPS Growth
2. 3 Year EPS Growth > Indy. Avg. 3 Year EPS Growth
3. 5 Year EPS Growth > Indy. Avg. 5 Year EPS Growth
4. 3 Year EPS Growth > 5 Year EPS Growth
5. TTM EPS Growth > 3 Year EPS Growth

Growth Tests—Package D
1. Latest Quarter EPS Growth > 0
2. Latest Quarter Sales Growth > 0
3. Latest Quarter EPS Growth > Latest Quarter Sales Growth
4. TTM EPS Growth > TTM Sales Growth
5. 3 Year EPS Growth > 3 Year Sales Growth

These four growth-test packages illustrate an important point. It's a lot easier to say you're a growth investor than it is to find the collection of growth-oriented tests that's exactly right for you. You might be able to eliminate some choices by deciding, for example, to stress time series rather than cross-sectional comparisons. Others might narrow the field by focusing on EPS only and not sales. But even with these limitations, the number of possibilities remains huge. And the examples barely scratch the surface of all possible ways to screen for growth.

The reason it can be hard to choose the best, so to speak, growth screen has much to do with the fact that all the packages shown, as well as many others you can create, have merit. Each will produce lists that are different. But that doesn't mean one is necessarily better than the other. When the market favors growth stocks, many different kinds of growth screens will produce winners. And when growth is out of favor, you'll need to wait patiently regardless of what sort of growth screen you use.

Layered screening is a technique that allows you to say that although your goal is growth, you are not deeply committed to any specific set of growth tests. You can create as many different kinds of growth screens as you like, aggregate all the lists into a master growth stock list, and then create an entirely new screen (a second layer), to identify the best among your growth-oriented mini-universe.

I could again turn to the growth theme when I create my layer-two screen. But that's not the most effective way to use the process. (Any new growth screen I create now could just as easily have been added to the layer-one group.) The best way to use this strategy is to base the layer-two screen on a different goal or set of goals. For example, I might seek the best-of-the-best growth stocks by creating the following layer-two screen.

1. Analyst Mean Rating Now <= 1.75
2. Analyst Mean Rating Now < Analyst Mean Rating 4 Weeks Ago
3. EPS Estimate for Current Year > EPS Estimate for Current Year as of 4 Weeks Ago

If you're thinking that this is just a glorified version of a regular screen containing an alternative theme, you're right. But here's why it can be worthwhile to take the extra trouble to use the layered approach. If I combine all the growth tests used in the four packages with the three analyst-related tests into a single screen, it would produce just two names. However, the four growth packages combine to produce 1,175 names (after eliminating overlaps involving companies that appear in more than one package). When I apply the layer-two analyst screen to the growth mini-universe, I wind up with 34 names.

Considering that some ideas will fall by the wayside as we move to Step 2 (Analyze) and beyond, 34 is a more practical-sized result set than two. And remember the key motivation for layered screening—the fact that I seek growth stocks but am not hyperparticular about the exact way growth is defined. Given that I'm perfectly happy to have my stocks satisfy several growth tests but not necessarily all of them, I cannot say the 32 stocks eliminated by the one-screen approach were really dropped for good reason.

The other benefit to layered screening is flexibility. I can create and save different kinds of layer-two screens, based on value, company quality, price momentum, and so on to match with my growth universe. After having done that, I can easily go back and forth. For example, I might first try a layer-two screen based on price momentum. But if none of the names I see catches my fancy on this particular day, I can immediately switch to a different layer-two screen based on a different theme, such as value.

Note, though, that not every screener can fully accommodate every strategy. Layered screening requires programs that can handle user-defined portfolios. The Multex screeners and Stock Investor Pro allow you to create and load such custom universes. With Pro Search, MSN.Money, and Smart-MoneySelect, you cannot load user portfolios, but you can export your stock lists (to spreadsheets or text files). Those tickers can be copied into the former applications as user portfolios, so you can get substantial layered screening capability if you are willing to use more than one application.

CHAPTER **8**

Sharpening the Focus

Our efforts to this point have proceeded under the assumption that we wish to wind up with an evaluation list containing 15 to 50 companies, with a preference for the lower end of the range. But no matter what we do with our screen, we aren't going to buy any stock simply because the name appeared in a screen. Before buying, we'll want to complete Step 2 (Analyze), where we look at a variety of company-specific information in order to discover each stock's unique investment story. As you'll see when we reach that section, starting with Chapter 10, the process is very manageable. But even the most efficient analytic method can bog down if it has to be applied to more companies than you can fit within your time constraints.

So you will often find it necessary to narrow your efforts to fewer companies than appear on your screen, perhaps to no more than three or four. You could simply modify the screen by picking some tests and making them as stringent as necessary to drive the result set down to the desired number of companies. But that may not be the most productive approach. All we need do to see this is revisit the enough-is-enough logic presented in support of alternative screening. If you start with a database of, say, 9,500 stocks and screen your way down to 25, you've eliminated 99.74 percent of the database. If you use the same variables to go down to, say, four companies (i.e., you eliminate another 21 companies, or 0.22 percent of the universe), can you really have much faith that the companies eliminated by this final effort are worse than the ones left standing at the end?

There are two better ways to identify three or four stocks that you can plausibly describe as the highest analytic priorities. One is to sort the list based on one or more preferred criteria. The other is to score your results such as to spotlight those situations that have the most to offer in the criteria that are most important to you. This is better than merely increasing the stringency of the screen, because you can sort and score based on data items that never made it into your screen. This way, when you narrow the selection, say from 25 stocks to four, you are doing so on the basis of new information rather than a rehash of the data items you already used. In fact, as you gain proficiency in sorting and/or scoring, you'll find that you can easily work with screens that produce more than 50 names.

SORTING

Screening applications don't simply spit out lists of company names and/or tickers. Each presents company lists according to some kind of formatted report that looks something like a spreadsheet.

There's always a default layout. For example, in the Multex applications each company is listed along with the data items included in your screen. If, for example, your screen was built using variables for trailing 12-month EPS growth, three-year EPS growth, and three-year sales growth, your report will show, for each company, what its TTM and three-year EPS growth rates were and what its three-year sales growth rate was. Other applications default to the standard default data layouts regardless of which screening variables you used.

Obviously, you can pick a data item (report column) to use as a basis for best-to-worst sorting and start analyzing companies from the top of the list, working your way down through as many as you wish or have time to look at. But this isn't really the good part of the process. If you're sorting within the default layouts in the Multex screeners, you're still beating to death at least one of the same data items used in the screen. If your application uses a standard default layout for all screens, you may find that you aren't especially interested in companies that rank at or near the top in any of the available categories. Sorting becomes most useful after you adapt the report layout to something more to your liking.

Each application has its own set of layout-related features. Some offer a variety of preset sortable layouts from which you can choose. MSN.Money goes a step further and allows you to customize the report layout by deleting data items and adding any others you wish from among those that are used as screening variables. But you cannot save your custom layouts for future use, so you'll have to keep re-creating them. Meanwhile, the Multex screeners balance the scales differently. As of this writing, there are no preset layouts. You always start with the default (the one that mimics the data items you used as screening variables). But you are perfectly free to create as many custom layouts as you wish and save them for future use.

Figure 8.1 shows a layout I created for the free Multex application. I

Ticker	Name	Current Price	Price 12 Month High	Price 12 Month Low	Price % Change 4 Weeks	PEG Ratio	Average Recmnd.	Market Capitalization
ASW	A.C.L.N. Limited	31.060	50.000	18.750	13.86	0.292	1.00	443.692
ACRT	Actrade Financial Tech.	28.900	44.300	15.250	10.52	0.442	1.00	292.844
ICTG	ICT Group, Inc.	15.980	17.990	8.000	13.90	0.933	1.20	195.292
MNTG	MTR Gaming Group, Inc.	13.640	14.200	4.000	29.91	0.575	1.25	352.117
ADVP	AdvancePCS	27.200	40.150	14.500	-10.27	0.885	1.33	2,506.126
DFXI	Direct Focus, Inc.	27.000	33.500	11.611	14.41	0.653	1.33	942.732
FOSL	Fossil, Inc.	21.100	23.350	13.000	17.42	0.730	1.33	636.587
SHFL	Shuffle Master, Inc.	17.600	23.300	7.250	43.09	1.109	1.33	317.997
ANSI	Advanced Neuromodulation	27.150	29.900	5.000	9.92	2.926	1.33	242.477
CPN	Calpine Corporation	22.380	58.040	18.900	-9.02	0.402	1.35	6,833.017
CHS	Chico's FAS, Inc.	32.020	39.000	11.583	26.76	0.793	1.36	856.311
MIR	Mirant Corporation	25.400	47.200	19.250	3.88	0.651	1.40	8,651.748
IFIN	Investors Financial Ser.	66.490	96.000	46.000	24.28	1.558	1.40	2,121.230
NRG	NRG Energy, Inc.	16.990	37.700	13.100	-5.87	0.594	1.50	3,373.110
POOL	SCP Pool Corporation	26.250	27.200	17.083	13.64	0.956	1.50	655.305
AXCA	Axcan Pharma Inc.	12.250	12.700	8.313	15.68	0.754	1.63	422.870
HCOW	Horizon Organic Holdings	13.250	13.300	4.000	16.43	2.478	1.67	133.878
CDIS	Cal Dive Int'l, Inc.	21.150	32.000	15.560	2.92	0.776	1.71	688.961
ACF	AmeriCredit Corp.	22.800	64.900	14.000	43.22	0.250	1.75	1,923.043
NSIT	Insight Enterprises, Inc.	19.850	29.938	12.860	18.86	0.766	1.75	826.951
HOTT	Hot Topic, Inc.	28.200	38.200	14.125	5.62	0.883	1.78	584.812
BJS	BJ Services Company	28.400	43.100	14.550	9.02	0.731	1.81	4,655.612

FIGURE 8.1 Data Layout Created for Multex Screener, Sorted by Average Recommendation from Most to Least Bullish
Fundamental data supplied by Market Guide. © 2001, Multex.com. All rights reserved.

chose to set it such that when it is accessed, the stocks will always be sorted based on mean analyst rating. Hence if I'm unable to properly analyze all stocks on the list, I'll be giving top preference to those for which analysts are most bullish. (To avoid overkill, if mean rating figures prominently in my screen I can easily, and often do, sort the report based on a different column, such as PEG ratio.)

SCORING

Scoring is a turbocharged version of sorting. Thus far, we've been assuming each data item we use is equally important to us. We edge away from that when we pick certain items we want to see in the report and one or two that will serve as bases for sorting. Scoring carries this idea to its logical conclusion. We expressly identify some items as being more important than others and say exactly how important or unimportant each item is.

If you use the Morningstar Premium Stock Selector, scoring is easy, since the capability is built directly into the results reports. Here's a value screen (including an alternate test based on the profitability grade) I created.

1. Forward P/E <= Industry Average Forward P/E
2. Price/Sales <= Industry Average Price/Sales
3. Price/Cash Flow <= Industry Average Price/Cash Flow
4. PEG Ratio <= 1.00
5. Profitability Grade >= A

The screen yields 91 names, far too many for me to analyze. Figure 8.2 shows what I see after I click the link in the report that says "Score These Results."

The companies at the top of the priority list are based on the scores derived from the default preferences established in the application, as shown in the left side of Figure 8.2. Notice, too, that Morningstar treats each data item as being of equal importance (i.e., each is scored 5, the middle of a 1 through 10 worst-to-best scale). The scores aren't being applied directly to the data items. In other words, we wouldn't multiply a score of 5 by a 13 percent growth rate to produce a component equal to 65. The data items are ranked by Morningstar, and in each case, Morningstar's data rank is multiplied by your score. If a 13 percent growth rate is in the middle of the pack, its rank of 5 is multiplied by your score of 5 to get 25, a number that is added to others calculated based on similar score/data rank combinations.

Notice the Customize Criteria button in the bottom left-hand corner. Figure 8.3 shows the results of my customization efforts. I changed the data items that will be used, and I altered the scoring. The result is a new priority list for Step 2 (Analyze).

The good part of the Morningstar scoring feature is that it is effective and easy to use. The negative aspect is that as of this writing it can be used only on lists generated with the Morningstar Premium Stock Selector (Morningstar allows me to add individual tickers. But it does not allow me to copy and paste large user universes, so it is not practical to import and score lists produced by other screeners). So if you aren't using Morningstar, you have only two scoring options: (1) skip it entirely or (2) create your own spreadsheet scoring template.

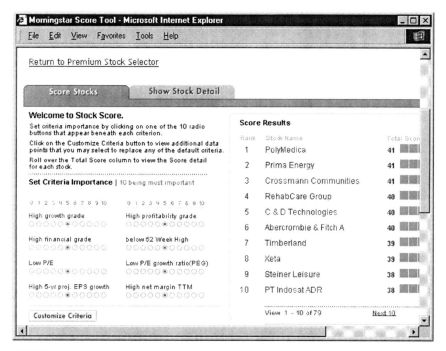

FIGURE 8.2 Scoring Area of the Morningstar Premium Stock Selector, Showing the Default Scoring Categories and Scores
Source: Morningstar.com (www.morningstar.com). © 2001 Morningstar, Inc. All rights reserved. Reprinted with permission.

Most will probably choose the first option. And that's exactly what I recommend if you read on and find the do-it-yourself approach cumbersome or confusing. Sorting is a perfectly fine way to sharpen your focus, so don't feel pressured to deal with another procedure that doesn't appeal to you. But many investors are proficient in using spreadsheets, and some actually consider it fun to design interesting spreadsheets. For those in this category, here is an example.

I started with the "Industry Leaders" stock screen I created for the MultexInvestor.com site. (TTM means trailing 12 months.)

1. TTM P/E <= (Industry Average TTM P/E) * 1.1
2. 5 Year Sales Growth >= (Industry Average 5 Year Sales Growth) * 1.1
3. 5 Year EPS Growth >= (Industry Average 5 Year EPS Growth) * 1.1
4. Net Margin >= (Industry Average Net Margin) * 1.1

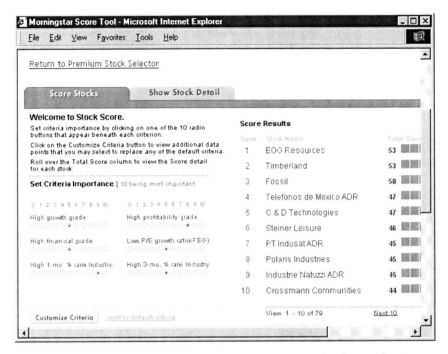

FIGURE 8.3   Scoring Area of the Morningstar Premium Stock Selector, Showing Scoring Choices

Source: Morningstar.com (www.morningstar.com). © 2001 Morningstar, Inc. All rights reserved. Reprinted with permission.

5. Debt/Equity Ratio <= Industry Average Debt/Equity Ratio
6. Stock Price % Change Last 4 Weeks >= (Industry Average Price % Change Last 4 Weeks) * 1.1

(*Notes:* Tests 2, 3, and 6 require negative number adjustments as described in Chapter 5. For the sake of simplicity, they are not reproduced here. Also, be aware that test 1 really does allow a stock to have a P/E as much as 10 percent above the industry average. You aren't seeing a mirage. This compensates for the fact that other tests require at least 10 percent company-to-industry superiority.

As of this writing, 61 companies passed the screen. That's too big a list, so I need to do some sorting and/or scoring. Figure 8.4 shows how a portion of the Excel spreadsheet I downloaded looks after choosing the data items I want to see in the report.

	Microsoft Excel - indyld basic.xls							_ □ ×

File Edit View Insert Format Tools Data Window FactSet Help

	A	B	C	D	E	F	G	H
1	Ticker	Name	Price	Price % Chg	Cur Fiscal	Cur Fiscal	5 Yr.	5 Yr Avg
2			% Change	4 Weeks	Year EPS	Year EPS	Return On	ROI
3			4 Weeks	Industry	Mean	4 Wks Ago	Investment	Industry
4	AAON	AAON, Incorporated	8.77	7.32	1.57	1.60	17.91	11.45
5	AT	Alltel Corporation	-3.30	-9.98	2.86	2.87	10.68	8.04
6	SAT	Asia Satellite Telecomm.	7.03	-9.98	1.90	1.90	18.82	8.04
7	APL	Atlas Pipeline Partners	12.19	4.38 NA	NA		11.66	8.13
8	BJS	BJ Services Company	17.46	4.38	1.74	1.99	5.34	8.13
9	CDIS	Cal Dive Int'l, Inc.	5.24	4.38	0.86	0.86	14.51	8.13
10	CEC	CEC Entertainment, Inc.	11.16	2.75	2.23	2.22	14.77	9.82
11	CCF	Chase Corporation	7.83	4.57 NA	NA		20.16	9.04
12	PLCE	Children's Place, The	37.95	4.32	1.68	1.67	46.59	25.78
13	COCO	Corinthian Colleges, Inc.	20.46	0.36	1.52	1.49	12.63	15.62
14	CW	Curtiss-Wright Corp.	-2.55	-3.19	3.98	4.03	10.95	8.10
15	DVN	Devon Energy Corporation	0.90	-2.03	5.02	5.05	-2.57	4.11
16	DCO	Ducommun Incorporated	4.19	-3.19	1.38	1.38	17.37	8.10
17	DYII	Dynacq International Inc.	-4.54	-8.06 NA	NA		17.39	4.94
18	ECTX	ECtel Ltd.	5.44	-9.98	0.85	0.85	4.82	8.04
19	EXM	Excel Maritime Carriers	0.00	-2.36 NA	NA		-69.09	6.19
20	FOSL	Fossil, Inc.	2.63	-1.62	1.45	1.45	25.03	14.75
21	GDT	Guidant Corporation (New)	9.43	-0.64	1.66	1.65	14.40	11.90
22	HNI	HON INDUSTRIES, Inc.	20.69	2.55	1.52	1.38	17.17	12.65
23	HMC	Honda Motor Co., Ltd.	10.30	0.14	5.98	6.11	9.22	5.91

FIGURE 8.4 Spreadsheet Downloaded for the Industry Leaders Stock Screen, Showing Data Display Choices

Figures 8.5 and 8.6 show what the spreadsheet looks like after I added scoring capabilities. As you can see, I decided to score based on three data items.

1. I gave top priority to the relationship between the company's four-week share price percent change and that of its industry average. If the company's stock performed more than 5 percentage points better than the industry, I gave it a score of +8; if not, it scored –8.

2. The next priority went to estimate revision. If the consensus EPS estimate was increased in the past four weeks, I gave the company a score of +5; if not, I assigned a score of –5.

3. Finally, I compared the company's five-year average return on investment to the average for its industry over that same period. If the company was more than 5 percentage points better than the industry, the score was +3; if not, the score was –3.

Microsoft Excel - indyld scoring.xls

File Edit View Insert Format Tools Data Window FactSet Help

A1   =

Ticker	Name	Price % Change 4 Weeks	Price % Chg 4 Weeks Industry		Cur Fiscal Year EPS Mean	Cur Fiscal Year EPS 4 Wks Ago	5 Yr. Return On Investment	5 Yr ROI Indu
	Score			8			5	
PLCE	Children's Place, The	37.95	4.32	8	1.68	1.67	5	46.59
OCLR	Ocular Sciences, Inc.	9.49	-0.64	8	1.40	1.34	5	23.27
PCAR	PACCAR Inc.	22.13	0.14	8	2.09	2.02	5	11.19
SRNA	SERENA Software, Inc.	42.99	16.05	8	0.68	0.66	5	37.79
WCST	Wescast Industries Inc.	2.11	-3.13	8	4.62	4.61	5	20.38
CEC	CEC Entertainment, Inc.	11.16	2.75	8	2.23	2.22	5	14.77
COCO	Corinthian Colleges, Inc.	20.46	0.36	8	1.52	1.49	5	12.63
GDT	Guidant Corporation (New)	9.43	-0.64	8	1.66	1.65	5	14.40
HNI	HON INDUSTRIES, Inc.	20.69	2.55	8	1.52	1.38	5	17.17
THX	Houston Exploration, The	11.78	4.38	8	4.14	4.11	5	2.37
KSWS	K-Swiss Inc.	18.87	3.70	8	2.16	2.03	5	13.10
KPN	Koninklijke KPN N.V.	58.21	-9.98	8	-0.17	-0.18	5	7.61
KTC	Korea Telecom Corp.	9.66	-9.98	8	1.34	1.20	5	1.56
LTBG	Lightbridge, Inc.	10.06	-9.98	8	0.61	0.59	5	7.38
TLD	TDC A/S	7.65	-9.98	8	0.88	0.86	5	10.76
TYC	Tyco Int'l Ltd. (NEW)	13.23	4.84	8	3.55	3.42	5	4.11
VLKAY	Volkswagen AG	8.67	0.14	8	1.28	1.15	5	2.50

scoring template

FIGURE 8.5   Industry Leaders Spreadsheet with Scores Added In

Note the use of subtraction for share price performance and return on investment. Mathematically speaking, I really should have divided the two numbers to produce a proportionate (percentage) comparison. But some cells have negative numbers, and when those are incorporated into division operations I may get unintended results. For example, I want to give good scores to stocks that outperformed their industry averages. Suppose XYZ has a four-week price change of –10 percent while the industry average is –5 percent. A division-based formula would read the answer as +2 and assume, incorrectly, that XYZ was a better-than-average stock. A subtraction-based formula gives an answer of –5, correctly recognizing XYZ as a poor performer. We could address this by creating more complex formulas (probably involving Excel's Absolute Value function), but it's not worthwhile to complicate the process. We're just picking a group of stocks that warrant further review. We're not taking a math test.

I could easily have scored based on a greater number of data items. I held back so the illustration would be clearer. Even so, I am still able to identify 5 companies out of the 61 that get my highest priority for Step 2

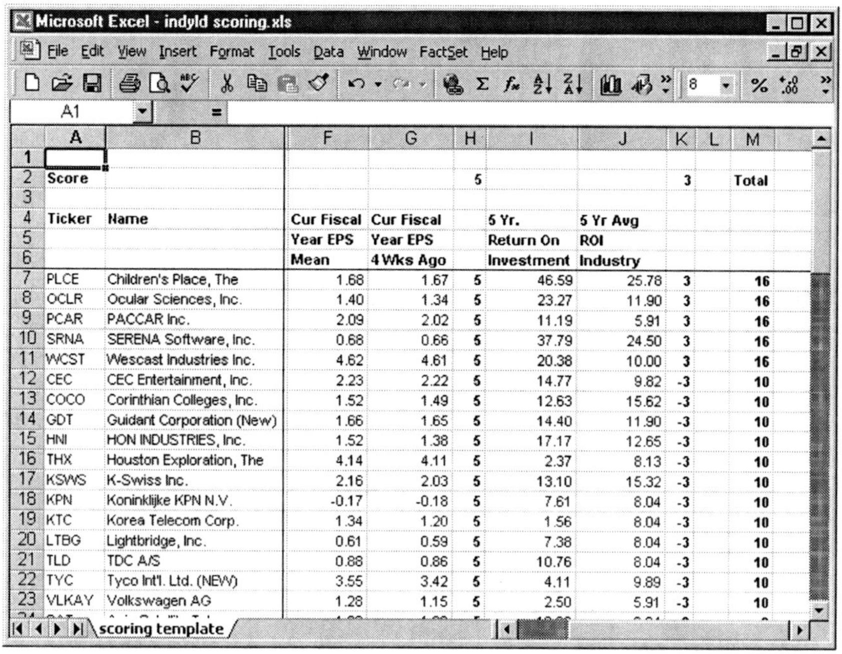

	A	B	F	G	H	I	J	K	L	M
1										
2	Score				5			3		Total
3										
4	Ticker	Name	Cur Fiscal	Cur Fiscal		5 Yr.	5 Yr Avg			
5			Year EPS	Year EPS		Return On	ROI			
6			Mean	4 Wks Ago		Investment	Industry			
7	PLCE	Children's Place, The	1.68	1.67	5	46.59	25.78	3		16
8	OCLR	Ocular Sciences, Inc.	1.40	1.34	5	23.27	11.90	3		16
9	PCAR	PACCAR Inc.	2.09	2.02	5	11.19	5.91	3		16
10	SRNA	SERENA Software, Inc.	0.68	0.66	5	37.79	24.50	3		16
11	WCST	Wescast Industries Inc.	4.62	4.61	5	20.38	10.00	3		16
12	CEC	CEC Entertainment, Inc.	2.23	2.22	5	14.77	9.82	-3		10
13	COCO	Corinthian Colleges, Inc.	1.52	1.49	5	12.63	15.62	-3		10
14	GDT	Guidant Corporation (New)	1.66	1.65	5	14.40	11.90	-3		10
15	HNI	HON INDUSTRIES, Inc.	1.52	1.38	5	17.17	12.65	-3		10
16	THX	Houston Exploration, The	4.14	4.11	5	2.37	8.13	-3		10
17	KSWS	K-Swiss Inc.	2.16	2.03	5	13.10	15.32	-3		10
18	KPN	Koninklijke KPN N.V.	-0.17	-0.18	5	7.61	8.04	-3		10
19	KTC	Korea Telecom Corp.	1.34	1.20	5	1.56	8.04	-3		10
20	LTBG	Lightbridge, Inc.	0.61	0.59	5	7.38	8.04	-3		10
21	TLD	TDC A/S	0.88	0.86	5	10.76	8.04	-3		10
22	TYC	Tyco Int'l. Ltd. (NEW)	3.55	3.42	5	4.11	9.89	-3		10
23	VLKAY	Volkswagen AG	1.28	1.15	5	2.50	5.91	-3		10

FIGURE 8.6 Continuation (the Right-Hand Portion) of Scored Industry Leaders Spreadsheet

(Analyze), 12 more for the next priority group, and 9 for the third group. If I stop there, at 26 companies, I probably have more than enough to look at. In fact, just quickly eyeballing the top 26 shows eight companies whose shares I either own as of this writing or am seriously considering.

Here's how the template was built.

- I started with the spreadsheet I downloaded from the Multex screener (Figure 8.4).
- I inserted some blank rows at the top of the spreadsheet to make room for the scores I'll be assigning.
- I inserted blank columns after each data set. These will hold component scores (in cells E2, H2, and K2).
- In column M, I created a formula that adds each of the component scores. For cell M7, the formula is:

  =E7+H7+K7

- In columns E, H, and K, each company row holds an IF-THEN formula.

The formula in E7 (that is copied down to other cells in the column) is as follows:

$$=IF(C7-D7>5,E\$2,E\$2*-1)$$

■ Similar formulas are created for columns H and K.

Let's take a closer look at the IF-THEN formula. (All other aspects of the spreadsheet are self-evident.) An Excel IF-THEN statement uses the format that can be summarized as follows: IF(A,B,C). A, B, and C, separated by commas, are parameters. A is the condition being evaluated as true or false. If A is true, then the answer is B. If A is false, the answer is C. Spreadsheet devotees recognize the dollar signs placed into the formula causing cell E2 to now be identified as E$2. That means it can be included in formulas copied down to other cells in the column without interfering with our desire to always have it refer back to row 2. So now, we can see that the formula says "if C7 minus D7 is greater than 5, the value of cell E7 is the same as the number that's sitting in E2; otherwise, if C7 minus D7 is not greater than 5, the value of E7 will be the negative of whatever number is in E2."

Obviously, there are many ways you can adjust this template. I assumed that for each data set you would use the score as a positive or negative number based on whether your IF-THEN condition is satisfied. You could, of course, vary that. Perhaps a good answer gets the positive number score and a bad answer gets a zero. Or a good answer might get the score multiplied by 2, and a bad answer gets the numeric score multiplied by −5. And there's nothing sacred about the scores 8, 5, and 3. These simply reflected my weighting preferences. You could adjust them however you choose; in fact, the template is designed such that you can always see the scores (they are placed near the top of the spreadsheet), thereby making it easy for you to decide whether you want to change them in a particular case. You could also rank the data points, as Morningstar does, and multiply ranks (make sure high numbers are associated with good ranks) by scores. The template is only a suggestion to help launch your imagination.

There's just one more item of housekeeping we need to cover here: storing a copy of your template in such a way that it truly is a template, something that could be used frequently with ever-changing company lists and data items. Figure 8.7 shows what my scoring spreadsheet looks like when stored as a master template. Here's how the update procedure would work.

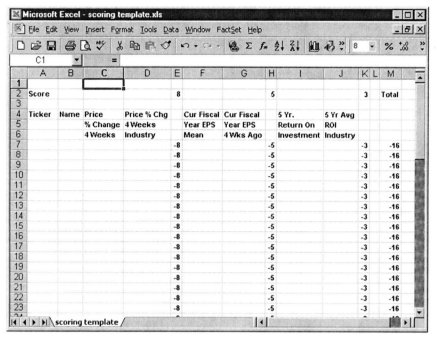

FIGURE 8.7 Spreadsheet Scoring Template

■ Start with the spreadsheet as shown in Figure 8.4. This is the way it looks when it's downloaded from my screener.

■ Copy columns A and B from Figure 8.4 (starting on row 4) to equivalent places in the template illustrated in Figure 8.7 (note that in the scoring template, the starting point drops to row 7 because I inserted some rows at the top when I created the template based on the Figure 8.4 spreadsheet that I downloaded directly from the screener).

■ Copy columns C and D from Figure 8.4 (starting on row 4) into the equivalent places in the Figure 8.7 template (the block that begins at cell C4 in the original spreadsheet is copied into the template in an area that starts with cell C7).

■ Copy columns E and F from Figure 8.4 (starting on row 4) into the equivalent places in the Figure 8.7 template (cell E4 in the original spreadsheet is equivalent to cell F7 in the template; besides shifting rows, by now we also have shifted columns so that E and F in the original sheet become F and G in the template).

■ Copy columns G and H from Figure 8.4 (starting on row 4) into the equivalent places in the Figure 8.7 template (cell G4 in the original spreadsheet is equivalent to cell I7 in the template; columns G and H in the original sheet become I and J in the template).

Needless to say, you may be constantly adjusting the template to different numbers of variable groups, or different ways of using the variables (e.g., sorting instead of comparing). Once again, though it bears repeating, simple sorting is a perfectly adequate solution. So if you find the do-it-yourself scoring material cumbersome, skip it.

## CHAPTER 9

Your Virtual Research Staff

Imagine you are in charge of an investment research group at a large firm. Perhaps you are a research director, a vice president for investment strategy, or an investment committee chairperson for a money management organization. You are in conference with your staff. The agenda is simple: select some stocks to recommend to clients or buy for your clients' accounts.

Now think about the job titles of the people sitting before you. In some cases, the organization chart might classify the meeting participants based on their expertise in different industries or sectors. In other words, there would be a technology analyst, an energy analyst, a capital goods analyst, and others. Another organizational structure might feature a roster that includes a technical analyst, a value specialist, an economist, and so forth.

Our efforts here will be more closely analogous to the latter. Each member of your research staff is expert in a particular investment style. Some will favor momentum. Others will favor value. Some will focus on large-cap stocks in general. Others will spend all their time examining small-cap and micro-cap stocks. One or two might base their methods on the teachings of well-known investment gurus such as Warren Buffett, T. Rowe Price, or Peter Lynch. Everybody who attends the meeting will have a buy list ready to present should you ask to see it. Each analyst also will have brought a written explanation of how the stocks were selected and why he/she believes this particular method has merit. That pretty much sums up what preset screens are all about.

OFF-THE-SHELF STOCK SCREENS

All the screening applications discussed in this book are accompanied by a set of preset screens. These consist of up-to-date stock lists and articles explaining the rationale behind the screen and how it was created.

On one level, preset screens can be viewed as an instructional device. Nobody likes to read manuals that tell you how to use a software application. Users typically prefer hands-on demonstrations that show them what they can do. Preset screens definitely fulfill this function. You can often assume that each collection of screens will show off the strengths of the application. Usually you can modify these screens and save them, under new names, as your own personal screens. That makes for a great way to get started with a new program.

Preset screens can also be valuable on an ongoing basis even to experienced users. Take seriously the aforementioned analogy comparing preset screens to staff reports you would receive if you were chairing an investment strategy meeting. All of the screens accompanying all of the screening applications discussed in this book are acceptable approaches. Some are better than others. But I haven't seen any I consider utterly unacceptable. In other words, suppose I were to cut up little pieces of paper and on each write the name of a preset screen and throw them all (or at least all that are somewhat compatible with my investment philosophy) into a hat. I would rather close my eyes, draw one slip, and analyze the stocks on the list produced by that screen than work with what Chapter 4 referred to as popular lists. If you chose to work this way, you'd already be ahead of many others who chase tips from friends, media hype, and so on. (Remember, I'm presupposing that you at least took the trouble to skim over the explanations and decided the screen is reasonably consistent with your investment preferences before throwing the name into the hat.)

It would be as if you were an ultra-easygoing research director. But not many executives, in any profession, are really that laid-back. A danger to the draw-from-a-hat management style is that you might get lulled into assuming that just because all options are generally acceptable today, the same will hold true six months from now. My statement about the widespread acceptability of the preset screens I see accompanying the applications covered here is based on what I'm observing as of the date of this writing. Things change. It's reasonable for me to assume that in the future new screens will be added and some existing screens will vanish.

This is why it is not worthwhile for me to give specifics about today's offerings. It's more important that we discuss how you can evaluate any preset screen you encounter, whether it's one that exists now or one that gets introduced after this book is published. So let's assume that you are going to be an active research director. You're going to look closely at the reports submitted by your staff, accept some as is, discard some, and mark up others, so to speak, to be returned to the analysts with instructions for revision. (This is why it's a good idea to have read Chapters 6 and 7 even if you would rather use preset screens than create your own.) When you evaluate preset screens (the virtual staff reports), consider three factors: the capabilities of the screener (how talented a group of virtual analysts is), the story behind each screen (the theme each virtual analyst is pursuing), and the specific screening tests (how each virtual analyst goes about implementing his/her strategy).

The Capabilities

Every real-world boss knows that most employees tend to be better at some things than others. It's unlikely that anyone is great at everything. But if the organization has been effectively built, you should expect that there will always be at least one person on the staff who can address any problem that may arise. The same holds true of your virtual research staff (the preset screens).

As with human staffers, each screening application has its own strengths and weaknesses. So even before you start to examine individual screens, you ought to be able to expect that certain applications are more likely to give you what you want than others.

If you favor technical analysis, start with ProSearch. (The preset screens aren't easily visible based on the site's layout at the time this is being written. You can find them by clicking on the Stocks tab, and then on the link to the Commentary Archives located near the bottom of the page. The screens are contained in the three categories grouped under the heading ProSearch Commentary Archives.) To be sure, that application offers a good number of fundamental screens. For example, as of this writing, there are more than 30 screens in the value category, not all of which include technical tests. But remember, you're like a virtual research director who can edit the reports submitted by your analysts. Each screen explanation tells you the exact tests being used, so you can easily re-create and then edit the screen. If your inclination is to add technical tests, ProSearch is the place to be because that's the program that offers the greatest capabilities in this area. (Put another way, the ProSearch virtual analyst is your best chartist.)

If you like analytics, Morningstar and ProSearch should get special attention. As a matter of fact, proprietary analytics (and proprietary Morningstar category labels that, from a screening standpoint, function similarly to ratings) are the main ingredients in its preset screens. And watch the evolution of MSN.Money. As of this writing, its StockScouter rating system is still fairly new. I wouldn't be surprised to see an increase in the availability of preset screens using it as time passes.

If you want screens based on comparative testing and that take advantage of the functional themes described in Chapter 7, check the preset screens offered on the MultexInvestor.com web site (all of which are detailed in the appendix to this chapter). They were created with Multex's premium screener, so you won't be able to edit them in the free application. But the use of comparative screening is extensive (especially cross-sectional comparison), so those lists can certainly position you well for Step 2 (Analyze).

If you like the idea of relative strength percentile tests, the preset screens that come with Stock Investor Pro and SmartMoneySelect deserve close attention. Many use such tests. And if they aren't used exactly the way you want them used, you can edit the screens. Stock Investor Pro is also a fertile source of preset screens based on year-by-year data trends.

The Stories

Use what you learned in Chapter 7 to evaluate the "story" serving as the foundation for the preset screens you examine. The title of the screen will suggest what you can expect to see in terms of primary theme. The preset screens presented on MultexInvestor.com are the ones that most closely work with the secondary/alternate themes in the manner described in Chapter 7, so you should easily be able to identify which role each test is playing.

With preset screens available elsewhere, it won't always be easy to recognize different themes. Usually, themes other than primary will be present. In some cases, though, they will be so numerous as to make it seem hardly worthwhile to bother analyzing the screen this way. But it can be worth your while to take the trouble to go through the screen, test by test, and identify which theme each represents. This exercise will lead to one of two outcomes. You may decide that you like the generalist approach (i.e., lots of one-test secondary or alternative themes) taken by the screen. The other possibility is that you may decide some tests aren't really contributing to the screen in a way you deem worthwhile. If this occurs, delete the test.

Don't worry if removing a test increases the list from, say, 15 stocks to 70. From a time management standpoint, it's good to narrow a list. But it doesn't help to do so based on criteria that are of questionable relevance. You'd be better off either editing the screen to increase the stringency of another test that's more relevant to your goals or accepting the oversized list and using the sorting or scoring techniques described in Chapter 8 to narrow the list in a more constructive manner.

Guru Screens   One widely available preset screen story line is based on guru methodology. These gurus are widely recognized successful investors (past and present), such as Peter Lynch, Warren Buffett, William O'Neil, T. Rowe Price, Martin Zweig, and Benjamin Graham.

On the whole, these so-called gurus achieved powerful reputations based on perceived merit. It's not always easy to quantifiably demonstrate that their methods will produce market-beating returns. Some were active in a previous generation, so we can't be absolutely certain that the methods for which they are noted still work. And even those who are active today don't necessarily invest under conditions that require them to regularly report their results publicly. (For example, it's been more than a decade since Peter Lynch, one of the most revered gurus, stepped down from the helm at Fidelity Magellan.) Nevertheless, guru screens are accompanied by good explanations of why the screen has been built as it has. Hence it's easy for you to determine whether the screen is compatible with your style. Sometimes the commentary is written by the gurus (if not on the sites that present the guru screen, then elsewhere in books, articles, etc.), and other times we're dealing with text written by people who closely study the gurus' methods.

Among the applications covered here, there are two sources of guru content. One of them, Quicken.com, offers analytic data reports based on guru methodology, but does not use guru concepts in its preset screens. So we'll postpone consideration of that site's content until the appropriate point in Step 2 (Analyze). At this time, we'll confine consideration to use of guru concepts in Step 1 (Find). Preset screens based on this theme are included with Stock Investor Pro.

Not every Stock Investor Pro preset screen is guru-based. But most of them are. The menu includes Warren Buffett (a company quality theme), David Dreman (a contrarian theme), Richard Driehaus (a momentum theme), Philip Fisher (a quality/growth theme), Benjamin Graham (a value theme), Josef Lakonishok (a value theme), Peter Lynch (a quality/growth/value theme), Michael Murphy (a technology theme), the National Association of Investors Corporation (a company quality theme), John Neff (a contrarian theme), James O'Shaughnessy (a growth/value theme), T. Rowe Price (a growth theme), John Templeton (a safety/value theme), Ralph Wagner (a small company theme), and Geraldine Weiss (a blue-chip theme).

This roster is impressive. But an important question quickly comes to mind. Did the gurus really create, or even approve, any of these screens? The articles accompanying the screens (in the help material built into the program and in the Stock Investor section of the AAII.com web site) feature extensive attributions to the gurus and make it clear that these screens are based on the AAII's interpretation of each guru's approach. This makes sense. Many of the guru philosophies were conceived and disseminated before stock screening and Internet data reports became widespread. And nonnumeric considerations are often important to the decision-making processes of these well-known investors. So it seems inevitable that these screens would reflect interpretation of the gurus' work, rather than actual dictates from the gurus themselves.

But do the gurus endorse these interpretations? On a human level, one might view the situation this way: A living guru who saw his/her name attached to a screen that was wholly inadequate as a representation of his/her ideas would likely contact AAII and object. If that happens, it's hard to imagine AAII persisting in publishing a guru screen under such conditions. Therefore, we can assume the guru at least acquiesces to the screen that purports to be based on his/her ideas. As logical as this might sound, I have to confess that a good lawyer would be horrified at such reasoning, and would object vigorously if such an argument were presented in a courtroom. And you can be sure any judge would sustain the objection. It's tempting to think famous people monitor and endorse or refute what others say about them. But I wouldn't invest real-world money based on an assumption this is really so. Public figures are well within their rights to ignore what is said about them.

Fortunately, for our purposes, we really don't have to take a position one way or the other on this issue. All we need do is read the explanations and look at the screening tests as well as the back-test results posted for each screen on the AAII.com web site. If you like the screen, use it. If you don't like it, don't use it or modify it. In fact, that's the approach you should take even if the guru publicly states he/she saw the screen and loves it.

Data Mining   Be careful about stories built around a "what works" plot line that looks something like this:

> *This screen was created in consultation with or based on the work of so-and-so, who studied such-and-such number of data items over this many years and concluded, to an impressive degree of statistical significance, that certain factors are closely associated with superior share price performance. The tests used in this screen are those identified by so-and-so's research as the most productive.*

It's easy to get lulled into believing this is a guru screen. But it's not. In truth, you're looking at something that might help you if you get lucky, but can just as easily prove damaging to your financial health: data mining. Here's how you can tell the difference. Explanations accompanying legitimate guru screens focus on *why* one ought to be able to assume a particular strategy should work. Data miners, on the other hand, stick to *what*. If you are able to ask them why a method should work, they are likely to dodge the question and instead produce lots of data showing that the method actually did work during a particular sample period in the past.

I have to confess that this section poses a diplomatic dilemma for me. A lot of excellent reputable research is conducted by studying historical relationships between data items and stock price performance. In fact, that's the only kind of research that can be done (since the past is all that's available to us). I've done a lot of it myself.

The term *data mining* is used to disparage research that is seen by knowledgeable experts as lacking in credibility. The best way to drive home the point is to show you a real-life example of data mining in action. I paused from writing this for about two minutes (you should already be starting to shudder) to do a study. I examined the following ratio:

Current Dividend Yield/5 Year Industry Average Return on Assets

During the 52-week period I examined, all stocks in Multex's approximately 9,000-company database experienced a median return of –0.46 percent. I looked separately at the stocks above and below the overall median. Shares of companies with the higher yield to five-year industry ROA ratio posted a median return of +6.07 percent. Shares of companies with lower ratios had a median return of –2.35 percent. That's a noteworthy difference. I didn't bother to perform the statistical significance computations (my two minutes had elapsed), but my gut tells me it's probably significant under standard statistical tests. So I could plausibly hunt down some movers and shakers at BogusDataMining.com and persuade them to build a preset screen based on Gerstein's research into the relationship between dividend yield and long-term return on assets for the industry in which the company is classified.

Would you actually use such a screen? Don't count play-money office stock-picking contests. (If Multex runs one in the near future, I think I might give this screen a try, unless somebody else sees the manuscript and steals my hot new what-works idea.) I mean, would you use it with your own real money, your retirement account?

I think you get the idea. If you feel averse to using this method, you are correctly perceiving that there is a big difference between correlation and causation. Correlation refers to things that tend to happen together.

You might observe that every time you stick your hand into a flame you are burned. So you would say that sticking your hand into fire is closely correlated with a burning sensation. Does sticking your hand into fire *cause* the burning sensation? Yeah. We have correlation and causation. Let's go further. Suppose somebody in your house always has a view out the window as you're conducting your research, and notes that every time you stick your hand in the flame a car with an even-numbered license plate passes by. Again we have a great correlation. But did sticking your hand into fire cause the cars with even-numbered tags to drive by (or vice versa)? Stop laughing! This is what data miners do. They rely on correlation alone without giving proper attention to the difference between correlation and causation.

So don't use a preset "what works" screen until you have reviewed it and satisfied yourself that you believe the tests relate to factors that really can be said to cause superior share price performance. You don't have to conduct your own studies. Common sense will suffice.

Is it reasonable to assume earnings and/or sales growth have some causal relationship with superior investment performance? Yes (assuming you understand all the issues that arise when you use past performance to assess future prospects). That was easy. Let's try another example. Can you assume large company size has some causal relationship with superior investment performance? I warn you, this is a trick question. Data miners can produce reams of vintage 1980s–1990s data showing powerful correlation. But what about causation?

From a pure theory standpoint, it's hard to argue there's a causal relationship between size and market capitalization. But the world doesn't always work exactly as theory suggests. In the 1980s and 1990s, there was an increasing tendency of investors to index (create or add funds to portfolios built to mimic the S&P 500), and many overseas investors who put money into the U.S. markets tended to favor large companies they had heard of whose shares were highly liquid. These trends boosted demand for big-company shares, and probably account for some degree of causation between large size and superior share price performance.

So now we can accept large size as a legitimate test in a "what works" preset screen. Right? Remember, I told you this was a trick question. Indexing and liquidity weren't the only factors that impacted big-cap stocks during those decades. In the late 1970s, following a prolonged period of lackluster performance for the big caps (and strong performance for what were then called secondary stocks), blue-chip valuations were extremely low. That's not the case as this is written. Also during the 1980s and 1990s, large companies made considerable headway focusing on core operations and making themselves more cost efficient. Profit gains achieved this way cannot persist indefinitely. At some point, sales growth has to become the primary driver.

So what's ahead for big-cap stocks? The valuation and cost efficiency underpinnings that stimulated share price performance in the 1980s and 1990s are, arguably, gone. The liquidity argument is probably alive, but how long will investors index this way if share prices keep rising at a pace that is disproportionate to earnings growth? It's hard to imagine mega-sized funds pumping massive amounts of money into small stocks. But they might move more money into overseas markets in the years ahead (especially if economic systems there continue to open and if non-U.S. companies improve their efficiencies).

Don't take this as a forecast that big-cap U.S. stocks will turn into laggards. Maybe enough of what drove them in the recent past will persist and enable them to continue leading the way. Or they might really run out of steam. Each investor should come up with his/her own answer. I raise the issue as an example of the way you have to approach a "what works" preset screen. First, ask yourself whether the relationships are causal or nothing more than correlation. If a cause-and-effect relationship is present, go to the next question. Ask why the causal relationship existed in the past, and decide whether you expect those factors to persist in the future. This thought process is what separates legitimate research from data mining.

The Tests

Even if you like a story, it's still possible you may find that a preset screen isn't quite to your liking because of one or more specific tests. So if the application allows you to edit the screen, go for it. You will have your own preferences as to certain kinds of tests you'll dislike and want to eliminate or modify. To help you get started in your own critical screen-editing endeavors, I'll share three categories of personal pet peeves, tests I often see in preset screens that drive me crazy.

Size   As you might have guessed from the preceding section, I'm not impressed by the so-called research that suggests big cap is the place to be (there seems to be a lot of data mining mixed in). If anything, I'm slightly biased against large stocks as of the time this is written. I don't expect all the factors that contributed to past successes to continue, and many of those stocks are richly valued. For me, the main downsides to small company investing are lack of trading liquidity and hopeless obscurity. So I'll accept a volume- or exchange-based test from time to time. But for the most part, I'd rather deal with such issues in Step 2 (Analyze). You might think I'd be inclined to add company-size tests designed to spotlight smaller companies. But there's really no reason to do that. My skepticism toward big caps isn't so severe as to make me want to completely bar them from view. I'll go for an individual blue chip that strikes me as reasonably valued in light of my assessment of overall fundamentals. Bottom line: When I'm investing my own money (as opposed to creating a theme-oriented screen based on some sort of on-the-job need), I see no constructive purpose to having size tests. In preset screens, I delete tests relating to sales levels or market capitalization.

Numerical Debt Ratios I want to scream when I see a test requiring debt-to-capital ratios to be below 50 percent or 40 percent or any specific number. The authors of these screens claim this helps you mitigate risk. I vehemently disagree. Those tests systematically eliminate many moderate-to low-risk companies in industries that normally utilize high debt (such as banking). And they aren't even protecting you against true financial danger. It's better to screen debt ratios based on comparison to industry averages. Other helpful risk gauges are interest coverage and liquidity ratios. If your screener doesn't offer variables that let you build proper financial risk tests, at least delete the bogus ones and confine your risk assessment to Step 2 (Analyze). This, by the way, is one example of why it's good to see screening as just one part of a comprehensive four-step method. Our ability to address financial risk in Step 2 (Analyze) means we can afford to reject the bad-test-is-better-than-no-test logic that might be put forth to justify the debt measures often used in preset screens.

Meager Performance Hurdles A few hours before writing these words, I had occasion to notice a preset screen accompanied by an explanation that made reference to, among other things, a desire to find strong companies. So what kind of test does it use? One was a requirement that operating margin be above 1 percent. *Yawn!* One measly little percent? That's all? Even if this screener was restricted to numeric comparisons (in fact, the one I was looking at was quite able to handle more complex tests), how about something that is at least close to the S&P 500 (for which the operating margin has been running in the mid-teens). I feel the same way about tiny return on equity hurdles (like 5 percent or 10 percent, well below the S&P 500 average, which has been hovering near 20 percent). I can see good reasons for setting hurdles below the S&P 500 averages (i.e., there may be tougher tests elsewhere in the screen). But at least get somewhere in the ballpark if you really are trying to find superior investment opportunities.

MEETING OF THE MINDS

Let's go back to the research meeting scenario at the opening of this chapter. It assumed you were the kind of research director who collects input from each of your analysts, retires to the privacy of your office, reviews everything, and selects one or two (perhaps even three) sets of recommendations that will serve as a basis for action. The rest are discarded.

Now, let's change the management style to a more collaborative approach. No longer will some staff buy lists be accepted and others rejected in their entirety. Now everybody is going to participate. All stocks suggested by all the analysts will be aggregated into a single master list, and then you'll narrow it down to an elite best-of-the-best listing.

This is very similar to the layered screening technique discussed in Chapter 7. But there's good reason to treat this as a separate topic. In Chapter 7, we assumed all the screens in the first layer were based, more or less, on the same primary theme. Now we're dropping that assumption. These layer-one screens can consist of any possible combination of themes. You can mix and match styles at will.

The reason I discuss this technique here is because it lends itself especially well to working with preset screens. In fact, that's exactly how I came upon this method; it was developed as a technique to help me work efficiently with the 19 preset screens I maintain on the MultexInvestor.com web site. Before you read about the benefits of this technique, it's important that you understand exactly what is being done. So in the next section, I'll explain more fully how to use this collaborative effort to produce best-of-the-best stock lists. You'll see that it requires some work. But in the final section of this chapter, I'll explain the benefits so you can judge for yourself whether it is worth the effort.

I will, however, reiterate that the technique I describe is something I do every week in the real world. It's how I narrow the several hundred stocks appearing each week in the 19 preset MultexInvestor.com screens to a manageable number from which I'll select, using Step 2 (Analyze) and Step 3 (Buy), the ones I write about as feature recommendations. And for the past few months, *Forbes* magazine's Forbes.com web site has recognized MultexInvestor.com as a "Best of the Web *Forbes* Favorite" in three categories. In the "Stock Pickers" category, *Forbes* described the best stock picking feature of MultexInvestor.com as follows: "Download all of the 700-odd stocks appearing on the weekly screens into a portfolio, which you can then run through custom screen." The feature cited by *Forbes* is the one that will be described here.

The Best of the Best

I'll illustrate this technique two ways. First, we'll look at the easy way, an approach the average real-world investor can implement with little effort. Then I'll show you how I actually go about combining all my screens in such a way as to allow me to efficiently identify stocks that might be worthy of being featured on MultexInvestor.com. I don't imagine you will use the hard way. Presumably, you only need to select stocks for your own portfolio or for your clients. My task on MultexInvestor.com is broader. I search for stocks that would be of interest not just to me, but to our user base as a whole, which includes many investors whose goals and styles differ from mine. Nevertheless, I'll show you the hard way so you can see how far you can go with this method.

The Easy Way   Start by creating a master list of tickers that will (going back to the earlier analogy) serve as the sum total of all ideas put forth by all analysts on your virtual research staff. If you want to use all the tickers in all the preset screens on MultexInvestor.com, much of the grunt work has been done for you. As noted by *Forbes*, a master list is made available on the site. Download it, and copy the tickers to your clipboard, paste it into the user-portfolio area of the free Multex application, and save it under a name like Select or Master List. Then go into the program's screening area and switch out of the 9,000-plus stock Active Company database and into your Select portfolio, which will number about 400 stocks, depending on market conditions. Create some layer-two screens to run against this smaller, more elite data universe. Here are some suggestions.

The following screen sifts through the elite group and searches for those most heavily favored by analysts. (Even if you are generally skeptical about analyst recommendations, it becomes a lot easier to get comfortable with them if this screen is run only against a small database consisting of stocks that have been prequalified, so to speak, through other screens.)

1. Mean Rating <= 1.25
2. Current Price >= (52-Week High Price) * .90
3. EPS Surprise Latest Quarter > 0

The first test directly measures analyst ratings. The others are secondary themes. The second test, seeking stocks trading near 52-week highs, confirms that the market in general is as bullish as the analysts. The third test seeking positive earnings surprise addresses a factor that may be contributing to the general analyst bullishness.

Here's another elite screen seeking stocks that are well regarded by a variety of investment community constituencies.

1. Institutional Buy Transactions (Net of Sells) Latest Quarter > 0
2. Institutional % Ownership > 50
3. Insider Buy Transactions (Net of Sells) Latest Quarter > 0
4. Short Interest Ratio Now < Short Interest Ratio Prior Month
5. Mean Rating <= 1.75

Note that the analyst rating test is less stringent than in the preceding screen. I can afford to relax that one here, because I add tests seeking bullishness by other groups. Note, too, the absence of a secondary or alternative theme. I don't need one now because this screen is a layer-two screen for the Select group. Other themes were addressed via the screens that produced this elite universe.

Here's a screen that searches the Select group for stocks with positive price trends.

1. Share Price % Change Last 13 Weeks > 0
2. Share Price % Change Last 26 Weeks > 0
3. Share Price % Change Last 4 Weeks > Share Price % Change Last 13 Weeks
4. Share Price % Change Last 4 Weeks > Share Price % Change Last 26 Weeks

The absence of industry comparison (a feature not readily available in the free Multex offering) would make me reluctant to apply a screen like this against a full database. But in this context, I can relax since all stocks in the elite group were prequalified via other screens that did use the kinds of tests I prefer (including, in many cases, company-industry share price performance comparisons).

The Hard Way On MultexInvestor.com, I maintain 19 preset screens (that, as of this writing, are updated weekly via downloadable Excel spreadsheets). They were all created using our premium screener. I cannot promise that the preset screen collection existing as of this writing will remain exactly as is forever (or even through the publication date of this book). The world evolves, and it's reasonable to expect my screen roster to evolve along with it, albeit at a more measured pace, to guard against erratic shifting in response to the short-term fads. But we can effectively examine the meeting-of-the-minds approach using this specific group of screens. (Today's collection is presented in the appendix to this chapter.)

Once per week, I download the result set for each screen into an Excel spreadsheet. This takes just a couple of minutes. I copy the tickers from the first screen-spreadsheet into my Windows clipboard and then paste it into a new "master" spreadsheet I name Select.xls. After doing that, I go into my next screen-spreadsheet and copy those tickers into Select.xls just below the first list. I continue on with each screen-spreadsheet in turn. After I've gone through all 19 screen-spreadsheets, column A in Select.xls will contain one long list of all the tickers copied from all the other spreadsheets. Next, I import (via conventional clipboard copy-and-paste) that big ticker list into the Multex screener as a user-portfolio that I name Select. I don't even have to worry about duplicates, tickers that appear in more than one screen. The application's user-portfolio feature will eliminate them for me. (I also make the master ticker list available on the MultexInvestor.com site so users can create their own Select portfolios in the free application.)

The next thing I do is switch from the 9,000-plus Active Company database to the Select user portfolio (custom-created mini-database). Using this elite universe of about 400 stocks, I run four layer-two "super-screens" I created. Here they are.

Analyst Favorites
1. Current Year Consensus EPS Estimate Now >= Estimate as of 8 Weeks Ago
2. Current Quarter Consensus EPS Estimate Now >= Estimate as of 4 Weeks Ago
3. Long-Term EPS Growth Projected 4 Weeks Ago >= Estimate as of 8 Weeks Ago
4. Long-Term EPS Growth Projected 8 Weeks Ago >= Estimate as of 13 Weeks Ago
5. EPS Surprise Latest Quarter >= 0
6. # Strong Buy Ratings > # Buy Ratings
7. # Strong Buy Ratings > # Hold Ratings
8. # Underperform Ratings = 0
9. # Sell Ratings = 0

Industry (Cross-Sectional) Comparison
1. EPS % Growth Latest Quarter >= Industry Average EPS % Growth Latest Quarter
2. EPS % Growth Trailing 12 Months >= Industry Average EPS % Growth TTM

3. EPS % Growth Last 3 Years >= Industry Average EPS % Growth Last 3 Years
4. EPS % Growth Last 5 Years >= Industry Average EPS % Growth Last 5 Years
5. TTM Return on Investment >= Industry Average TTM ROI
6. 5 Year ROI >= Industry Average 5 Year ROI

Historical (Time Series) Comparison
1. EPS % Growth Last 3 Years >= EPS % Growth Last 5 Years
2. EPS % Growth TTM >= EPS % Growth Last 5 Years
3. EPS % Growth Latest Quarter >= EPS % Growth TTM
4. Operating Margin TTM >= 5 Year Average Operating Margin
5. ROI TTM >= 5 Year Average ROI

Market Factors
1. 4 Week Share Price % Change >= Industry Average 4 Week Share Price % Change
2. Current Price >= (52 Week High Price) * .85
3. Institutional % Ownership < 90
4. Institutional % Ownership <= (Industry Average Institutional % Ownership) * 1.5
5. Institutional Net Shares Purchased Latest Quarter > 0
6. Institutional Net Shares Purchased Latest Quarter >= Institutional Net Shares Purchased Prior Quarter
7. Short Interest 1 Month % Change <= 0

That gives me four best-of-the-best lists. But as long as I'm sharing the details of my work methods, let's take it all the way home.

I repeat the procedure I used to create Select.xls using just the four super-screen spreadsheet downloads. I create another master list from which I create another portfolio; this one is lovingly named Ultimate. Using the premium Multex screener, I download the Ultimate portfolio into a single spreadsheet (Ultimate.xls) formatted based on my favorite data items, which I sort or score as described in Chapter 8. This is how I identify stocks I consider featuring on MultexInvestor.com. The final decision is made after I look at those stocks based on Step 2 (Analyze) and Step 3 (Buy).

Why Bother?

As noted, you probably won't need to go as far as I do with the "hard way" (since the method was designed to help me pick stocks that would be interesting to a broader audience consisting of many who don't share my investment philosophies). But even the easy way requires some commitment, at the very least a willingness to choose screening programs that allow you to screen on a universe you custom create (a user-defined portfolio). I hope more screeners will add that functionality in the future, but as of this writing only three of the programs discussed in this book have full portfolio-import capability: the two Multex screeners and Stock Investor Pro. So it is incumbent upon me to explain why you may find it worthwhile to try this procedure.

Application Limitations   The fact that some screeners have limited capabilities is more than a roadblock. It is also an incentive. There are more programs that allow you to download spreadsheets than import tickers. Hence you might want to download result sets from a variety of technical screens created in ProSearch and import them into a Multex screener as an elite universe for layer-two screens based on the latter's strong fundamental comparison and analyst data categories. You might also import a set of layer-one Stock Investor Pro screens (which may consist of or include that program's impressive array of guru-based preset offerings) into the free Multex application. In the latter program, create layer-two screens based on more time-sensitive data items (remember, Stock Investor Pro is a monthly CD accompanied by weekly downloadable updates, while Multex is updated daily).

Educational Safety Net   Many would love to create their own screens but are reluctant to use them to invest real money due to lingering fears they might have done something wrong and have lists that aren't really all that good. It's understandable that a novice could feel uncomfortable when working with a database containing many thousands of companies. This technique can help you get past beginner's block by serving as a safety net. If you use an elite list based on preset screens, such as those available on MultexInvestor.com or through Stock Investor Pro, you are less likely to get burned even if your initial efforts at screening are faulty. You can't wander too far astray since every stock in the select portfolio has already been prequalified through the screening talents of experienced professionals.

Prequalified Stock Market   This is the substantive benefit to the meeting of the minds or collaborative approach. In a sense, it represents the flip side of much of what we've discussed so far. Our work to this point has assumed we want to concentrate our efforts in creating the best screens possible to search for a manageable number of winning stocks buried in an overwhelming data universe consisting of thousands of the best gems, the worst dogs, and everything in between. Because the database is so vast and so varied when it comes to investment merit, we think carefully about the screening tests we create. Now we turn the tables. If we use a prequalified data universe that presumably has a far higher gem-to-dog ratio than the full database, we can afford to be casual about the screening tests we now employ.

Let's illustrate by looking at another screen I created, using the free Multex application, for the Select universe. It's a value-growth screen.

1. Projected P/E Based on Estimated EPS/Projected Long-Term Growth <= 1
2. Trailing 12 Month EPS Growth >= 20
3. 3 Year EPS Growth >= 20
4. 5 Year EPS Growth >= 20
5. Projected Long-Term Growth >= 20

The growth tests should raise an eyebrow in light of what I said elsewhere in this book. Recall, from Chapter 6, that numeric tests such as these are my least favorite. I cited them again earlier in this chapter when I discussed my preset screen pet peeves. Under normal circumstances, I'd rather hunt for a new program than stick with one that doesn't allow for comparative screening and forces me to rely on numeric tests. But the situation is different now. This is not a normal screen. It's a special screen created for the elite group comprised of stocks uncovered in my other screens. A company can't make it into this prequalified group unless it passes a reasonable number of the more sophisticated tests I prefer to use.

This sounds like a roundabout way to achieve the same result that would have occurred had I simply switched to a more robust program and created a screen with the kinds of tests I prefer to use. But that assumes I have access to such an application. Many don't want to pay high prices for top-of-the-line programs. Running simple screens that can be created using the free Multex application against the Select portfolio based on the preset screens I created in the premium screener is an indirect way for anyone to tap into the power of the pricier product.

But there's more. As we discussed in Chapter 7 in connection with layered screening, it's one thing to say you're a growth investor but another to articulate exactly how to define growth. In that chapter, we solved the problem by suggesting you define growth in as many ways as you can conceive, creating a series of lists that will then be aggregated and narrowed to a manageable number of stocks through a layer-two screen. This chapter offers a flip side. If you establish a smaller but superior data universe, you can afford to define growth less precisely than would otherwise be the case. Indeed, lines 2 through 5 of the preceding value-growth screen would suffice quite well for growth investors using a prequalified select universe, but not as a basic screen run against a full database.

Remember, too, that this material is included in the chapter dealing with preset screens. I am assuming most readers who work with an elite universe will create one based on a series of preset screens. So, in fact, you're really doing exactly what I suggested with the research meeting analogy. You aren't rolling up your sleeves and doing the heavy screening work yourself. You're relying on your virtual staff to do that for you. Then you aggregate the results and create a best-of-the-best screen that blends your generally articulated goals with the efforts of those who created the preset screens. You really are acting as a manager using your own methods to pick among the best suggestions presented to you by your staff, or, put another way, to achieve a meeting of the minds.

APPENDIX TO CHAPTER 9:
MULTEXINVESTOR.COM PRESET SCREENS

This is the group of preset screens that is available, as of this writing, on the MultexInvestor.com web site. All the screens were created using the premium Multex screener. Note that changes may have occurred by the time this book is published, and more may occur in the future.

As is done elsewhere in this book, the tests are described in a generic language that's broadly similar to the one used with the premium Multex screener but modified to be understandable at a glance even to those who aren't familiar with that application. Note that in several instances (wherever I combine a multiplication factor with a "greater than" comparison to a number that could conceivably be negative, such as a growth rate), the actual screen adds the negative number adjustment explained in Chapter 5.

The following abbreviations are used throughout this appendix:

MRQ	Most recent quarter
PYQ	In comparison with the prior year quarter (the same quarter a year ago)
TTM	Trailing 12 months
Indy. Avg.	Industry average

ROA	Return on assets
ROE	Return on equity
ROI	Return on investment
LTDebtRatio	Ratio of long-term debt to equity
TotalDebtRatio	Ratio of total debt to equity
CurrYr Est	Consensus estimate of EPS for the company's current fiscal year
CurrQtr Est	Consensus estimate of EPS for the company's current fiscal quarter
NextQtr Est	Consensus estimate of EPS for the company's next fiscal quarter
NextYr Est	Consensus estimate of EPS for the company's next fiscal year
ProjPE CurrYr	P/E calculated using estimate of EPS for current fiscal year
ProjPE NextYr	P/E calculated using estimate of EPS for next fiscal year
LT Growth	Consensus projection of long-term (three- to five-year) EPS growth
OTC	Over the counter

GROWTH CATEGORY

These screens reflect a variety of growth-oriented methods that can be used to select stocks.

Accelerating EPS Growth

Primary Theme: Find companies whose EPS is growing at an accelerating pace. Make sure, in Step 2 (Analyze), to check company life cycle issues to assess the likelihood that the rapid growth isn't about to end. Note the use of a numeric test in line 1 to set a floor for other time series comparisons. Lines 4 and 5 are supporting themes.

1. 3 Year % EPS Growth >= 15
2. TTM % EPS Growth >= 3 Year % EPS Growth
3. PYQ % EPS Growth >= TTM % EPS Growth

4. CurrYr Est Now > CurrYr Est 8 Weeks Ago
5. Share Price % Change Last 4 Weeks > Indy. Avg. Share Price % Change Last 4 Weeks

Relative Growth

Primary Theme: Seek growth companies, with growth measured based on a series of cross-sectional, time series, and line item comparisons. Line 7 is an alternative earnings-quality test.

1. PYQ EPS % Change > Indy. Avg. PYQ EPS % Change
2. PYQ EPS % Change > TTM EPS % Change
3. TTM EPS % Change > TTM Sales % Change
4. 3 Year EPS % Change > 3 Year Sales % Change
5. TTM Sales % Change > Indy. Avg. TTM Sales % Change
6. TTM Sales % Change > 3 Year Sales % Change
7. Tax Rate >= 25

Relative Momentum

Primary Theme: Find stocks/companies that have been beating their industry peers by wide margins in terms of sales growth and share price performance. Lines 7 and 8 are secondary tests. Line 7 is behavioral in nature, assuming a high PEG ratio is evidence of favorable expectations for the future.

1. PYQ Sales % Change > (Indy. Avg. PYQ Sales % Change) * 1.5
2. TTM Sales % Change > (Indy. Avg. TTM Sales % Change) * 1.5
3. Share Price % Change Last 4 Weeks > 0
4. Share Price % Change Last 4 Weeks > (Indy. Avg. Share Price % Change Last 4 Weeks) * 1.5
5. Share Price % Change Last 52 Weeks > 0
6. Share Price % Change Last 52 Weeks > (Indy. Avg. Share Price % Change Last 52 Weeks) * 1.5
7. ProjPE NextYr > LT Growth
8. CurrYr Est Now >= CurrYr Est 8 Weeks Ago

Rising Expectations

Primary Theme: Find situations where analysts are raising estimates to try to catch up to companies that habitually outperform consensus expectations. Lines 7 to 9 are secondary tests.

1. EPS Surprise Latest Quarter > 0
2. EPS Surprise 2 Quarters Ago > 0
3. EPS Surprise 3 Quarters Ago > 0
4. EPS Surprise 4 Quarters Ago > 0
5. CurrYr Est Now > CurrYr Est 4 Weeks Ago
6. CurrYr Est 4 Weeks Ago > CurrYr Est 8 Weeks Ago
7. Institutional (Net) Shares Purchased Latest Quarter > 0
8. Institutional (Net) Shares Purchased Latest Quarter > Institutional (Net) Shares Purchased Prior Quarter
9. Share Price % Change Last 4 Weeks > Indy. Avg. Share Price % Change Last 4 Weeks

Sales Growth Leaders

Primary Theme: Recognizing that good EPS growth cannot persist indefinitely absent healthy sales growth, this screen focuses on the latter. Lines 4 and 5 are secondary tests. Line 6 is an alternative test.

1. PYQ Sales % Change > 0
2. PYQ Sales % Change > Indy. Avg. PYQ Sales % Change
3. Consecutive Quarter Sales % Change > 0
4. CurrYr Est Now > CurrYr Est 4 Weeks Ago
5. CurrYr Est 4 Weeks Ago > CurrYr Est 8 Weeks Ago
6. Insiders (Net) Shares Purchased Latest Quarter > 0

VALUE CATEGORY

These screens reflect a variety of value-oriented methods that can be used to select stocks.

Catching Up

Primary Theme: Work with the market's tendency to rotate. Find stocks that have been outside the spotlight but deserve better and may be ready to move to center stage. Lines 1 to 3 establish lackluster, but not horrible, share price performance within an industry that is faring at least respectably. The other lines identify fundamentals suggesting the company's stock deserves to catch up with the pack. Lines 4 to 8 are secondary tests, since the growth themes are more directly related to share price performance. Line 9 could be considered an alternative test, since the link between return on capital and share price performance is not usually seen as being immediate.

1. Share Price % Change Last 4 Weeks < Indy. Avg. Share Price % Change Last 4 Weeks
2. Share Price % Change Last 52 Weeks > 0
3. Indy. Avg. Share Price % Change Last 4 Weeks Relative to S&P 500 > 0
4. LT Growth >= 20
5. PYQ % EPS Growth >= Indy. Avg. PYQ % EPS Growth
6. TTM % EPS Growth >= Indy. Avg. TTM % EPS Growth
7. 3 Year % EPS Growth >= Indy. Avg. 3 Year % EPS Growth
8. CurrYr Est Now >= CurrYr Est 4 Weeks Ago
9. (5 Year ROA > Indy. Avg. 5 Year ROA) OR (5 Year ROI > Indy. Avg. 5 Year ROI) OR (5 Year ROE > Indy. Avg. 5 Year ROE)

Contrarian Opportunities

Primary Theme: Focus on good companies whose stocks have in the short term been moving the wrong way due to temporary problems. Notice that the company-quality tests focus on the long term and avoid the more recent period, which, presumably, has been troublesome.

1. Share Price % Change Last 4 Weeks < Indy. Avg. Share Price % Change Last 4 Weeks
2. Share Price % Change Last 4 Weeks < –15
3. 3 Year % EPS Growth > Indy. Avg. 3 Year % EPS Growth
4. 5 Year % EPS Growth > Indy. Avg. 5 Year % EPS Growth
5. 5 Year Operating Margin > Indy. Avg. 5 Year Operating Margin
6. 5 Year ROE > Indy. Avg. 5 Year ROE
7. 5 Year ROI > Indy. Avg. 5 Year ROI

Credible Expectations

Primary Theme: Look for favorable growth forecasts, but take company life cycle considerations into account to make sure analysts aren't projecting more growth than the company has already shown itself capable of delivering.

1. LT Growth >= 20
2. LT Growth <= 3 Year % EPS Growth

3. LT Growth <= 5 Year % EPS Growth
4. EPS Surprise Latest Quarter >= 0
5. EPS Surprise 2 Quarters Ago >= 0
6. EPS Surprise 3 Quarters Ago >= 0
7. EPS Surprise 4 Quarters Ago >= 0
8. CurrYr Est Now >= CurrYr Est 4 Weeks Ago
9. CurrYr Est Now >= CurrYr Est 8 Weeks Ago
10. Share Price % Change Last 4 Weeks Relative to S&P 500 >= 0
11. ProjPE NextYr <= LT Growth

Growth at a Reasonable Price

Primary Theme: Focus on reasonable PEG (price/earnings-to-growth) ratios. Be especially attentive to the secondary company-quality and growth themes in lines 4 through 7. Line 8 is an alternative theme. Notice, too, the growth floor established by the numeric test in line 1. Line 7 compares ROE to ROI to measure financial aggressiveness (the extent to which return on capital is enhanced by use of debt); one way to do this is numeric, while the other checks to see that company financial aggressiveness is no worse than industry average financial aggressiveness. With secondary and alternative tests like these, it's a lot harder for the dogs that usually wind up in value screens to make the cut here.

1. LT Growth >= 20
2. ProjPE NextYr/LT Growth <= 1
3. TTM P/E <= 3 Year % EPS Growth
4. Tax Rate >= 25
5. 3 Year % EPS Growth >= Indy. Avg. 3 Year % EPS Growth
6. 3 Year % EPS Growth > 5 Year % EPS Growth
7. 5 Year ROE/5 Year ROI <= 1.2 OR (5 Year ROE/5 Year ROI) <= (Indy. Avg. 5 Year ROE/Indy. Avg. 5 Year ROI)
8. Share Price % Change Last 4 Weeks > Indy. Avg. Share Price % Change Last 4 Weeks OR Share Price % Change Last 4 Weeks > 0

Relative Value

Primary Theme: Find value stocks with value defined in terms of cross-sectional comparison. Note especially the secondary growth theme. Like the preceding growth at a reasonable price (GARP) screen, this one makes aggressive use of secondary and alternate tests to block as many dogs as possible, an especially important issue for value screens. Fewer such tests are used, but the multiplication factors add punch to the ones that are here. Note line 4's tolerance of a very high PEG ratio. The primary theme establishes value based on peer comparison, not growth. The PEG ratio is a secondary test that guards against extremes.

1. TTM P/E <= (Indy. Avg. TTM P/E) * 1.1
2. TTM Price/Sales <= (Indy. Avg. TTM Price/Sales) * 1.1
3. TTM Price/Free Cash Flow <= (Indy. Avg. TTM Price/Free Cash Flow) * 1.1
4. ProjPE NextYr <= (LT Growth) * 2
5. TTM % EPS Growth >= (Indy. Avg. TTM % EPS Growth) * 1.25
6. 3 Year % EPS Growth >= (Indy. Avg. 3 Year % EPS Growth) * 1.25
7. Share Price % Change Last 4 Weeks > Indy. Avg. Share Price % Change Last 4 Weeks

QUALITY CATEGORY

These screens present companies that are superior in various fundamental categories.

Fastest Turnover

Primary Theme: All else being equal, the higher the margins, the better the company. But all else is rarely equal. Use turnover to uncover attractive companies others might brush aside because of low margins. Line 4 is a secondary test. Line 5 is an alternative test.

1. TTM Asset Turnover > (Indy. Avg. TTM Asset Turnover) * 1.25
2. TTM Inventory Turnover > (Indy. Avg. TTM Inventory Turnover) * 1.25
3. TTM Receivables Turnover > (Indy. Avg. TTM Receivables Turnover) * 1.25
4. 5 Year ROI >= Indy. Avg. 5 Year ROI
5. CurrYr Est Now >= CurrYr Est 8 Weeks Ago

Industry Leaders

Primary Theme: Find companies that excel under a variety of fundamental cross-sectional comparisons.

1. 5 Year Sales % Change >= (Indy. Avg. 5 Year Sales % Change) * 1.1
2. 5 Year EPS % Change >= (Indy. Avg. 5 Year EPS % Change) * 1.1
3. 5 Year EPS % Change >= 5 Year Sales % Change
4. TTM Net Margin >= (Indy. Avg. TTM Net Margin) * 1.1
5. MRQ TotalDebtRatio <= Indy. Avg. MRQ TotalDebtRatio
6. TTM P/E <= (Indy. Avg. TTM P/E) * 1.1
7. Share Price % Change Last 4 Weeks > (Indy. Avg. Share Price % Change Last 4 Weeks) * 1.1

Strong Operating Margins

Primary Theme: Find good-quality companies using operating margin as the benchmark of quality.

1. TTM Operating Margin > Indy. Avg. TTM Operating Margin
2. 5 Year Operating Margin > Indy. Avg. 5 Year Operating Margin
3. TTM Operating Margin > Operating Margin Prior Year
4. Operating Margin Prior Year > Operating Margin 2 Years Prior
5. Operating Margin 2 Years Prior > Operating Margin 3 Years Prior
6. TTM Operating Margin >= (5 Year Operating Margin) * 1.25
7. NextYr Est Now > NextYr Est 4 Weeks Ago

Strong Return on Investment

Primary Theme: Find high-quality companies, with ROI being the main indicator of quality. Lines 5 and 6 are alternative themes.

1. TTM ROI > (5 Year ROI) * 1.2
2. TTM ROI > (Indy. Avg. TTM ROI) * 1.2
3. 5 Year ROI > (Indy. Avg. 5 Year ROI) * 1.2
4. (TTM ROI/Indy. Avg. TTM ROI) > (5 Year ROI/Indy. Avg. 5 Year ROI) * 1.2
5. CurrQtr Est Now >= CurrQtr Est 8 Weeks Ago
6. Institutional (Net) Shares Purchased Latest Quarter > 0

SENTIMENT CATEGORY

In these screens, investment opportunities come to light through evidence of favorable sentiment on the part of an important segment of the investment community.

Analyst Favorites

Primary Theme: Select stocks based on what brokerage house analysts like.

1. # Strong Buy Ratings >= 5
2. # Buy Ratings <= 3
3. # Strong Buy Ratings >= (# Buy Ratings) + 5
4. # Hold Ratings = 0
5. # Underperform Ratings = 0
6. # Sell Ratings = 0
7. Mean Rating Now <= Mean Rating 4 Weeks Ago

High P/E Multiples

Primary Theme: The above line does not contain a typographical error! This P/E-oriented "best in class" screen really is designed to seek stocks selling at high multiples (subject to the line 3 test that prevents things from getting completely ridiculous), not low ones. Here, high P/E tests are behavioral. (So, too, is the alternative short interest test.) Key, here, are tests addressing the question of whether the stock deserves a high P/E.

1. TTM P/E > Indy. Avg. TTM P/E
2. TTM P/E > Prior 12 Month P/E
3. TTM P/E < 200
4. PYQ % EPS Growth > Indy. Avg. PYQ % EPS Growth
5. 3 Year % EPS Growth > Indy. Avg. 3 Year % EPS Growth
6. PYQ % EPS Growth > 0
7. # Analysts Publishing EPS Estimates for Next Quarter > 3
8. Short Interest 1 Month % Change < 0

Institutional Ownership

Primary Theme: Look for companies ripe for greater attention from institutions. Modest institutional ownership is the primary theme. Lines 4 and 5 establish, as a secondary theme, that the obscurity is not so excessive as to pose trading liquidity problems. Lines 6 to 10 are behavioral tests that also play secondary roles.

1. Institutional % Share Ownership > 10
2. Institutional % Share Ownership < Indy. Avg. Institutional % Share Ownership

3. Institutional (Net) Shares Purchased Latest Quarter > 0
4. Exchange Not OTC
5. 10 Day Average Trading Volume (in Millions) > .02
6. # Analysts Publishing EPS Estimates for Next Quarter >= 2
7. Insiders (Net) Shares Purchased Latest Quarter > 0
8. Short Interest 1 Month % Change < 0
9. Share Price % Change Last 4 Weeks > 0
10. Share Price % Change Last 4 Weeks > Indy. Avg. Share Price % Change Last 4 Weeks

Lesser-Known Stocks

Primary Theme: Look for obscure stocks. (*Note:* Float refers to shares in the hands of the public, shares not owned by insiders or others holding especially large blocks of stock.) The screen uses secondary tests designed to identify stocks that don't deserve to be obscure and may be starting to shed their obscurity. Notice that when we're dealing with obscure firms, we cut some slack and establish more lenient share price performance tests than is normally the case.

1. Institutional # Shares Owned/Float <= .5
2. Institutional % Share Ownership < (Indy. Avg. Institutional % Share Ownership) * .8
3. Institutional (Net) Shares Purchased Latest Quarter >= 0
4. # Analysts Publishing EPS Estimates for Next Quarter < 6
5. 10-Day Average Trading Volume (in Millions) >= .02
6. Share Price % Change Last 52 Weeks >= 0
7. Share Price % Change Last 4 Weeks > –10
8. PYQ EPS % Change > 0
9. PYQ EPS % Change > Indy. Avg. PYQ EPS % Change

Technology Favorites

Primary Theme: Look for reasonably valued technology stocks. Because so much of what happens at such companies defies numeric analysis, the screen makes extensive use of a secondary set of (behavioral) analyst sentiment tests.

1. Company in Technology Sector
2. ProjPE NextYr/(LT Growth) <= 2

3. # Strong Buy Ratings >= 3
4. # Strong Buy Ratings – # Buy Ratings >= 2
5. # Hold Ratings <= 1
6. # Underperform Ratings = 0
7. # Sell Ratings = 0
8. CurrQtr Est Now >= CurrQtr Est 4 Weeks Ago

Analyze . . . a Specific Company and Its Stock

Managing the Unmanageable

In Step 1 (Find), you sifted through 9,000 to 10,000 stocks and identified the ones most likely to be of interest to you. But you won't want to buy a stock simply because it appears in a screen. The data may be impacted by unusual factors that aren't really consistent with what you had in mind (e.g., EPS growth resulting from cost cuts that can't continue forever as opposed to increasing demand for the company's products). Also, screens can include only a small number of tests. Stock market performance, however, is influenced by many factors.

Step 2 (Analyze) is where you broaden your inquiry to incorporate all available relevant information, regardless of whether it relates to the goals you articulated through your screening. Now you look at each company on your evaluation list one at a time to get the full investment story. The rest of this chapter and Chapter 11 will describe how you can use data presentations readily available on the Internet.

Generally, the material presented here will be familiar to most investors. But it may not have been optimally utilized in the past, due to excess drudgery. For example, you may realize that you can benefit from knowing how a company's present operating margin compares with its past margins and with peer-group averages. But to get all this, you'd have to go way beyond the company's latest annual report. You'd need dozens, or perhaps hundreds, of reports before you could extract the information you'd need.

But nowadays, data providers do all the grunt work for you. As you move through Chapter 11, you'll see that the analytics you always wanted but couldn't plausibly create are there for your viewing. In fact, we give very little attention to the financial statements traditionally regarded as the heart of investment analysis. Instead, most of the focus is on analytics prepared based on the statements.

GETTING ORGANIZED

As you undoubtedly know, the amount of information available on any company is enormous, so much so that successfully organizing your effort can be more crucial than gathering information. Let's start by dividing all kinds of information into three categories: primary, secondary, and general.

Primary Information

This is information that is most directly related to your specific investment goals. If you are a value investor, valuation ratios will be considered primary information. If you are a growth investor, growth rates will be primary information. For momentum investors, price and volume data will constitute primary information.

But you need not define primary information so narrowly. A skilled value investor knows that he/she cannot select stocks based solely on low P/E, low price/sales, and so on. It's also important to look at growth rates, expectations, and other aspects to see if the company has poor prospects and, hence, deserves low valuation metrics. Conceivably, then, just about anything could be considered primary information. And if that's the case, we're back to square one staring at a huge pile of information that somehow needs to be organized.

The screening method provides a simple solution to this dilemma. Primary information will be based on the variables used in your screen. Consider a value screen that looks like this.

P/E-to-Growth Ratio <= 1.00
Price/Sales <= Industry Average Price/Sales
Current Price >= (52 Week High Price) * .85
3 Year Average Return on Equity >= Industry Average 3 Year ROE

Obviously, a value investor will recognize the PEG and price/sales ratios as directly related to the specific investment goals and hence consider them primary information, as are other valuation ratios not included in the screen.

For our purposes, we're also going to consider the stock price trend and ROE as primary information because these are included in the screen. And as long as we're considering ROE, it also makes sense to consider other information that is closely related to ROE, such as return on investment (ROI) and return on assets (ROA). It's not necessary that you spend a lot of time thinking about what information is related to your screening variables. For the most part, all you need do is look at other information in the same data table. ROE, ROI, and ROA usually appear together on financial web sites in a single table. So, too, do all the valuation ratios.

Meanwhile, you will also want to examine growth rates. But since no such variables were included in your screen, these would not qualify as primary information.

Secondary Information

This consists of any other information that is important to you that is not primary. Growth, financial strength, and short interest data may be important investment considerations to the creator of this value screen. Yet there are no variables based on them. No screen can incorporate every possible fact that you might see as relevant. If you were to try to put everything into a screen, no companies will pass. But the omission could also reflect the limitations of the screener that was used. For example, many screeners do not include comprehensive short interest variables. As was stated many times in Chapter 6, if your screener doesn't allow you to create variables to measure something you consider important, at least make sure you address it in Step 2 (Analyze).

All such situations give rise to secondary information. Put another way, secondary information is that which you might include in other screens, or would have included in this screen had the software allowed for it.

You'll note that institutional buying/selling was not included in the discussion so far as an example of secondary information. That's because I'm assuming the hypothetical creator of the sample value screen is not interested, one way or the other, in what institutions are doing. The idea of secondary information is that it be something that you, individually, consider worthwhile.

That's not to say our hypothetical value screener shouldn't at least glance at the institutional data. Modern Internet data presentations are so easy to use, I suggest all investors look at all the data tables. This is a matter of seconds, not hours. But if you take the trouble to identify certain kinds of information as being secondary (important to you, even though it didn't make this particular screen), you will have positioned yourself well for Step 3 (Buy), where you balance all the pros and cons to reach a final decision.

General Information

This is the catch-all category that includes any information that is not primary or secondary. The most important kind of general information consists of qualitative content that can't fit into screens or data tables: business descriptions, news items, analyst research, and any visual impressions one can glean from looking at a stock price chart.

Beyond that, general information consists of data items that aren't primary or secondary. Continuing with the example, institutional trading data would be general information. By so classifying it, I'm acknowledging that it doesn't play a noteworthy role in forming my opinion of a stock, while at the same time noting it as something I should at least glance quickly at to allow for the possibility of something unexpected catching my eye.

THE ROAD MAP

The labels primary, secondary, and general information might suggest a preferred sequence for looking at information—start with primary information, move on to secondary information, and wrap up with the general information. But the labels aren't meant to do that. Instead, they signify priority, different degrees of importance to the formation of an investment decision.

Even so, you could, if you like, follow a primary-to-secondary-to-general sequence for viewing information. In fact, you can use any sequence you like. What's most important is that you choose some sequence and more or less stick with it. Nobody's going to penalize you if you go out of order. But if you maintain discipline, there's a better chance you'll eventually become so comfortable with the process that you'll be able to move through it quickly. And you'll be confident that you're seeing everything that is important in light of your investment style while at the same time leaving yourself open to notice important things outside the scope of what you were actively seeking. I know this sounds very touchy-feely. But it's important. You'd be amazed at how easy it is to make bad decisions because once you get immersed in the heat of battle you can miss important things right under your nose.

If you don't want to create your own road map, all you need do is follow the sequence prescribed by your favorite web site(s). You can't really know the extent, if any, to which investment professionals participated in the creation of the sequence. But I wouldn't worry about that. Remember that it's more important that you follow some sort of sequence than it is to follow one specific road map. And for the record, I have yet to see a web site whose proposed sequence struck me as objectionable.

Having said that, I'll now switch gears and share my favorite analysis sequence. I divide my road map into three parts. I could think of these as beginning, middle, and end. But in fact, I prefer more descriptive designations: "Getting Acquainted," "Exploring the Fundamentals," and "Finishing Touches." Here's a brief description of each phase.

- **Getting Acquainted:** I start by looking at information that gives me an initial sense of what kind of company I'm looking at. Since screening is so effective in calling one's attention to companies one hadn't previously heard of, this phase will often provide an initial sense of such basic issues as what the company does and whether there's any reason to expect that it's good at it.
- **Exploring the Fundamentals:** This is the meat of the process, where you look at data tables that show a wide variety of useful numeric information. Some will replicate the data relationships you built into your screen. Most will be relationships not part of the screen due to limitations of the application you used and/or the fact that there are just so many tests that can plausibly fit into any one screen. And as we'll see in the next chapter, this is where the classification of information as primary or secondary is most useful. The category will determine how exacting you are in interpreting what you see.
- **Finishing Touches:** Here, general information predominates. However comprehensive and well organized a data presentation may be, and however diligent you may be in reviewing it, there's always a chance that something unique or odd about a particular situation may slip between the cracks. You can guard against that by taking a quick look at the basic financial statements (the raw material from which the other data trends and relationships were drawn). And although you can't know members of the corporate management team as well as you might if you worked with them day in and day out, you can look at some data reports to see whether any red flags jump out at you.

NARROWING DOWN

How often have you shared an investment idea with a friend, a colleague, or a financial adviser and everyone agreed right away that you'd found a great opportunity? My guess is that it has happened rarely. More likely, the responses began with a phrase like "But what about. . . ." There are countless ways they can complete the question. They can refer to near-term earnings problems, management issues, or competition. It's always something. They aren't simply being cynical. They're reacting to the very real fact that few prospective investments are completely without blemish. Get used to the fact that sound analysis will usually reveal things you don't like seeing. The stocks you wind up buying won't be those that perfectly match your goals. Instead, they'll be the ones that look best after you balance a lot of pros against a lot of cons in Step 3 (Buy).

This raises an important question for Step 2 (Analyze). How lenient should you be about negatives as they surface? Should you take note of them and keep going all the way through the analytic process? Or is there a point at which you see enough negatives to warrant dropping the stock before you finish the rest of your analysis?

If you're too picky about this sort of thing, you'll wind up never investing in anything. Here's another troubling scenario. You are very quick to drop the stocks you examine early on. Suddenly, you find your list dwindling close to zero. Since you want to avoid winding up with nothing, you subconsciously move toward the other extreme and wind up being too tolerant of blemishes in the stocks at the bottom of the list.

I suggest a balanced approach. There probably are certain qualities that you absolutely, positively dislike. Some turnoffs may be automatic. Perhaps you have a personal policy of never investing in stocks with average daily trading volume below certain thresholds, or companies with multiple classes of common stock. Other types of turnoffs are less permanent. For example, if you expect oil prices to plummet, you may decide in advance to automatically bypass all energy companies, but you'd be open to such situations later on if your view of price prospects changes.

It's not necessary to take the trouble to list all of the things that would cause you to quickly eliminate a stock. All you need do is be able to recognize them when you see them. And you'll find that Step 2 (Analyze) is organized in such a way as to bring these to your attention as quickly as possible. Most will surface during the initial Getting Acquainted phase. Use this as an opportunity to eliminate prospects you know you won't like regardless of what the core fundamentals reveal. Once a company clears this hurdle, keep it under consideration throughout Step 2 (Analyze). And don't go overboard with early winnowing. If you find yourself thinking carefully about whether to eliminate the company during the Getting Acquainted phase, chances are that's a sign that the obstacle you're seeing isn't necessarily earth-shaking, and that you'd do best to let the company go through the full analytic process.

Different investors will wind up adopting different approaches to Step 2 (Analyze) eliminations. The key is the number of companies you can comfortably deal with in Step 3 (Buy). You'll develop a feel for this as you gain experience with the process.

Let's proceed now to Chapter 11, where we'll look in more detail at how this road map can help us develop a unique investment story for each stock.

11

Developing the Investment Story

Chapter 10 introduced a three-phase approach to reviewing information in such a way as to develop a unique investment story for each stock you analyze. In the first phase, you assess background information to acquaint you with the company in a very general sense. The second phase involves a close examination of the fundamental data in a way that spotlights important trends and relationships between different data items. Finally you apply finishing touches to the process by hunting for red flags that may not have become visible as a result of your other efforts.

Within each phase, you'll be sensitive to distinctions between the three kinds of information. Primary information is most directly related to your screen. Secondary information is important to your investment philosophy but wasn't included in any screening variables. And general information covers any other kind of information that might impact your decision, especially qualitative factors that don't lend themselves to screening.

Housekeeping Notes We will focus primarily on the Market Guide brand data reports available on the MultexInvestor.com web site. This information can also be found on Yahoo! Finance and America Online (AOL)'s Personal Finance channel, both of which license data from Multex.com's Market Guide subsidiary. The MSN.Money investor site uses a similar format. We'll also touch on some different presentations available on the Morningstar.com and Quicken.com sites. As you examine different data sources, note that many terms can be defined in a variety of ways. Earnings per share (EPS) can differ depending on whether the number of shares used in the calculation reflects basic or diluted reporting, and what sort of unusual credits or charges are included in the computation. Operating profit can include or exclude depreciation. Even though the general terminology is familiar to you, make sure you understand the exact definitions used by whatever data sources you consult. Web sites usually provide this information in glossaries.

The appendix to this chapter provides a representative example of the information you can find on the Internet. The samples there are presented in the same order as they appear on the MultexInvestor.com web site. They give you a good sense of how the data is grouped together. You certainly can follow this sequence if you'd like. But when I go through the material, I use my own approach, often going back and forth from one report to another. As you go through this chapter, you'll see why I do that and how my custom sequence is specifically designed to provide the story I want to get.

GETTING ACQUAINTED

Just as nutritionists advocate the importance of starting the day with a good breakfast, the effectiveness of your analytic efforts will be enhanced by a good introduction. Give yourself a preview of the underlying investment story and decide quickly whether the company you're looking at is one you'd like to study in further detail. If so, get a sense of what's moving the stock and what you should be looking for as you move on to other sections.

First Impressions

Most financial web sites provide some sort of company introduction to jump-start the analytic process. These give you a basic sense of what the company does and a quick back-of-the-envelope idea of how well it's doing. On MultexInvestor.com it's called a snapshot (Appendix 11.A). You do not yet know the whys and wherefores behind what you see. But given that Step 1 (Find) focused entirely on numbers, it's a good idea to add qualitative judgment to the process as soon as you begin Step 2 (Analyze). Start considering now whether you want to drop the company from consideration. If you see something that looks bothersome on the surface but aren't sure that it is fatal, use that as a basis for prioritizing your next task. For example, I can accept companies with negative net income in certain instances, but if the company shows a negative operating margin on the snapshot, I'll put it on a very short leash. I'll bypass some other reports I routinely examine and go directly to content (such as the latest earnings release or financial strength data) most likely to help me decide whether to cross the company off my list or go on to the rest of the analysis.

Early Turnoffs

Few things can be more frustrating than thoroughly analyzing every number, news event, and aspect of the company's business only to see an investment turn out badly because you missed one of those tiny but often troubling details. And if you're pressed for time, as so many are, it's best to discover these before you go too far into your analysis.

The bottom of the MultexInvestor.com Highlights report is shown in Figure 11.1. The equity information section indicates the presence of major shareholders with controlling ownership blocks, multiple classes of common stock (with different classes having different voting powers), or convertible debt or preferred issues. Many investors automatically bypass companies with multiple stock classes (insiders usually hold all or most of the class with the strongest voting power) or complex capital structures (due to convertible issues). Many see heavy insider ownership as positive, but there can be too much of a good thing. Some are uncomfortable seeing too much stock ownership concentrated in too few hands. You might also note the public offering date. Has the company experienced both the ups and downs of business conditions as a publicly owned firm? Public corporations face different kinds of pressures than those of private businesses, so experience is relevant. Hence many investors prefer to exclude companies they deem unseasoned.

The Analyst Footnotes section describes things like stock splits, major acquisitions, divestitures, or changes in accounting practices. These signal

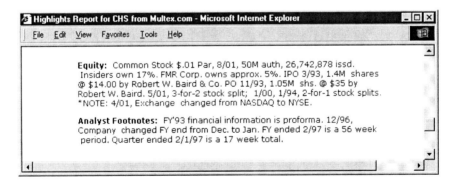

FIGURE 11.1   Equity Information and Analyst Footnotes Portions of Highlights Report Presented on MultexInvestor.com
Fundamental data supplied by Market Guide. © 2001, Multex.com, Inc. All rights reserved.

you when historic data might have unusually low predictive value about the future due to basic changes in the corporation itself. Some argue that the most bullish footnote you can see is one that is completely blank. At the very least, this area alerts you to the need to pay especially close attention to the qualitative information available to you.

The Company's Business

Snapshot reports give you a broad idea of what the company does. Sometimes that's all you need, especially if the nature of the business is self-evident, as might be the case for a bank, a grocery chain, or a home builder. On other occasions, you'll need to dig deeper. For example, it's not necessarily enough to know a company makes semiconductors. Does it specialize in chips for a particular type of application, such as personal computers or telecommunication equipment?

The ultimate business description is the one contained in 10-K documents filed annually by companies with the Securities and Exchange Commission (SEC). These descriptions have evolved beyond their traditional image as being barely intelligible even to the company's lawyers. The pace of improvement is varying from one company to the next, but on the whole they are becoming much more readable and useful. Regulation FD, which limits the ability of corporate executives to communicate one-on-one with investors, provides incentive for companies to present written communications that are as helpful as possible. Also, our increasingly litigious society makes investors more willing to sue for perceived falsehoods in corporate disclosures. Company annual reports and web sites still exhibit more of a cheerleading aura than do SEC filings. But again, due to increasing pressure to be truthful, they are becoming more informative than in the past. Major financial web sites usually offer links to SEC filings and company web sites. Also, some information providers, such as Multex's Market Guide subsidiary, prepare their own descriptive material, which is posted on free web sites (Appendixes 11.H and 11.I). Additionally, research reports prepared by Wall Street analysts can often be purchased for modest fees through sites like Multex Investor.com. Longer reports (10 or more pages) are the ones most likely to have good background information. Shorter reports tend to focus more on current earnings trends. But even this isn't a sure thing. Sometimes a large number of numeric tables will comprise the lion's share of a lengthy report. So look at the main headline to help get a sense of the report's main focus.

The Stock Price Chart

In past generations, one could argue that stock prices might not reflect underlying economic reality simply because many investors were not up to speed on what was happening. In today's information age, that's less plausible. Always assume there's a reason why a stock has been behaving as it has. You may ultimately choose to disagree with the consensus explanation. But it's naive to assume no reason exists. If you positively cannot find any explanation for a stock's price action, stay on the sidelines. The essence of the screening method is its rationality. You'll always be presented with enough attractive ideas consistent with this theme that you need not invest based on guesswork or conjecture.

As your analysis progresses, you'll encounter some things about the company you like and other things you dislike. It's likely others who have looked at the company spotted the same issues. A positive share price trend suggests, on balance, that the others placed greater emphasis on the positives. If the chart depicts a sudden break in a trend, you can proceed to the rest of your analysis knowing you need to look for something in the recent past (often a company announcement) that caused investors to ignore most of the other data items.

Even if you see yourself as being committed to fundamentals, it's still a good idea to have some awareness of technical indicators, since price/volume trends reflect the collective conclusions other investors reached from their own fundamental analysis. Chart study is also a good idea even for those whose screens are already based on the strong technical offerings of an application such as ProSearch. Technical analysis is a visual discipline, so no matter how carefully you screen, eyeballing the chart can always bring fresh insights. Most financial web sites feature interactive price charts that allow you to choose among several widely used graphing techniques and technical indicators.

There are many excellent sources you can consult if you'd like to study any of these topics in depth. For now, here's an overview of what you can learn from the kinds of price charts featured on financial web sites. We'll use, as an example, the charts MultexInvestor.com licenses from Stockpoint (Appendix 11.B). These are representative of what you'll see on other sites.

> **Price Plots Based on Trading Ranges:** This is the widely used graphing technique that features a vertical line marking the distance between the high and the low for the chosen period (usually a day, a week, or a month) and a short horizontal marking to signify the period's closing price.

Candlestick Price Plotting: These plots literally do look like candles. The thick part, like the wax portion of the candle, represents the distance between the opening and closing price for the day. If the stock moved up over the course of the trading session, the candle is usually green. If the stock moved down, the candle is red. Thinner lines, like candle wicks, jut out from the top and/or bottom of the main portion. These mark intraday highs and/or lows outside the opening/closing range depicted by the main portion of the candle.

Moving Average: This is the average stock price computed over a particular period of time. (See page 89.) Chartists typically compare moving averages computed using different time periods and consider the trend favorable if the shorter-period moving average is plotted higher than or crosses above the longer-period average.

Moving Average Convergence/Divergence (MACD): This is an important relationship comparing differing moving averages, one covering a shorter time frame than the other. (See pages 89–90.) The horizontal line on the chart depicts the point at which these two averages are equal. The trend line is an indicator of the difference between the short and long averages. The stock is deemed to be in an uptrend whenever the trend line is above the horizontal base.

Stochastic Oscillators: This shows the relationship of the recent stock price to a recent trading range. (See page 88.) Plots near the top of a visual channel indicate that the stock is highly priced relative to the trend and may suggest that it is overbought. Conversely, low plots can be construed as an indication of an oversold stock.

On Balance Volume (OBV): This is a measure of supply and demand for a stock that combines price change and volume. (See pages 91–92.) Technical analysts suggest that an OBV line moving in the opposite direction of the price trend signals a change in the trend.

Relative Strength: This traces comparisons between the performances of a stock and of a market index, often the S&P 500. A rising line means the stock is outperforming the index, while a falling line indicates that the stock is underperforming. Technical analysts maintain that relative strength peaks precede price peaks and can therefore forecast trend reversals.

Percent Rate of Change: For each day, this line plots the stock's percent change over a particular time period, such as the most recent 20 days. A rising line indicates that the percentage changes are widening; that is, the stock price is accelerating. This is considered bullish. A falling line is deemed bearish.

Bollinger Bands: These are two lines that mark the boundaries of a price range that is one standard deviation above and one standard deviation below the stock's average price for a chosen time period, say 30 days. Standard deviation is an important indicator of volatility. For example, the numbers 7, 8, and 9 average out to 8; so, too, do the numbers –7, 8, and 23. But the second, more volatile sample has a higher standard deviation. Within the total 30-day sample, about two-thirds of the prices should fall within the Bollinger bands. Technical analysts suggest that a narrowing of the bands means a price movement, one way or the other, will soon occur. Also, they believe that tops or bottoms outside the bands followed by tops or bottoms within the bands signify that the trend is about to change.

Each indicator, in its own way, represents a picture that helps you see whether a stock is attracting a noteworthy degree of buying or selling interest. Looking at these in the early stage of your analysis is like reading a review before seeing a movie. It can be useful to go in with a general sense of what the film is about and what others thought about it, even though you'll ultimately form your own opinion.

What's Happening?

Now that you have a general sense of what the company does, how successful it has been, and how investors feel about it, it's time to start looking at details. Begin by finding out what's going on right now. Given the market's present-day preoccupation with near-term trends, this inquiry should, at the very least, make it clear to you why the stock is behaving as it is. You can also tune in to key qualitative investment considerations such as future prospects, new products, acquisitions, and so on.

Company Announcements   The most important item here is the earnings announcement. The numbers disseminated in these are generally the same ones you'll see later on when the company files its official earnings documents (the annual 10-K and quarterly 10-Q reports) with the SEC. Company announcements give you all the key information several weeks before the formal documents are filed. Also, companies issue preannouncements whenever management believes events have developed in such a way as to make it unlikely the company can meet prevailing investment community expectations. And on occasion, companies will issue preannouncements confirming prior expectations. Corporate announcements also can cover any other important topic, such as mergers and acquisitions, new products, or major changes in management ranks. When in written form, company announcements are usually issued through one or two wire services: PR Newswire and/or Business Wire. They can be retrieved through News links available on financial web sites.

The most important events will be accompanied by conference calls in which participation is typically limited to management and Wall Street analysts. But you can usually hear the calls over the phone (in listen-only mode) and/or through live webcasts of the calls (replays are usually available for varying periods after the call). Yahoo! Finance provides links to live webcasts and archived replays. So, too, do company web sites. Relying on company-prepared information is a double-edged sword. It's negative in the sense that it's likely to be as self-serving as possible consistent with legal requirements that disclosures be truthful. It's positive in the sense that it gives access to management's exact words with no filtering by analysts or reporters. If you listen in on a conference call, you can even judge for yourself whether analysts are properly interpreting what management tells them.

External Content   The most basic kind of external content is the Significant Developments reports you can find for each company on MultexInvestor.com (Appendix 11.C). These are prepared by Market Guide analysts, who look at all corporate announcements and separate that which is important from that which is not. When a report is deemed significant, the Market Guide analyst will digest it into a brief paragraph. These are combined onto a single web page you can quickly scan to identify important events. At the next level, the financial media often treat company announcements as newsworthy events and cover them accordingly (especially with larger firms). Sometimes a story in the media will do little more than parrot the company verbiage. But business reporters will often add value by consulting with and quoting other sources (analysts, competitors, customers) who add their assessments of what the announcement means for investors. The highest level of external content consists of analyst reports. These reiterate events but also go further to suggest how investors should react vis-à-vis the stock. The value of these reports isn't based on whether you wish to follow the analyst's recommendation. What you seek, here, is direct exposure to a knowledgeable source of opinion.

EXPLORING THE FUNDAMENTALS

By now, you have a broad understanding of what kind of company you're looking at and what has happened to it recently. Many investors stop here and make their buy-hold-sell decisions. You can see that in the speed with which stock prices react to major announcements, especially those relating to earnings. But in fact all we've done is establish a framework for the meat of the evaluation process, which begins right now.

In the Getting Acquainted stage, I suggested you drop stocks from your list if something rubs you the wrong way. So by now, each company still under consideration passed your screen, may have fared well in any sorting or scoring you did pursuant to Chapter 8, and made it through the Getting Acquainted stage intact. That is a hefty showing of merit. Even so, few, if any, opportunities are perfect. But given the process that's occurred to this point and the fact that your workload has been whittled to a much more manageable level, it's now time to let companies stay on the list even if you see some negatives. Put another way, we can say the remaining stocks have earned enough respect to be brought to Step 3 (Buy), where the blemishes you discover from this point on will be weighed and balanced against those of all the other companies that still remain under consideration.

As noted, the appendix to this chapter shows the MultexInvestor.com first-to-last report sequence. If you haven't looked at it yet, I suggest pausing and doing so now. That will enable you to understand the nature of the custom sequence I created for myself and will describe now. My sequence is based on the following themes:

- **What is the rationale for the current stock price?** I look at data that shows me whether the stock is a value play, a momentum play, or one that combines elements of both approaches.
- **What do analysts expect from the company, and are their expectations credible?** I look at forecasts and compare them to what the company has done in the past. I also note the extent to which past expectations turned out to be accurate.
- **What is the general sentiment surrounding this stock?** After having looked at what analysts think, I examine the behavior of other investment community constituencies.
- **What kinds of footprints of success are visible?** I develop a sense of overall company quality by examining important time series and peer group comparisons.

Next, we'll look more closely at how each topic is addressed. Before doing that, I want to reiterate two important points that were previously made.

1. All the concepts we'll examine are consistent with the screening ideas described in Chapter 6. In some instances, you'll find yourself revisiting data relationships you built into your screen. More often, though, you'll wind up considering ideas you could have added to your screen but didn't because they weren't top priority according to your investment philosophy, or for the practical reason that no single screen can encompass every important investment consideration.
2. Rarely, if ever, will an investment candidate be perfect. Before looking at the data, make sure you recall what was central to your screen. How you classify a particular item of information—as primary, secondary, or general—will impact your eventual willingness to tolerate imperfect answers.

Stock Price Rationale

Check the forward-looking P/E ratios and the consensus long-term EPS growth forecast. These are shown in Figure 11.2. Get a general sense of the price/earnings-to-growth (PEG) ratio. You don't need to be precise; eyeballing is fine. (We are, after all, dealing with the future, something that can never be known with precision.)

Determine whether forward-looking P/E ratios are based on EPS levels that are more or less normal. Compare the consensus EPS estimates (Figure

Earnings Estimates for CHS from Multex.com - Microsoft Internet Explorer						
File Edit View Favorites Tools Help						

Earnings Per Share Estimates						
In US Dollar						
	# of Ests.	Mean Est.	High Est.	Low Est.	Std. Dev.	Proj- P/E
Quarter Ending 10/01	10	0.32	0.32	0.31	0.00	--
Quarter Ending 01/02	10	0.24	0.28	0.20	0.03	--
Year Ending 01/02	10	1.41	1.44	1.37	0.03	22.42
Year Ending 01/03	10	1.78	1.88	1.68	0.06	17.74
LT Growth Rate	7	28.29	35.00	25.00	3.73	--

FIGURE 11.2 Earnings per Share Estimates table from Earnings Estimates Report Presented on MultexInvestor.com
Fundamental data supplied by Market Guide. © 2001, Multex.com, Inc. All rights reserved.

11.2) with the recent results (Figure 11.3). If the EPS figure used in the P/E calculation is depressed by factors you deem temporary (e.g., weakness in the business cycle), you can tolerate higher P/E and PEG ratios than would normally be the case. If EPS trends seems unusually hot (possibly because the company is approaching a major cyclical peak), reduce your thresholds of acceptability for P/E and PEG.

Look at the valuation ratio comparisons. An example is shown in Figure 11.4. Be especially attentive to company-to-industry P/E and price/sales comparisons. You're seeking one of two kinds of value: growth-based value (a P/E ratio that seems near or below the projected growth rate) or relative value (company valuation ratios that appear reasonable relative to industry benchmarks). Don't assume a stock should be avoided if it appears highly valued. It's most important to recognize the extent, if any, to which an investment case can be supported by valuation. This seems so simple, but many invest without considering these relationships. One wonders how many investors would have gotten out of new-economy technol-

---

Highlights Report for CHS from Multex.com - Microsoft Internet Explorer

File   Edit   View   Favorites   Tools   Help

REVENUE

Quarters	1999	2000	2001	2002
APR	25,896	36,425	56,692	93,233
JUL	27,359	36,771	60,638	89,491
OCT	26,754	40,009	68,990	
JAN	26,732	41,798	73,126	
Totals	106,741	155,003	259,446	182,724

Note: Units in Thousands of U.S. Dollars

EARNINGS PER SHARE

Quarters	1999	2000	2001	2002
APR	0.093	0.160	0.280	0.450
JUL	0.107	0.147	0.273	0.400
OCT	0.093	0.153	0.287	
JAN	0.067	0.120	0.207	
Totals	0.360	0.580	1.047	0.850

Note: Units in U.S. Dollars

FIGURE 11.3   Quarterly Sales and Earnings per Share Tables from Highlights Report Presented on MultexInvestor.com
Fundamental data supplied by Market Guide. © 2001, Multex.com, Inc. All rights reserved.

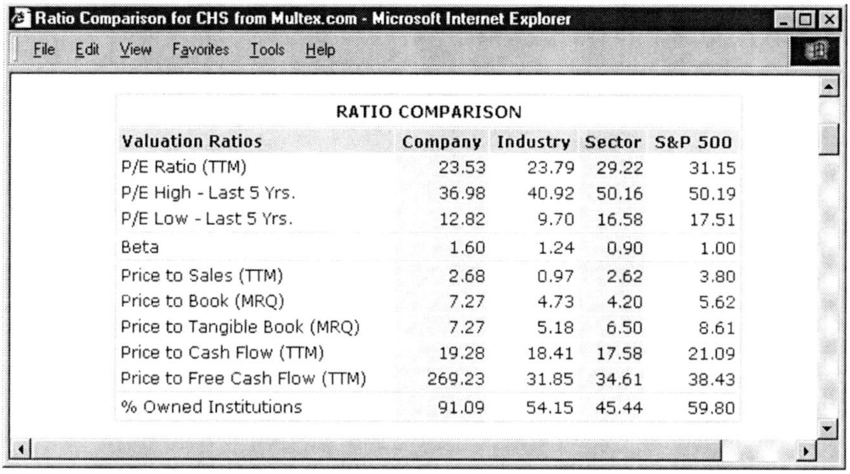

FIGURE 11.4 Valuation Comparisons from Ratio Comparison Report Presented on MultexInvestor.com
Fundamental data supplied by Market Guide. © 2001, Multex.com, Inc. All rights reserved.

ogy before the bubble burst had they noticed that forward-looking P/E ratios were three to four times greater than long-term growth projections. If you choose to own such stocks, knowing the numbers puts you on notice of the need to be extra vigilant regarding momentum-oriented signals, especially technical indicators you can see in the interactive price charts. Investors who were sensitive to new-economy overvaluations were probably the first ones to get out once momentum started to falter; they were most aware that without great momentum readings, there were no reasons to own the stocks.

Potential differences in relative and growth-based value present a good example of how the distinction between primary and secondary information can help you. For example, if you screened based on relative value, appealing metrics there could make you more willing than you might otherwise be to tolerate a high PEG ratio.

If dividend income is important to you, examine the dividend ratio comparisons. Figure 11.5 shows an example. Above-average dividend growth rates and below-average payout ratios are likely to be bullish. Don't assume likewise when it comes to yield. A very high yield relative to industry peers could reflect concerns about a possible cut in the payment. Be especially sensitive to this issue if the spread between the stock's yield

```
 Ratio Comparison for CHS from Multex.com - Microsoft Internet Explorer        _ □ ✕
  File   Edit   View   Favorites   Tools   Help                                     

        Dividends                      Company  Industry  Sector  S&P 500
        Dividend Yield                    0.00      1.12    1.97     1.75
        Dividend Yield - 5 Year Avg.      0.00      0.74    1.29     1.26
        Dividend 5 Year Growth Rate         NM     10.93    4.02     9.13
        Payout Ratio (TTM)                0.00     16.03   20.96    28.29
```

FIGURE 11.5   Dividend Comparisons from Ratio Comparison Report Presented
on MultexInvestor.com
Fundamental data supplied by Market Guide. © 2001, Multex.com, Inc. All
rights reserved.

and the industry average is significantly higher at present than it had been,
on average, over the past five years.

Additional Topics   The steps outlined in the preceding paragraphs are
based on the content you can find on MultexInvestor.com. Similar data tables are available on other major finance sites such as Yahoo! Finance,
America Online's Personal Finance channel, and MSN.Money. But there
are three noteworthy kinds of presentations that are not available on these
sites.

▦ Precalculated PEG Ratios: You may have noticed that Multex
  Investor.com does not actually present PEG ratios. Instead, it offers the
  data (P/E ratios and growth rates) from which you can calculate PEG
  on your own. At first glance, this may seem off-putting and you might
  be inclined to look at conveniently precalculated ratios available on
  many other sites. This can be beneficial, especially if you'd like to compare company PEG ratios to industry, sector, or S&P 500 averages. But
  be careful. An important part of our work in the next section will involve assessing the credibility of growth rate assumptions. You cannot
  benefit from the convenience of precalculated PEGs or benchmark
  comparisons until you have satisfied yourself regarding the reasonable-
  ness of the growth forecasts used in the calculations.
▦ Sequential Valuation Histories: These provide context for the stock's
  present valuation status by showing you where average annual ratios stood for each of several past years. If such information is of interest to you, check the Morningstar Stock Valuation Ratios report

(Figure 11.6). It features numeric and graphic presentations of year-by-year price/earnings, price/book, price/sales, and price/cash flow ratios going back five fiscal years and culminating in the TTM (trailing 12-month) period. More interesting, perhaps, than the valuations themselves are the ratios comparing each company metric to the S&P 500 average. Eyeballing trends in these relative ratios shows how the stock evolved into its current stature—gradually, suddenly, or erratically.

■ **Intrinsic Value:** Except for occasional asset plays (e.g., an acquisition candidate or a company likely to be liquidated with the per-share sale price of its assets minus liability repayments hopefully exceeding the stock price), investors don't usually think in terms of a stock having an objectively ascertainable intrinsic value. Instead, the focus is usually on the likelihood that the stock will outperform the overall market. But finance textbooks do present intrinsic value theories, and some investors are curious to see how the stocks they look at measure up under such approaches. The intrinsic value section of Quicken.com's Stock Evaluator (Figure 11.7) lets you do just that. Bear in mind, however, that the two essential inputs to its model, the five-year growth projection and

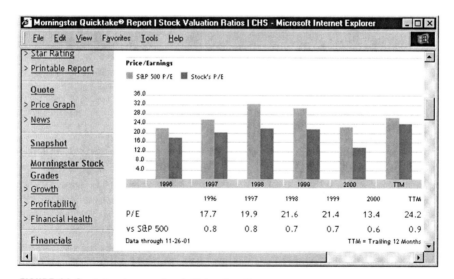

FIGURE 11.6 Morningstar Stock Valuation Report
Source: Morningstar.com (www.morningstar.com). © 2001 Morningstar, Inc. All rights reserved. Reprinted with permission.

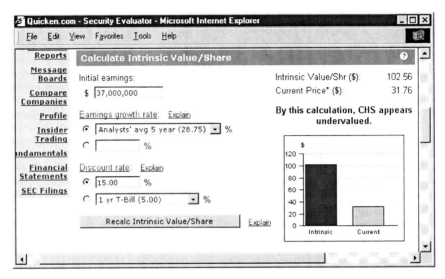

FIGURE 11.7   Intrinsic Value Report from the Quicken.com Stock Evaluator
Source: Quicken.com. Reprinted with permission.

the discount rate, are both extremely difficult to forecast with any reasonable degree of accuracy (a major reason why most investors don't calculate intrinsic value). The best way to use this content is to make lots of changes to the inputs to see what sort of discount rate/growth combinations are implied in the stock's current price.

Expectations and Credibility

Check the number of analysts issuing long-term growth forecasts and the range of forecasts. (See Figure 11.2.) The narrower the range and/or the greater the number of analysts, the more you can rely on the forecast, to the extent that any such projections can be relied upon (obviously, no such predictions can ever be treated as if carved in stone).

Compare the long-term growth forecast to historic growth rates. See if the growth projection (Figure 11.2) is in line with historic growth rates (Figure 11.8). What you see here is tantamount to a statement about where the company is within its corporate life cycle (see pages 53–57) and/or an assertion that the company is changing in a way contrary to what life cycle considerations alone would suggest. EPS numbers are always prone to un-

Growth Rates Table

GROWTH RATES			
	1 Year	3 Years	5 Years
Sales %	67.38	51.01	33.87
EPS %	78.60	108.54	70.21
Dividend %	NM	NM	NM

FIGURE 11.8   Growth Rates Table from Highlights Report Presented on
MultexInvestor.com
Fundamental data supplied by Market Guide. © 2001, Multex.com, Inc. All
rights reserved.

usual items that can temporarily distort growth trends. So look at sales
growth as well.

Stock investments ultimately succeed or fail based on the future, something that cannot be known. So don't focus on mechanical growth thresholds or specific number-to-number comparisons. Instead, eyeball all the sales and EPS growth rates presented in Figure 11.8 to develop a general feel for the situation. Remember, this is one step in a four-step method. If specific growth comparisons or thresholds are important to you, they belong in the screens you create in Step 1 (Find). Step 2 (Analyze) involves more of a blend between qualitative judgment and quantitative rigor. This is an example of how screening and human judgment work as allies, as opposed to being adversaries.

If a growth forecast seems too high in light of the corporate life cycle status and you see no credible explanation why the company should be able to step out of character in the future, you'd be well within your rights to brace yourself for some event that will force analysts to lower not just long-term forecasts, but also near-term estimates and stock recommendations. Conversely, if you think analysts are too conservative, you could legitimately anticipate that something in the future will cause them to turn more bullish.

Check the number of analysts issuing near-term estimates and the range of forecasts. (See Figure 11.2.) Since companies and analysts communicate in greater detail about near-term quarterly and annual forecasts than they do about long-term projections, you can be more tolerant, here, about a smaller number of analysts. But you should also expect a narrower range between high and low estimates.

Assess how the near-term estimates mesh with recent quarterly growth trends. Compare the near-term estimates (Figure 11.2) to recent quarterly sales and EPS performance (Figure 11.3). The nature of the forecasting process is such that prognosticators typically anticipate that past trends will persist unless they see a good reason to assume otherwise. The greater the extent to which estimates represent a break from recent trends, the greater will be your need to focus on specific explanations (usually contained in company news releases, archived conference call replays, or analyst research reports).

Assess the extent to which analysts have a handle on the situation. Look at the trend of earnings surprises (Figure 11.9) and estimate revisions (Figure 11.10). Estimates are continually being changed. Usually stocks perform well when analysts find it necessary to chase reality upward by increasing their estimates. Poor performance tends to occur while analysts are reducing estimates in an effort to chase reality downward. Take another look at the stock price chart. Decide whether you believe the market's reaction to the most recent revisions is reasonable.

Note the distribution and trend of analyst recommendations. (See Figure 11.11.) As discussed in Chapter 6, top-heavy rating profiles and low mean rating scores are bullish. Also, stocks tend to perform well relative to the market when analyst ratings are becoming more bullish. Hence this

	Estimate	Actual	Difference
July 2001	0.38	0.40	0.02
April 2001	0.43	0.45	0.02
January 2001	0.20	0.21	0.01
October 2000	0.27	0.28	0.01
July 2000	--	0.27	--

FIGURE 11.9 Earnings Surprises Table from Earnings Estimates Report Presented on MultexInvestor.com
Fundamental data supplied by Market Guide. © 2001, Multex.com, Inc. All rights reserved.

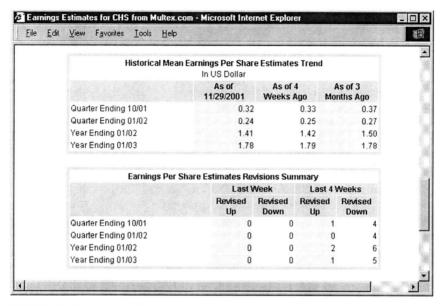

FIGURE 11.10 Historical Mean Earnings per Share Estimates Table and Earnings per Share Estimates Revisions Summary Table from Earnings Estimates Report Presented on MultexInvestor.com
Fundamental data supplied by Market Guide. © 2001, Multex.com, Inc. All rights reserved.

Earnings Estimates for CHS from Multex.com - Microsoft Internet Explorer

File   Edit   View   Favorites   Tools   Help

Analyst Recommendations and Revisions

	As of 11/29/2001	As of 4 Weeks Ago	As of 8 Weeks Ago	As of 12 Weeks Ago
(1) Strong Buy	7	7	9	10
(2) Buy	4	4	4	6
(3) Hold	0	0	1	1
(4) Underperform	0	0	0	0
(5) Sell	0	0	0	0
No Opinion	0	1	1	1
Mean Rating	1.36	1.36	1.43	1.47

FIGURE 11.11 Analyst Recommendations and Revisions Table from Earnings Estimates Report Presented on MultexInvestor.com
Fundamental data supplied by Market Guide. © 2001, Multex.com, Inc. All rights reserved.

data table is especially important to any sort of momentum-oriented investment case.

Don't feel you need to agree with the recommendation profile. As was the case with stock valuation information, it's more important to know where a stock stands than it is to follow any simple buy-or-don't-buy formula. Extremely attractive buying opportunities can occur when analysts are bearish. This isn't due to a lack of skill on their part. Instead, it relates to agenda. For better or worse, many of the institutional clients they serve are extremely sensitive to near-term corporate earnings trends, increasing or decreasing their percentage stakes in shares of companies they perceive to be performing better or worse than average on the bottom line. If your investment philosophy is such that you feel comfortable getting into or out of a stock early (before the positives become manifest in EPS trends), don't hesitate to continue to invest that way. But knowing that you are proceeding contrary to analyst opinion is important, if for no other reason than to give you the intellectual fortitude to stick with your decisions when media hype points the other way.

General Sentiment

Get a sense of whether the stock is generally in or out of favor compared to key benchmarks. Look at the Price Performance table in Figure 11.12. It's

		Price Performance		
Period	Actual(%)	vs. S&P 500(%)	In Industry	Industry Rank
4 Week	5.0	2.0	46	81
13 Week	-11.9	-8.2	45	23
26 Week	1.9	14.5	75	17
52 Week	41.3	66.8	76	34
YTD	126.3	162.8	93	48

Note: Rank is a Percentile that Ranges from 0 to 99, with 99 = Best

FIGURE 11.12   Price Performance Table from Performance Report Presented on MultexInvestor.com
Fundamental data supplied by Market Guide. © 2001, Multex.com, Inc. All rights reserved.

tempting to assume that any stock going up is in favor. But don't underestimate the power of a general bull market to lift many not-so-meritorious stocks. Take note of the column that compares the stock's performance to the S&P 500 over a variety of time periods. And be especially attentive to the two rightmost columns on that table. The one headed "In Industry" presents percentile ranks (with 0 being worst and 99 being best) showing how this stock has fared relative to others in its own industry. The last column, labeled "Industry Rank," gives a percentile rank showing how the stocks in the industry have performed over various time periods compared with all other industries.

Among the most interesting relationships you can see on this table are discrepancies in the two percentile rank columns. A high "In Industry" rank coupled with a low "Industry Rank" could signify a hot stock in a cold industry. This is of great interest to a bottom-up investor. It suggests that the investment community as a whole picked this company out as being particularly attractive. This can be especially rewarding later on, when the industry as a whole moves into favor. The reverse, a cold stock in a hot industry, is also noteworthy. It can help you distinguish between stocks moving up because of company-specific merit and those that rise simply because the industry is currently in favor (the rising tide that lifts all boats).

Determine whether institutions have a significant presence in the stock. In the institutional/insiders table in Figure 11.13, check the number of in-

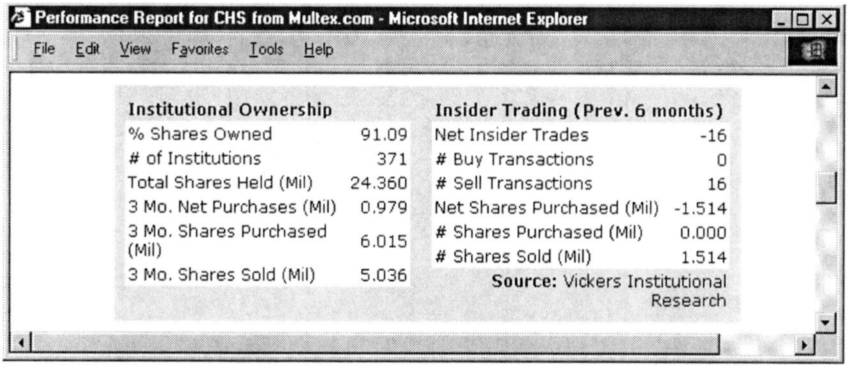

FIGURE 11.13 Institutional Ownership and Insider Trading Tables from Performance Report Presented on MultexInvestor.com
Fundamental data supplied by Vickers Institutional Research. © 2001, Multex.com, Inc. All rights reserved.

stitutional shareholders. Look at the valuation ratio comparison table in Figure 11.4 and compare institutional percent ownership to the industry average. Low levels of institutional presence can present opportunities; you may have found a heretofore undiscovered gem. But you may have to be patient, until the larger investors take notice. If institutional presence is too low, double-check other company quality data to make sure you didn't miss one or more important negatives that may be causing institutions to avoid the stock.

Look at the recent trends in institutional and insider trading. (See Figure 11.13.) As noted in Chapter 6, it's worthwhile to know what institutions are doing (regardless of whether you are inclined to follow them) simply because they are so big. In the short term, stocks will perform well if institutions are buying, and poorly if they are selling. Meanwhile, insider buying can be interpreted as a bullish signal (insider selling, on the other hand, has less value as a true indicator of sentiment for the reasons mentioned in Chapter 6).

Take note of significant levels of and changes in short interest. When creating screens for Step 1 (Find), you usually work with short interest (the number of shares sold short). In Step 2 (Analyze), you have an opportunity to view related data that is not generally available as a screening variable. In Figure 11.14, check the rightmost column of the table, labeled "Days." This establishes an important context for short interest (the number of shares sold short). It tells you how many days it would take for all short positions to be covered if recent trading volume levels persist. The larger the number, the greater the chance of a short squeeze (a rally that

Performance Report for CHS from Multex.com - Microsoft Internet Explorer
File   Edit   View   Favorites   Tools   Help

	Short Interest			
Month	Shares (Mil)	% Outs.	% Float	Days
10/08/01	6.449	24.115	30.856	6.868
09/10/01	6.898	25.794	33.005	14.584
08/08/01	7.643	28.579	36.569	13.432
07/09/01	6.613	24.728	31.641	14.861

FIGURE 11.14   Short Interest Table from Performance Report Presented on MultexInvestor.com
Fundamental data supplied by Market Guide. © 2001, Multex.com, Inc. All rights reserved.

occurs when short sellers rush to buy a less liquid stock, fearing exorbitant losses they might incur if they wait too long and the stock rises too much further).

Footprints of Success

Review data relating to growth rates, financial strength, profitability, management effectiveness, and efficiency, all of which are available on the Ratio Comparison report. These tables (Figures 11.15 to 11.19) compare company performance to industry averages, sector averages, and the S&P 500 average. The growth and company quality screening ideas discussed in Chapter 6 draw heavily on the relationships depicted in these data tables.

Earlier, we looked at the stock valuation ratio comparisons (Figure 11.4) and the dividend comparisons (Figure 11.5). Footprints of success can be discovered in the comparison tables entitled Growth Rates (Figure 11.15), Financial Strength (Figure 11.16), Profitability Ratios (Figure 11.17), Management Effectiveness (Figure 11.18), and Efficiency (Figure 11.19).

The Ratio Comparison report lets you address all the factors that did not find their way into your screen (because your screener was unable to accommodate them and/or because you could fit just so many tests into your screen). But the way you think about the data now is different. The

Growth Rates(%)	Company	Industry	Sector	S&P 500
Sales (MRQ) vs Qtr. 1 Yr. Ago	47.58	-4.34	8.82	-0.51
Sales (TTM) vs TTM 1 Yr. Ago	63.12	8.21	14.77	7.68
Sales - 5 Yr. Growth Rate	33.87	17.62	20.23	15.21
EPS (MRQ) vs Qtr. 1 Yr. Ago	46.32	13.55	-11.09	-12.05
EPS (TTM) vs TTM 1 Yr. Ago	62.11	-17.51	-8.19	-2.66
EPS - 5 Yr. Growth Rate	70.21	29.68	19.55	17.08
Capital Spending - 5 Yr. Growth Rate	107.70	24.16	21.74	12.57

FIGURE 11.15 Growth Rates Comparison from Ratio Comparison Report Presented on MultexInvestor.com

Ratio Comparison for CHS from Multex.com - Microsoft Internet Explorer

File Edit View Favorites Tools Help

Financial Strength	Company	Industry	Sector	S&P 500
Quick Ratio (MRQ)	1.29	0.42	0.74	1.14
Current Ratio (MRQ)	2.70	1.70	1.30	1.68
LT Debt to Equity (MRQ)	0.04	0.26	0.87	0.70
Total Debt to Equity (MRQ)	0.05	0.41	1.02	0.99
Interest Coverage (TTM)	NM	18.65	5.70	8.41

FIGURE 11.16   Financial Strength Comparison from Ratio Comparison Report Presented on MultexInvestor.com
Fundamental data supplied by Market Guide. © 2001, Multex.com, Inc. All rights reserved.

Ratio Comparison for CHS from Multex.com - Microsoft Internet Explorer

File Edit View Favorites Tools Help

Profitability Ratios (%)	Company	Industry	Sector	S&P 500
Gross Margin (TTM)	59.05	33.90	41.13	48.24
Gross Margin - 5 Yr. Avg.	57.70	34.55	40.75	48.89
EBITD Margin (TTM)	20.74	10.25	22.62	20.80
EBITD - 5 Yr. Avg.	14.25	13.53	21.65	22.34
Operating Margin (TTM)	18.25	8.10	10.61	15.99
Operating Margin - 5 Yr. Avg.	11.75	10.52	11.45	18.26
Pre-Tax Margin (TTM)	18.37	8.03	8.98	13.98
Pre-Tax Margin - 5 Yr. Avg.	11.55	10.31	12.53	17.67
Net Profit Margin (TTM)	11.39	4.73	5.22	9.09
Net Profit Margin - 5 Yr. Avg.	7.10	6.44	7.70	11.41
Effective Tax Rate (TTM)	38.00	43.07	37.32	33.70
Effective Tax Rate - 5 Yr. Avg.	38.80	38.62	39.45	35.54

FIGURE 11.17   Profitability Comparison from Ratio Comparison Report Presented on MultexInvestor.com
Fundamental data supplied by Market Guide. © 2001, Multex.com, Inc. All rights reserved.

FIGURE 11.18 Management Effectiveness Comparison from Ratio Comparison Report Presented on MultexInvestor.com
Fundamental data supplied by Market Guide. © 2001, Multex.com, Inc. All rights reserved.

FIGURE 11.19 Efficiency Comparison from Ratio Comparison Report Presented on MultexInvestor.com
Fundamental data supplied by Market Guide. © 2001, Multex.com, Inc. All rights reserved.

relationships that were incorporated into your screen (primary information) are the ones most important to you. Your expectations for these will be most exacting. You can be less stringent regarding the rest of the data.

Suppose, for example, your screen was based on the theme of relative growth (company growth rates in excess of industry averages). If your tests were based on EPS growth, you know the companies fare well in this area based simply on the fact that they passed the screen and are on your list. But recall, from Chapter 10, that our definition of primary information extends beyond the exact data items referenced in the screen, and includes all related items. You can see that the growth rates table (Figure 11.15) also covers sales growth. This, too, is primary information. You needn't be as exacting as a computer executing a screen, so you might tolerate some degree of company shortfall below the industry averages. But relative growth is your primary theme, and we know strong EPS growth can't persist indefinitely without good sales growth. So before you move to the other comparison tables (secondary information), investigate any shortfall in sales growth.

Note, too, some of the so-called little things you can check. One is the five-year capital spending growth rate. On a year-to-year basis, growth in capital spending can be erratic as programs ramp up or wind down. But over a long period, it is reasonable to expect capital spending growth to more or less keep pace with sales growth. Figure 11.15 enables you to compare five-year capital spending and sales growth. If sales growth is significantly higher, that might mean that capital spending may accelerate in the next few years. Conversely, if capital spending has been growing faster than sales, the company may be entering into a period where it can afford to lighten is expenditure program. You can gain additional context by comparing the relationship between company sales and capital spending growth to that of the industry.

Another little thing is the nature of the company-to-industry tax rate comparison. At first glance, it may seem as if a below-average company rate is desirable. But often, this sort of thing happens because a company is taking advantage of special benefits that often won't persist indefinitely. That could give rise to a future situation in which company pretax earnings grow briskly but net income falls as the company returns to a more normal tax rate. Hence you may wish to favor companies whose tax rates are more or less in line with historic averages and industry comparisons.

In an ideal world, even a growth screen could include requirements that returns on capital be above industry averages and improving over time, that all categories of profit margin be above average and improving, that turnover be faster than average, and that financial strength ratios be better than average. But in the real world any screen that demanding, assuming your application has the ability to create it, would have no passing companies. The key to Step 2 (Analyze) is the opportunity you get to give less precise consideration to important issues that were omitted from your screen. That's the essence of secondary information. It's important, but not so much so as to warrant automatic exclusion of any company not meeting the sort of precise threshold you would build into a screen. Look at all of these data tables and consider the relationships described in Chapter 6 (relative comparison, time series comparison, etc.). But in this context, assume the company will pass some tests with flying colors, barely get by in some instances, come close in others, and falter more significantly in some areas. Each company on your list will have a different set of pros and cons, and you'll weigh each against the others in Step 3 (Buy).

FINISHING TOUCHES

However comprehensive and well organized a data presentation may be, there's always a chance that something unique about a particular situation may slip through the cracks. You can guard against that by looking at the following types of information.

Analyst Research Reports

Financial theory tells us share prices are somehow related to the value of a stream of future economic benefit (dividends, cash flow, net income, retained earnings). Hence predictions about the future are of paramount importance. As we've seen, looking at expectations is easy given the availability of data showing consensus earnings forecasts and stock recommendations. The challenge is to assess the credibility of these expectations.

The most basic way to learn more is, of course, to read the research reports analysts write. Some are available only to clients of the brokerage firms for which the analysts work. But many nowadays can be purchased individually on MultexInvestor.com and affiliated sites such as Yahoo! Finance and Quicken.com. Most reports sell for $25 or less.

Analysts are, perhaps, the single most controversial group of people in today's investment landscape. On the one hand, these are intelligent, highly educated, hardworking people who are often generously compensated to know and communicate things about companies we all need to know but aren't able to find out on our own. On the other hand, they are criticized for being overly optimistic in order to curry favor with companies to help their firms earn investment banking fees.

Realistically, some analysts who regularly follow a company might be shy about exposing its warts. But here's a simple trick. Read research reports written about the company's competitors. Analysts covering Motorola may not have been aggressive about exposing its market share losses in cellular handsets. But analysts pushing Nokia (the company that was beating Motorola) were speaking boldly about how much market share it was gaining.

Understand that analysts are human and do often serve more than one master. So don't adopt an attitude of blind faith toward their reports. But across-the-board cynicism is no better. There's much valuable information available here. It's best to follow a balanced approach. Use analyst research to fill in the gaps that will inevitably be left after even the most thorough review of numerical data.

Focus on the basic facts and the qualitative conclusions the analyst draws about the company. The attention you give to the estimates and investment recommendation depends on whether you are acquainted with the individual analyst's overall body of work. If the analyst is familiar to you and you have confidence in his/her opinions, then consider them. But if you do not have specific familiarity with and confidence in the analyst who wrote this particular report, which is often the case with individual investors, you will be better served by deemphasizing this analyst's estimates and recommendation and focusing instead on consensus data.

Independent Research When investors think about analyst research, they are usually thinking about sell-side analysts (those who work for brokerage firms). The work product of their usual counterparts, the buy-side analysts, is generally prepared for internal use only (for portfolio managers who work at the same firm) and, hence, not generally offered to the public. However, there is a third source that is readily available: the independents. The most accessible of these are Standard & Poor's and Morningstar. As is the case with other independent research organizations, they cover large numbers of stocks, feature proprietary ratings or grades, and produce reports that can be accessed via annual subscription or in Morningstar's case, premium web site membership. But these firms go a step further and make their analyst research available on a pay-per-view basis (costing $5 per report for S&P and $10 for Morningstar) on MultexInvestor.com and affiliated sites (such as Yahoo! Finance). Such commentary isn't as long or deep as are some sell-side reports. But the independents are objective and easy to understand. I especially like the format Morningstar is using at present for much of its analyst commentary: Many of the reports have a section entitled "The Bulls Say," another entitled "The Bears Say," and a third section entitled "Morningstar Take" devoted to a synthesis and recommendation by the Morningstar analyst. Whether you agree with the Morningstar conclusion or not, its analysts undeniably add value to your efforts by clearly articulating the issues you should be considering.

Financial Statements

You may have noticed that thus far we haven't looked at what so many others regard as the staple of investment analysis, company financial statements. Actually, the reports we've already seen draw very heavily from the statements. Instead of studying the statements in their raw form, we examined data tables that extracted key information from them and re-presented it in more usable formats. So by now we already know most of the important information that can be gleaned from the financials.

Even so, every investment story is unique and it's always possible something important wasn't captured by the main data presentation. That's why major financial web sites include the statements themselves. Use them as safety valves to see whether there's anything important the data tables missed. Here are the main kinds of things you should be looking for.

Sequential Trends Most data presentations focus on long-term averages, usually over three-, five-, or ten-year periods. A company going from $1.00 EPS in year 0 to $1.61 in year 5 would show a 10 percent cumulative average annual growth rate. That would be the case with a perfectly smooth five-year EPS progression (1.00, 1.10, 1.21, 1.33, 1.46, and 1.61) as well as if the year 0 through year 5 progression was choppy (1.00, 1.75, –2.55, –0.50, 1.61). The latter pattern is obviously more risky. The most thorough view of a trend can be seen in the financial statements themselves. You can look beyond the erratic trend in EPS and examine each line of the income statement to see exactly why that's occurring. Such detail can help you make a thoughtful assumption as to whether the volatility is likely to persist in the future.

Another way to examine sequential trends is to consult year-by-year (an in some cases, quarter-by-quarter) summary data. Besides examining sequential trends in raw numbers (sales, EPS, long-term debt, etc.), you can study period-by-period trends in key ratios, such as those dealing with stock valuation or company quality. Basic presentations along these lines are available in the MSN.Money Ten Year Summary (Figure 11.20) and various reports contained within the Quicken.com Stock Evaluator (Figure 11.21).

My favorite is the Morningstar.com Stock Grades report (Figure 11.22), which shows annual trends in key analytics (growth rates, quality ratios, debt ratios) rather than raw numbers. It also presents year-by-year industry percentile rankings for return on assets and return on equity as

CHS Financial Results Key Ratios: Investing - MSN Money - Microsoft Internet Explorer

File   Edit   View   Favorites   Tools   Help

Quotes
Charts
Recent News

Research
Company Report
SEC Filings
Advisor FYI
Stock Rating
Earnings Estimates
Analyst Ratings
Financial Results
  Highlights
  Key Ratios
  Statements
Insider Trading
Ownership
Community

Guided Research
Research Wizard

Find Stocks
Stock Screener
Top Rated Stocks

Chico's FAS, Inc.: Key Ratios

Growth Rates
Price Ratios
Profit Margins
Financial Condition
Investment Returns
Management Efficiency
▶ Ten Year Summary

	Avg P/E	Price/ Sales	Price/ Book	Net Profit Margin (%)
1/01	16.80	2.22	6.76	10.9
1/00	17.60	1.63	4.80	10.0
1/99	17.50	2.40	7.48	8.5
1/98	17.30	0.75	2.62	3.7
1/97	32.60	0.49	1.76	3.0
12/95	29.80	0.57	2.11	2.8
12/94	25.60	0.66	2.73	5.6
12/93	21.20	2.82	12.33	10.5
12/92	NC	NC	NC	8.3

	Book Value/ Share	Debt/ Equity	Return on Equity (%)	Return on Assets (%)	Interest Coverage
1/01	3.25	0.08	33.3	24.1	NC
1/00	2.05	0.13	29.5	22.0	NC
1/99	1.36	0.20	26.5	18.6	75.5
1/98	0.90	0.31	13.0	8.1	12.5
1/97	0.76	0.39	10.6	6.1	9.0
12/95	0.69	0.37	10.6	6.3	5.8
12/94	0.61	0.33	23.2	12.0	57.0
12/93	0.46	0.06	45.8	29.5	81.0
12/92	0.23	0.15	56.3	30.7	NC

FIGURE 11.20   Ten-Year Financial Summary Report from MSN.Money
Source: MSN.Money (http://moneycentral.msn.com). Reprinted with permission.

well as year-by-year comparisons between company balance sheet ratios and S&P 500 averages.

Unusual Income/Expenses   Reporting income can sometimes seem as much an art as a science. Indeed, in the aftermath of the Enron situation, many who for years barely, if ever, thought about this have become hypersensitive to the kinds of reporting decisions made by companies and endorsed by accountants. An important decision category relates to the treatment of various kinds of unusual, or nonrecurring, income and expenses. Certain items, such as those that reflect discontinued operations or changes in accounting methods, are widely accepted as being of little relevance to investment analysis. The official accounting label for these is "extraordinary," and the investment community makes a standard practice of analyzing EPS

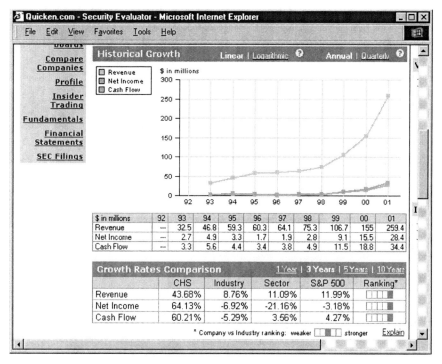

FIGURE 11.21   Historical Growth Report from Quicken.com Stock Evaluator
Source: Quicken.com. Reprinted with permission.

"before extraordinary items." Earnings-related data on Web-based analytic reports is typically calculated on this basis.

But there are other kinds of unusual items about which there is much difference of opinion. Examples include gains/losses on the sale of assets, write-offs to reflect reduced value of assets such as stale inventory, plant closing costs, severance costs relating to layoffs, and so on. You will see differences in earnings-related data depending on the data provider's choices regarding treatment of such issues. It's not really possible to objectively say that any particular analytic response is right or wrong. What's most important is that you understand the presence of unusual items (which you can see by looking at the income statement) and make your own decision as to how you wish to interpret the information.

Here's a general guide that will help you decide how to assess unusuals. They are relevant when you are studying a track record to assess the general level of success achieved by the company. Journalists and financial

Morningstar Quicktake® Report I Morningstar Stock Grades I CHS - Microsoft Internet Explorer

File   Edit   View   Favorites   Tools   Help

Analysis

> Analyst Report

> Star Rating

> Printable Report

Quote

> Price Graph

> News

Snapshot

Morningstar Stock
Grades

> Growth

> Profitability

> Financial Health

Financials

> Sales Graph

> Income Statement

> Cash Flows

> Balance Sheet

> Quarterly Income

> Segment/Region

Profitability Grade: A+   What is this?

Fiscal year-end: January

TTM = Trailing 12 Months

	1997	1998	1999	2000	2001	TTM
Return on Assets %	6.2	8.0	18.7	22.0	24.1	27.1
Industry Rank	58	44	17	8	---	4
Return on Equity %	10.7	12.9	26.6	29.4	33.3	36.5
Industry Rank	53	52	25	22	---	13

Industry Rank (100=Worst)

ROE Breakdown

Net Margin%	3.0	3.7	8.6	10.0	10.9	11.4
Asset Turnover	2.1	2.2	2.2	2.2	2.2	2.4
Financial Leverage	1.7	1.6	1.4	1.3	1.4	1.3

View company's full financials

Financial Health Grade: A   What is this?

Fiscal year-end: January

Qtr = Current Quarter

	1997	1998	1999	2000	2001	Qtr
Long-Term Debt $Mil	7	7	7	7	7	7
Total Equity $Mil	18	21	34	53	85	101
Debt/Equity	0.4	0.3	0.2	0.1	0.1	0.1
S&P 500	0.5	0.8	1.8	0.9	0.9	1.1
Financial Leverage	1.7	1.6	1.4	1.3	1.4	1.3
S&P 500	4.0	4.6	4.7	4.6	4.8	4.8
Current Ratio	1.8	2.4	3.5	3.4	2.0	2.3
S&P 500	1.3	1.7	1.7	1.7	1.8	1.8

View balance sheet

Internet

FIGURE 11.22   Stock Grades Report for Chico's FAS, Inc. from Morningstar.com
Source: Morningstar.com (www.morningstar.com). © 2001 Morningstar, Inc. All
rights reserved. Reprinted with permission.

writers often do this. So they argue that unusuals should be considered,
and their articles tend to criticize analysts who think otherwise. But if you
are studying historic data relationships (inventory-to-sales, gross margin,
etc.) in order to help you formulate forecasts for the future, unusuals are
not directly relevant. Their main role is to provide a very broad guidance
about the sustainability of historic relationships. For example, if a company had a major inventory write-down, it would not be plausible for you
to assume that such charges will recur in the future. But it could suggest
that future inventory-to-sales ratios will probably be lower than those calculated in recent years. This is the way analysts work and is an important

reason why they tend to exclude unusuals and work with presentations of operating, or recurring earnings.

Nonoperating Income/Assets In one sense, these are similar to unusuals in that they do not relate to the regular day-to-day activities of the company. However, it's hard even for analysts to brush them aside since, unlike unusuals, they are likely to be recurring from one period to the next. Looking directly at the income statement and/or balance sheet will tell you how big they are in relation to the entire company. Many investors see large nonoperating income/assets a negative. Some dislike companies that seem unfocused. Others are troubled by what they see as a greater burden of having to understand and become comfortable with matters that may be hard to predict. The latter concern might be alleviated somewhat if the financial statements show stable period-to-period trends in nonoperating items.

Cash Generation Investors who look at the statement of cash flows and see a stable and/or rising period-to-period trend of positive cash generation tend to look favorably on the company. But before drawing such a conclusion, examine the three components of cash flow: operations, financing, and investment. Positive cash flow from the operating component alone is considered most positive, since that relates most directly to the core business operations. It is normal to see the investment category show a net outflow, since it includes capital spending. Another key investing outflow here would be money spent for acquisitions. Investment inflows usually come from funds generated by asset divestitures. Looking directly at the statement of cash flows shows you how great a role acquisitions/divestitures play in the corporate strategy and performance. If you are worried about financial risk, be especially attentive to cash generation from the third category, financing (issuing or retiring debt or equity). Consistently positive cash generation is not bullish if the company relies too heavily on infusion of capital from outside sources.

Note, too, that excess cash generation isn't always a good thing. Back in the 1980s, junk bond investors referred to this as "event risk." The idea was that if companies are doing too well, there's an increasing probability they may do something, like make a big acquisition, that would cause them to borrow more, thereby increasing financial risk. Event risk is present for stocks, too, as corporations feeling a bit too flush can succumb to the temptation to make investments that ultimately prove unwise. What Peter Lynch referred to as "diworsification" falls under this category. Consistently heavy period-to-period cash generation, coupled with comparatively poor and/or deteriorating returns on capital (i.e., a track record of unproductive capital allocation) raises a red flag for event risk.

The Executive Suite

Finally, there's management itself. While it's not as possible to truly know management as well as some like to believe, there are some readily available facts that can provide important clues about the experience of key executives as well as the extent to which their interests are aligned with those of outside shareholders.

Resumes   On MultexInvestor.com, you can find out who the key officers and directors are, their respective ages and tenures with the firm (Appendix 11.J), and backgrounds (Appendix 11.K). An obvious way to use this information is to check to see what they bring to the table in terms of relevant career experience and accomplishments. Ironically, you can also make use of the fact that the public reporting of such information is inexact. A company can get by with skimpy and dry information about its officers and directors. But investors have a right to wonder about a corporation that decides to play close to the vest in an area like this. We can't say for sure it's a signal of a less qualified executive group. But it's reasonable to consider it and to allow relative silence to tip the balance in a close call between a buy/avoid investment decision.

Compensation   There are two categories of compensation: cash (salary, bonus, fringe benefits, etc.) and stock options. Information about these is available on MultexInvestor.com (Appendixes 11.L and 11.M). This information isn't easy to use, given conflicting considerations. On the one hand, shareholders ought not appreciate executives who are overpaid in relation to what they contribute. On the other hand, generous compensation is sometimes necessary to attract the most talented individuals who are best able to enhance long-term share value. Rather than attempting to analyze compensation numbers in detail and draw hard-and-fast conclusions, use these as broad contextual backdrops for the rest of what you have examined, and possibly, as tiebreakers when the investment decision is a close call.

   In any case, don't get caught up in occasional outbreaks of sometimes-righteous public rhetoric you see on this topic. Specifically, don't join those who try to relate compensation to short-term earnings or share price trends. Corporate executives cannot control many relevant factors (such as business or market cycles), and companies understand they will not be able to attract and retain talented executives if they start slashing compensation every time there's a stock market correction.

The best way to look at this data is by comparing a company to others in the same general business and of the same general size. When compensation viewed this way seems excessive, that might be a red flag, especially if insider share control is heavy. Also, be more willing to accept higher compensation when it is in the form of stock options. It is true that per-share results can eventually be diluted when these shares are issued. But it can help align the interests of management with those of shareholders. Note, though, that sometimes option-heavy employees don't necessarily see themselves as long-term investors in the company. Substantial share price declines can make options virtually worthless (unless the corporation is willing and able to readjust strike prices). Too, as soon as the options become exercisable, many employees exercise and sell at the first available opportunity. But even this situation isn't black-and-white. Often, a generous option package allows a company to recruit talent at lower salaries than might otherwise be required. Again, don't hinge a major part of your investment case on stock options. Just be aware of the facts, and possibly allow option-heavy compensation practices to help tilt you one way or the other in a close decision.

APPENDIX TO CHAPTER 11: KEY MULTEXINVESTOR.COM DATA REPORTS

This Appendix presents a comprehensive picture of how the content described in Chapter 11 looks on the MultexInvestor.com web site. The content (Appendixes 11.A to 11.P) is shown in the same sequence you would experience if you went through the menu step by step. You can decide for yourself whether you'd like to stick with this "official" sequence, use the one I proposed in Chapter 11, or design your own approach.

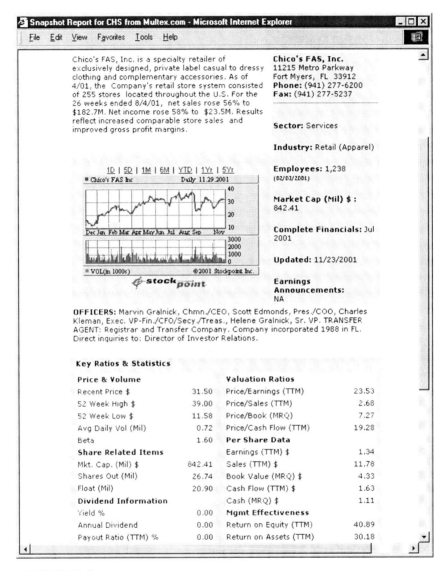

Chico's FAS, Inc. is a specialty retailer of exclusively designed, private label casual to dressy clothing and complementary accessories. As of 4/01, the Company's retail store system consisted of 255 stores located throughout the U.S. For the 26 weeks ended 8/4/01, net sales rose 56% to $182.7M. Net income rose 58% to $23.5M. Results reflect increased comparable store sales and improved gross profit margins.

Chico's FAS, Inc.
11215 Metro Parkway
Fort Myers, FL 33912
Phone: (941) 277-6200
Fax: (941) 277-5237

Sector: Services

Industry: Retail (Apparel)

Employees: 1,238
(02/03/2001)

Market Cap (Mil) $:
842.41

Complete Financials: Jul 2001

Updated: 11/23/2001

Earnings Announcements:
NA

1D | 5D | 1M | 6M | YTD | 1Yr | 5Yr
■ Chico's FAS Inc   Daily 11.29.2001
■ VOL(in 1000s)   ©2001 Stockpoint Inc.

OFFICERS: Marvin Gralnick, Chmn./CEO, Scott Edmonds, Pres./COO, Charles Kleman, Exec. VP-Fin./CFO/Secy./Treas., Helene Gralnick, Sr. VP. TRANSFER AGENT: Registrar and Transfer Company. Company incorporated 1988 in FL. Direct inquiries to: Director of Investor Relations.

Key Ratios & Statistics

Price & Volume		Valuation Ratios	
Recent Price $	31.50	Price/Earnings (TTM)	23.53
52 Week High $	39.00	Price/Sales (TTM)	2.68
52 Week Low $	11.58	Price/Book (MRQ)	7.27
Avg Daily Vol (Mil)	0.72	Price/Cash Flow (TTM)	19.28
Beta	1.60	**Per Share Data**	
Share Related Items		Earnings (TTM) $	1.34
Mkt. Cap. (Mil) $	842.41	Sales (TTM) $	11.78
Shares Out (Mil)	26.74	Book Value (MRQ) $	4.33
Float (Mil)	20.90	Cash Flow (TTM) $	1.63
Dividend Information		Cash (MRQ) $	1.11
Yield %	0.00	**Mgmt Effectiveness**	
Annual Dividend	0.00	Return on Equity (TTM)	40.89
Payout Ratio (TTM) %	0.00	Return on Assets (TTM)	30.18

APPENDIX 11.A Snapshot
Price Chart Source: Copyright 2001 Stockpoint, Inc. (a Screaming Media Co.). All rights reserved. Fundamental data supplied by Market Guide. © 2001, Multex.com, Inc. All rights reserved.

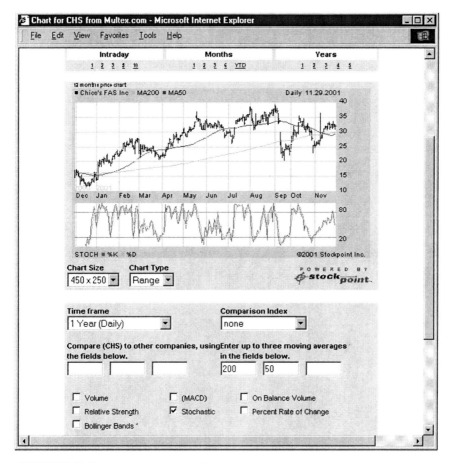

APPENDIX 11.B   Interactive Price Chart

Source: Copyright 2001 Stockpoint, Inc. (a Screaming Media Co.). All rights reserved. © 2001, Multex.com, Inc. All rights reserved.

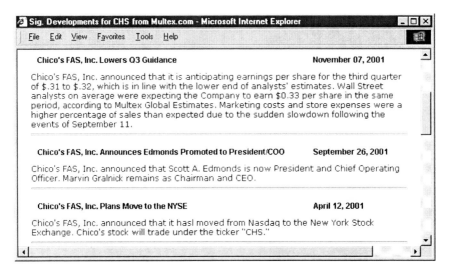

APPENDIX 11.C   Significant Developments

Source: MultexInvestor.com. Fundamental data supplied by Market Guide. © 2001, Multex.com, Inc. All rights reserved.

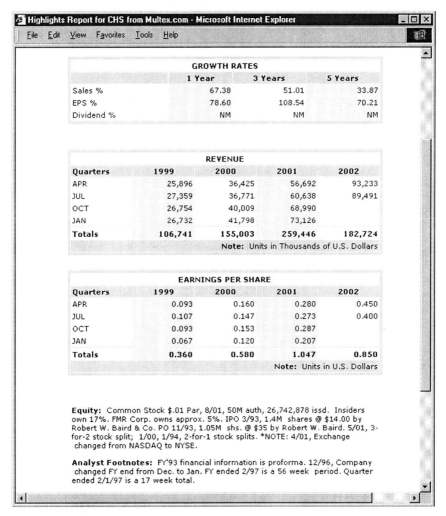

Highlights Report for CHS from Multex.com - Microsoft Internet Explorer

File Edit View Favorites Tools Help

GROWTH RATES

	1 Year	3 Years	5 Years
Sales %	67.38	51.01	33.87
EPS %	78.60	108.54	70.21
Dividend %	NM	NM	NM

REVENUE

Quarters	1999	2000	2001	2002
APR	25,896	36,425	56,692	93,233
JUL	27,359	36,771	60,638	89,491
OCT	26,754	40,009	68,990	
JAN	26,732	41,798	73,126	
Totals	**106,741**	**155,003**	**259,446**	**182,724**

Note: Units in Thousands of U.S. Dollars

EARNINGS PER SHARE

Quarters	1999	2000	2001	2002
APR	0.093	0.160	0.280	0.450
JUL	0.107	0.147	0.273	0.400
OCT	0.093	0.153	0.287	
JAN	0.067	0.120	0.207	
Totals	**0.360**	**0.580**	**1.047**	**0.850**

Note: Units in U.S. Dollars

Equity: Common Stock $.01 Par, 8/01, 50M auth, 26,742,878 issd. Insiders own 17%. FMR Corp. owns approx. 5%. IPO 3/93, 1.4M shares @ $14.00 by Robert W. Baird & Co. PO 11/93, 1.05M shs. @ $35 by Robert W. Baird. 5/01, 3-for-2 stock split; 1/00, 1/94, 2-for-1 stock splits. *NOTE: 4/01, Exchange changed from NASDAQ to NYSE.

Analyst Footnotes: FY'93 financial information is proforma. 12/96, Company changed FY end from Dec. to Jan. FY ended 2/97 is a 56 week period. Quarter ended 2/1/97 is a 17 week total.

APPENDIX 11.D   Highlights Report
Source: MultexInvestor.com. Fundamental data supplied by Market Guide. © 2001, Multex.com, Inc. All rights reserved.

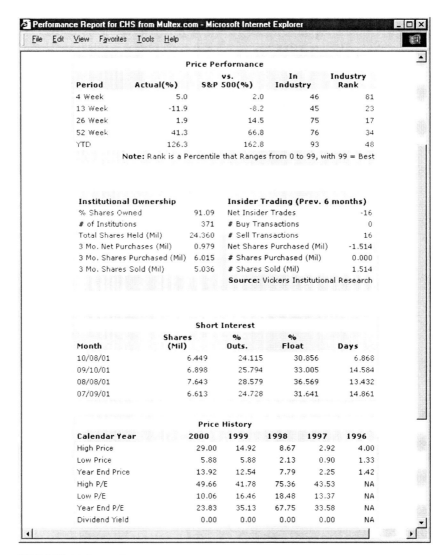

Performance Report for CHS from Multex.com - Microsoft Internet Explorer

File Edit View Favorites Tools Help

Price Performance

Period	Actual(%)	vs. S&P 500(%)	In Industry	Industry Rank
4 Week	5.0	2.0	46	61
13 Week	-11.9	-8.2	45	23
26 Week	1.9	14.5	75	17
52 Week	41.3	66.8	76	34
YTD	126.3	162.8	93	48

Note: Rank is a Percentile that Ranges from 0 to 99, with 99 = Best

Institutional Ownership

% Shares Owned	91.09
# of Institutions	371
Total Shares Held (Mil)	24.360
3 Mo. Net Purchases (Mil)	0.979
3 Mo. Shares Purchased (Mil)	6.015
3 Mo. Shares Sold (Mil)	5.036

Insider Trading (Prev. 6 months)

Net Insider Trades	-16
# Buy Transactions	0
# Sell Transactions	16
Net Shares Purchased (Mil)	-1.514
# Shares Purchased (Mil)	0.000
# Shares Sold (Mil)	1.514

Source: Vickers Institutional Research

Short Interest

Month	Shares (Mil)	% Outs.	% Float	Days
10/08/01	6.449	24.115	30.856	6.868
09/10/01	6.898	25.794	33.005	14.584
08/08/01	7.643	28.579	36.569	13.432
07/09/01	6.613	24.728	31.641	14.861

Price History

Calendar Year	2000	1999	1998	1997	1996
High Price	29.00	14.92	8.67	2.92	4.00
Low Price	5.88	5.88	2.13	0.90	1.33
Year End Price	13.92	12.54	7.79	2.25	1.42
High P/E	49.66	41.78	75.36	43.53	NA
Low P/E	10.06	16.46	18.48	13.37	NA
Year End P/E	23.83	35.13	67.75	33.58	NA
Dividend Yield	0.00	0.00	0.00	0.00	NA

APPENDIX 11.E   Performance Report

Source: MultexInvestor.com. Fundamental data supplied by Market Guide. © 2001, Multex.com, Inc. All rights reserved. Institutional and insider data supplied by Vickers Institutional Research.

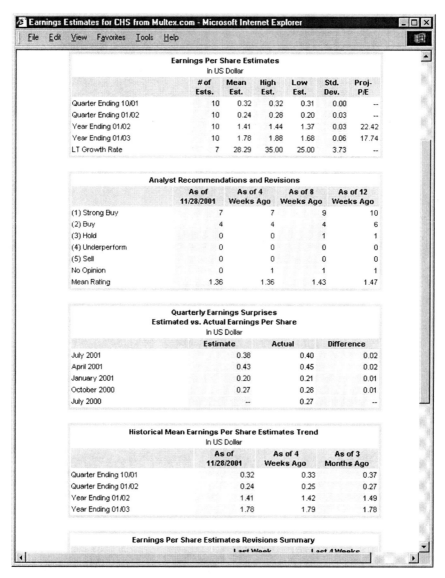

Earnings Estimates for CHS from Multex.com - Microsoft Internet Explorer

File   Edit   View   Favorites   Tools   Help

Earnings Per Share Estimates
In US Dollar

	# of Ests.	Mean Est.	High Est.	Low Est.	Std. Dev.	Proj- P/E
Quarter Ending 10/01	10	0.32	0.32	0.31	0.00	--
Quarter Ending 01/02	10	0.24	0.28	0.20	0.03	--
Year Ending 01/02	10	1.41	1.44	1.37	0.03	22.42
Year Ending 01/03	10	1.78	1.88	1.68	0.06	17.74
LT Growth Rate	7	28.29	35.00	25.00	3.73	--

Analyst Recommendations and Revisions

	As of 11/28/2001	As of 4 Weeks Ago	As of 8 Weeks Ago	As of 12 Weeks Ago
(1) Strong Buy	7	7	9	10
(2) Buy	4	4	4	6
(3) Hold	0	0	1	1
(4) Underperform	0	0	0	0
(5) Sell	0	0	0	0
No Opinion	0	1	1	1
Mean Rating	1.36	1.36	1.43	1.47

Quarterly Earnings Surprises
Estimated vs. Actual Earnings Per Share
In US Dollar

	Estimate	Actual	Difference
July 2001	0.38	0.40	0.02
April 2001	0.43	0.45	0.02
January 2001	0.20	0.21	0.01
October 2000	0.27	0.28	0.01
July 2000	--	0.27	--

Historical Mean Earnings Per Share Estimates Trend
In US Dollar

	As of 11/28/2001	As of 4 Weeks Ago	As of 3 Months Ago
Quarter Ending 10/01	0.32	0.33	0.37
Quarter Ending 01/02	0.24	0.25	0.27
Year Ending 01/02	1.41	1.42	1.49
Year Ending 01/03	1.78	1.79	1.78

Earnings Per Share Estimates Revisions Summary
Last Week   Last 4 Weeks

APPENDIX 11.F   Earnings Estimates Report
Source: MultexInvestor.com. Fundamental data supplied by Market Guide. © 2001,
Multex.com, Inc. All rights reserved.

```
┌─────────────────────────────────────────────────────────────────────────┐
│ Ratio Comparison for CHS from Multex.com - Microsoft Internet Explorer  _□✕│
├─────────────────────────────────────────────────────────────────────────┤
│  File   Edit   View   Favorites   Tools   Help                          ▓ │
└─────────────────────────────────────────────────────────────────────────┘
```

RATIO COMPARISON

Valuation Ratios	Company	Industry	Sector	S&P 500
P/E Ratio (TTM)	23.53	23.79	29.22	31.15
P/E High - Last 5 Yrs.	36.98	40.92	50.16	50.19
P/E Low - Last 5 Yrs.	12.82	9.70	16.58	17.51
Beta	1.60	1.24	0.90	1.00
Price to Sales (TTM)	2.68	0.97	2.62	3.80
Price to Book (MRQ)	7.27	4.73	4.20	5.62
Price to Tangible Book (MRQ)	7.27	5.18	6.50	8.61
Price to Cash Flow (TTM)	19.28	18.41	17.58	21.09
Price to Free Cash Flow (TTM)	269.23	31.85	34.61	38.43
% Owned Institutions	91.09	54.15	45.44	59.80

Dividends	Company	Industry	Sector	S&P 500
Dividend Yield	0.00	1.12	1.97	1.75
Dividend Yield - 5 Year Avg.	0.00	0.74	1.29	1.26
Dividend 5 Year Growth Rate	NM	10.93	4.02	9.13
Payout Ratio (TTM)	0.00	16.03	20.96	28.29

Growth Rates(%)	Company	Industry	Sector	S&P 500
Sales (MRQ) vs Qtr. 1 Yr. Ago	47.58	-4.34	8.82	-0.51
Sales (TTM) vs TTM 1 Yr. Ago	63.12	8.21	14.77	7.68
Sales - 5 Yr. Growth Rate	33.87	17.62	20.23	15.21
EPS (MRQ) vs Qtr. 1 Yr. Ago	46.32	13.55	-11.09	-12.05
EPS (TTM) vs TTM 1 Yr. Ago	62.11	-17.51	-8.19	-2.66
EPS - 5 Yr. Growth Rate	70.21	29.68	19.55	17.08
Capital Spending - 5 Yr. Growth Rate	107.70	24.16	21.74	12.57

Financial Strength	Company	Industry	Sector	S&P 500
Quick Ratio (MRQ)	1.29	0.42	0.74	1.14
Current Ratio (MRQ)	2.70	1.70	1.30	1.68
LT Debt to Equity (MRQ)	0.04	0.26	0.87	0.70
Total Debt to Equity (MRQ)	0.05	0.41	1.02	0.99
Interest Coverage (TTM)	NM	18.65	5.70	8.41

Profitability Ratios (%)	Company	Industry	Sector	S&P 500

APPENDIX 11.G   Ratio Comparison Report

Source: MultexInvestor.com. Fundamental data supplied by Market Guide. © 2001, Multex.com, Inc. All rights reserved.

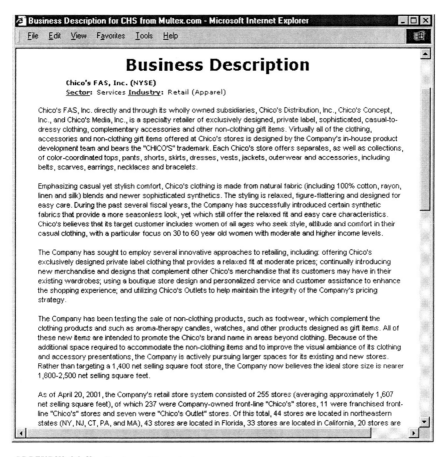

APPENDIX 11.H Business Description

Source: MultexInvestor.com. Fundamental data supplied by Market Guide. © 2001, Multex.com, Inc. All rights reserved.

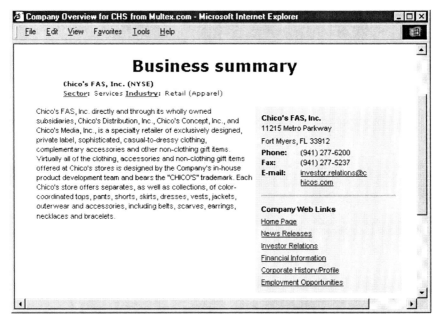

APPENDIX 11.I   Company Overview
Source: MultexInvestor.com. Fundamental data supplied by Market Guide. © 2001, Multex.com, Inc. All rights reserved.

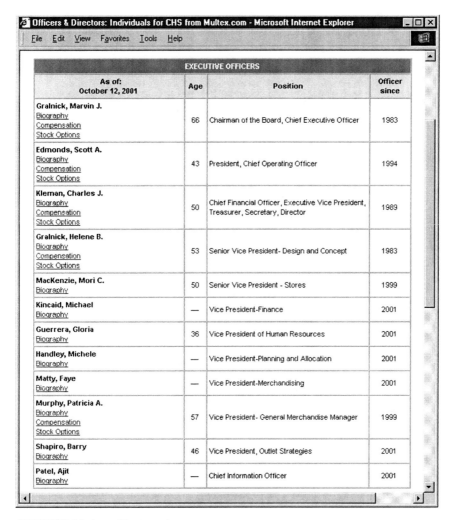

APPENDIX 11.J Officers and Directors
Source: MultexInvestor.com. Fundamental data supplied by Market Guide. © 2001, Multex.com, Inc. All rights reserved.

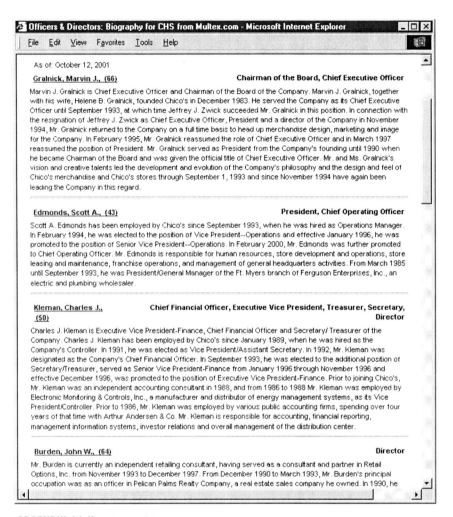

Officers & Directors: Biography for CHS from Multex.com - Microsoft Internet Explorer

File   Edit   View   Favorites   Tools   Help

As of: October 12, 2001

Gralnick, Marvin J., (66)   **Chairman of the Board, Chief Executive Officer**

Marvin J. Gralnick is Chief Executive Officer and Chairman of the Board of the Company. Marvin J. Gralnick, together with his wife, Helene B. Gralnick, founded Chico's in December 1983. He served the Company as its Chief Executive Officer until September 1993, at which time Jeffrey J. Zwick succeeded Mr. Gralnick in this position. In connection with the resignation of Jeffrey J. Zwick as Chief Executive Officer, President and a director of the Company in November 1994, Mr. Gralnick returned to the Company on a full time basis to head up merchandise design, marketing and image for the Company. In February 1995, Mr. Gralnick reassumed the role of Chief Executive Officer and in March 1997 reassumed the position of President. Mr. Gralnick served as President from the Company's founding until 1990 when he became Chairman of the Board and was given the official title of Chief Executive Officer. Mr. and Ms. Gralnick's vision and creative talents led the development and evolution of the Company's philosophy and the design and feel of Chico's merchandise and Chico's stores through September 1, 1993 and since November 1994 have again been leading the Company in this regard.

Edmonds, Scott A., (43)   **President, Chief Operating Officer**

Scott A. Edmonds has been employed by Chico's since September 1993, when he was hired as Operations Manager. In February 1994, he was elected to the position of Vice President--Operations and effective January 1996, he was promoted to the position of Senior Vice President--Operations. In February 2000, Mr. Edmonds was further promoted to Chief Operating Officer. Mr. Edmonds is responsible for human resources, store development and operations, store leasing and maintenance, franchise operations, and management of general headquarters activities. From March 1985 until September 1993, he was President/General Manager of the Ft. Myers branch of Ferguson Enterprises, Inc., an electric and plumbing wholesaler.

Kleman, Charles J., (50)   **Chief Financial Officer, Executive Vice President, Treasurer, Secretary, Director**

Charles J. Kleman is Executive Vice President-Finance, Chief Financial Officer and Secretary/ Treasurer of the Company. Charles J. Kleman has been employed by Chico's since January 1989, when he was hired as the Company's Controller. In 1991, he was elected as Vice President/Assistant Secretary. In 1992, Mr. Kleman was designated as the Company's Chief Financial Officer. In September 1993, he was elected to the additional position of Secretary/Treasurer, served as Senior Vice President-Finance from January 1996 through November 1996 and effective December 1996, was promoted to the position of Executive Vice President-Finance. Prior to joining Chico's, Mr. Kleman was an independent accounting consultant in 1988, and from 1986 to 1988 Mr. Kleman was employed by Electronic Monitoring & Controls, Inc., a manufacturer and distributor of energy management systems, as its Vice President/Controller. Prior to 1986, Mr. Kleman was employed by various public accounting firms, spending over four years of that time with Arthur Andersen & Co. Mr. Kleman is responsible for accounting, financial reporting, management information systems, investor relations and overall management of the distribution center.

Burden, John W., (64)   **Director**

Mr. Burden is currently an independent retailing consultant, having served as a consultant and partner in Retail Options, Inc. from November 1993 to December 1997. From December 1990 to March 1993, Mr. Burden's principal occupation was as an officer in Pelican Palms Realty Company, a real estate sales company he owned. In 1990, he

APPENDIX 11.K   Biographies

Source: MultexInvestor.com. Fundamental data supplied by Market Guide. © 2001, Multex.com, Inc. All rights reserved.

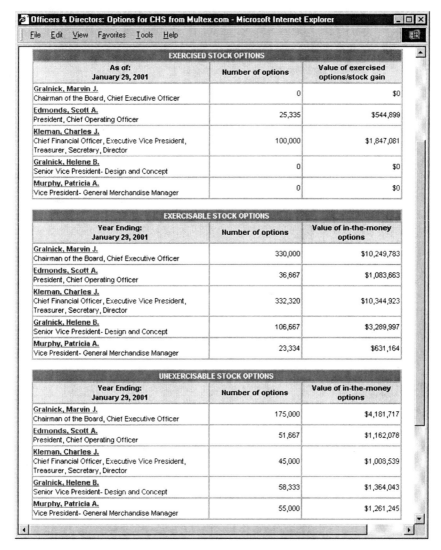

Officers & Directors: Options for CHS from Multex.com - Microsoft Internet Explorer

File   Edit   View   Favorites   Tools   Help

EXERCISED STOCK OPTIONS		
As of: **January 29, 2001**	**Number of options**	**Value of exercised options/stock gain**
Gralnick, Marvin J. Chairman of the Board, Chief Executive Officer	0	$0
Edmonds, Scott A. President, Chief Operating Officer	25,335	$544,899
Kleman, Charles J. Chief Financial Officer, Executive Vice President, Treasurer, Secretary, Director	100,000	$1,847,081
Gralnick, Helene B. Senior Vice President- Design and Concept	0	$0
Murphy, Patricia A. Vice President- General Merchandise Manager	0	$0

EXERCISABLE STOCK OPTIONS		
Year Ending: **January 29, 2001**	**Number of options**	**Value of in-the-money options**
Gralnick, Marvin J. Chairman of the Board, Chief Executive Officer	330,000	$10,249,783
Edmonds, Scott A. President, Chief Operating Officer	36,667	$1,083,663
Kleman, Charles J. Chief Financial Officer, Executive Vice President, Treasurer, Secretary, Director	332,320	$10,344,923
Gralnick, Helene B. Senior Vice President- Design and Concept	106,667	$3,289,997
Murphy, Patricia A. Vice President- General Merchandise Manager	23,334	$631,164

UNEXERCISABLE STOCK OPTIONS		
Year Ending: **January 29, 2001**	**Number of options**	**Value of in-the-money options**
Gralnick, Marvin J. Chairman of the Board, Chief Executive Officer	175,000	$4,181,717
Edmonds, Scott A. President, Chief Operating Officer	51,667	$1,162,078
Kleman, Charles J. Chief Financial Officer, Executive Vice President, Treasurer, Secretary, Director	45,000	$1,008,539
Gralnick, Helene B. Senior Vice President- Design and Concept	58,333	$1,364,043
Murphy, Patricia A. Vice President- General Merchandise Manager	55,000	$1,261,245

APPENDIX 11.L   Stock Options

Source: MultexInvestor.com. Fundamental data supplied by Market Guide. © 2001, Multex.com, Inc. All rights reserved.

Officers & Directors: Compensation for CHS from Multex.com - Microsoft Internet Explorer

File   Edit   View   Favorites   Tools   Help

OVERALL COMPENSATION

Fiscal Year Ending: January 29, 2001	Total Annual Comp.	Long- Term Incentive Plans	All Other	Fiscal Year Total
Gralnick, Marvin J. Chairman of the Board, Chief Executive Officer	$1,205,769	$0	$5,250	$1,211,019
Edmonds, Scott A. President, Chief Operating Officer	$497,788	$0	$5,250	$503,038
Kleman, Charles J. Chief Financial Officer, Executive Vice President, Treasurer, Secretary, Director	$517,019	$0	$5,250	$522,269
Gralnick, Helene B. Senior Vice President- Design and Concept	$417,269	$0	$5,250	$422,519
Murphy, Patricia A. Vice President- General Merchandise Manager	$429,500	$0	$5,250	$434,750

DETAILS OF ANNUAL COMPENSATION

Fiscal Year Ending: January 29, 2001	Salary	Bonus	Other	Total Annual Comp.
Gralnick, Marvin J. Chairman of the Board, Chief Executive Officer	$605,769	$600,000	$0	$1,205,769
Edmonds, Scott A. President, Chief Operating Officer	$277,788	$220,000	$0	$497,788
Kleman, Charles J. Chief Financial Officer, Executive Vice President, Treasurer, Secretary, Director	$289,019	$228,000	$0	$517,019
Gralnick, Helene B. Senior Vice President- Design and Concept	$233,269	$184,000	$0	$417,269
Murphy, Patricia A. Vice President- General Merchandise Manager	$240,000	$189,500	$0	$429,500

APPENDIX 11.M   Cash Compensation

Source: MultexInvestor.com. Fundamental data supplied by Market Guide. © 2001, Multex.com, Inc. All rights reserved.

```
Income Stmt: Annual for CHS from Multex.com - Microsoft Internet Explorer    _ □ ×
File   Edit   View   Favorites   Tools   Help
```

ANNUAL INCOME STATEMENT

In Millions of U.S. Dollars (except for per share items)	53 Weeks Ending 02/03/01	52 Weeks Ending 01/29/00	52 Weeks Ending 01/30/99	52 Weeks Ending 01/31/98	56 Weeks Ending 02/01/97
Revenue	259.4	155.0	106.7	75.3	67.8
Other Revenue	–	–	–	–	–
Total Revenue	**259.4**	**155.0**	**106.7**	**75.3**	**67.8**
Cost of Revenue	108.7	65.0	44.2	33.2	28.6
Gross Profit	**150.8**	**90.1**	**62.5**	**42.1**	**39.2**
Selling/ General/ Administrative Expenses	105.4	65.2	47.4	37.2	36.1
Research & Development	–	–	–	–	–
Depreciation/ Amortization	–	–	–	–	–
Interest Expense (Income), Net Operating	–	–	–	–	–
Unusual Expense (Income)	–	–	–	–	–
Total Operating Expense	**214.1**	**130.2**	**91.6**	**70.4**	**64.7**
Operating Income	**45.4**	**24.8**	**15.1**	**4.9**	**3.1**
Interest Income (Expense), Net Non-Operating	0.4	0.2	(0.2)	(0.4)	(0.4)
Gain (Loss) on Sale of Assets	–	–	–	–	–
Income Before Tax	**45.8**	**25.0**	**15.0**	**4.5**	**2.7**
Income Tax	17.4	9.5	5.8	1.8	1.1
Income After Tax	**28.4**	**15.5**	**9.1**	**2.8**	**1.6**
Minority Interest	–	–	–	–	–
Equity In Affiliates	–	–	–	–	–
Net Income Before Extra. Items	**28.4**	**15.5**	**9.1**	**2.8**	**1.6**
Accounting Change	–	–	–	–	–
Discontinued Operations	–	–	–	–	–
Extraordinary Item	–	–	–	–	–
Net Income	**28.4**	**15.5**	**9.1**	**2.8**	**1.6**
Preferred Dividends	–	–	–	–	–
Income Available to Common Excl. Extra. Items	**28.4**	**15.5**	**9.1**	**2.8**	**1.6**
Income Available to Common Incl. Extra. Items	**28.4**	**15.5**	**9.1**	**2.8**	**1.6**
Basic/ Primary Weighted Average Shares	26.03	25.41	24.50	23.74	23.59
Basic/ Primary EPS Excl. Extra. Items	**1.090**	**0.610**	**0.373**	**0.117**	**0.068**
Basic/ Primary EPS Incl. Extra. Items	**1.090**	**0.610**	**0.373**	**0.117**	**0.068**
Dilution Adjustment	–	–	–	–	–
Diluted Weighted Average Shares	27.22	26.52	25.59	24.10	23.93
Diluted EPS Excl. Extra. Items	**1.042**	**0.584**	**0.357**	**0.115**	**0.067**
Diluted EPS Incl. Extra. Items	**1.042**	**0.584**	**0.357**	**0.115**	**0.067**
Dividends per Share - Common Stock Primary Issue	0.000	0.000	0.000	0.000	0.000

APPENDIX 11.N   Income Statement

Source: MultexInvestor.com. Fundamental data supplied by Market Guide. © 2001, Multex.com, Inc. All rights reserved.

Balance Sheet: Annual for CHS from Multex.com - Microsoft Internet Explorer

File   Edit   View   Favorites   Tools   Help

ANNUAL BALANCE SHEET

In Millions of U.S. Dollars (except for per share items)	As of 02/03/01	As of 01/29/00	As of 01/30/99	As of 01/31/98	As of 02/01/97
Cash & Equivalents	3.9	4.0	14.5	2.9	0.8
Short Term Investments	14.2	14.0	–	–	–
Cash and Short Term Investments	18.1	18.0	14.5	2.9	0.8
Trade Accounts Receivable, Net	3.0	1.7	1.1	0.9	0.8
Total Receivables, Net	3.0	1.7	1.1	0.9	0.8
Total Inventory	24.4	14.8	10.1	9.5	7.8
Prepaid Expenses	2.3	0.7	0.5	0.7	0.5
Other Current Assets	3.0	2.0	1.6	1.3	1.3
Total Current Assets	**50.8**	**37.2**	**27.8**	**15.3**	**11.2**
Property/ Plant/ Equipment - Gross	80.2	41.2	27.7	23.6	22.3
Accumulated Depreciation	(14.6)	(9.9)	(8.0)	(6.6)	(5.1)
Property/ Plant/ Equipment, Net	65.6	31.3	19.7	17.0	17.2
Goodwill, Net	–	–	–	–	–
Intangibles, Net	–	–	–	0.0	0.0
Long Term Investments	–	–	0.0	1.0	1.6
Other Long Term Assets	1.4	1.7	1.5	1.2	1.2
Total Assets	**117.8**	**70.3**	**49.0**	**34.5**	**31.2**
Accounts Payable	13.8	6.0	4.0	3.5	3.3
Accrued Expenses	11.3	4.6	3.7	2.5	2.5
Notes Payable/ Short Term Debt	–	–	–	0.0	0.0
Current Port. LT Debt/ Capital Leases	0.3	0.3	0.3	0.3	0.5
Other Current Liabilities	–	–	–	0.0	0.0
Total Current Liabilities	**25.3**	**10.8**	**8.0**	**6.3**	**6.2**
Long Term Debt	7.2	6.8	6.7	6.7	7.0
Capital Lease Obligations	–	–	–	–	–
Total Long Term Debt	**7.2**	**6.8**	**6.7**	**6.7**	**7.0**
Total Debt	**7.4**	**7.1**	**7.0**	**7.0**	**7.5**
Deferred Income Tax	–	–	–	–	–
Minority Interest	–	–	–	–	–
Other Liabilities	–	–	–	0.0	0.0
Total Liabilities	**32.5**	**17.7**	**14.7**	**13.0**	**13.2**
Redeemable Preferred Stock	–	–	–	–	–
Preferred Stock - Non Redeemable, Net	–	–	–	–	–
Common Stock	0.2	0.2	0.1	0.1	0.1
Additional Paid-In Capital	18.9	14.7	11.9	8.2	7.6
Retained Earnings (Accum. Deficit)	66.2	37.8	22.3	13.2	10.4
Treasury Stock - Common	–	–	–	–	–
Other Equity	0.0	(0.0)	–	–	–
Total Equity	**85.3**	**52.6**	**34.3**	**21.5**	**18.0**

APPENDIX 11.0   Balance Sheet

Source: MultexInvestor.com. Fundamental data supplied by Market Guide. © 2001, Multex.com, Inc. All rights reserved.

```
┌─────────────────────────────────────────────────────────────────────┐
│ Cash Flow: Annual for CHS from Multex.com - Microsoft Internet Explorer  _ □ ✕ │
├─────────────────────────────────────────────────────────────────────┤
│  File   Edit   View   Favorites   Tools   Help                         │
```

ANNUAL CASH FLOW STATEMENT (Indirect Method)					
In Millions of U.S. Dollars (except for per share items)	53 Weeks Ending 02/03/01	52 Weeks Ending 01/29/00 Reclass. 02/03/01	52 Weeks Ending 01/30/99 Reclass. 02/03/01	52 Weeks Ending 01/31/98	56 Weeks Ending 02/01/97
Net Income	28.4	15.5	9.1	2.8	1.6
Depreciation/ Depletion	6.0	3.3	2.4	2.1	2.0
Deferred Taxes	(0.6)	(0.7)	(0.6)	0.0	(0.4)
Non-Cash Items	3.5	1.7	1.9	0.4	0.1
Changes in Working Capital	1.9	(2.7)	0.9	(1.7)	(0.2)
Total Cash from Operating Activities	**39.2**	**17.1**	**13.8**	**3.6**	**3.2**
Capital Expenditures	(40.5)	(15.2)	(5.0)	(2.0)	(2.9)
Other Investing Cash Flow Items	(0.2)	(14.0)	1.0	0.6	(1.6)
Total Cash from Investing Activities	**(40.6)**	**(29.2)**	**(4.0)**	**(1.4)**	**(4.5)**
Financing Cash Flow Items	(0.1)	0.0	(0.2)	(0.2)	(0.2)
Total Cash Dividends Paid	–	–	–	–	–
Issuance (Retirement) of Stock, Net	1.5	1.7	2.2	0.7	0.5
Issuance (Retirement) of Debt, Net	(0.1)	(0.2)	(0.1)	(0.6)	0.9
Total Cash from Financing Activities	**1.4**	**1.6**	**1.8**	**(0.1)**	**1.1**
Foreign Exchange Effects	–	–	–	0.0	0.0
Net Change in Cash	**(0.1)**	**(10.5)**	**11.5**	**2.1**	**(0.3)**
Cash Interest Paid	0.9	0.6	0.6	0.6	0.7
Cash Taxes Paid	15.8	9.4	4.9	1.8	1.8

APPENDIX 11.P　　Statement of Cash Flows

Source: MultexInvestor.com. Fundamental data supplied by Market Guide. © 2001, Multex.com, Inc. All rights reserved.

three

Buy . . . the Best of the Stocks That Pass Muster

## CHAPTER 12

The Learning Curve

We covered a lot of territory in Step 1 (Find) when we considered the different kinds of screens we could use. Then, in Step 2 (Analyze), we organized a massive quantity of facts in such a way as to tell a cohesive story with a clear beginning ("Getting Acquainted"), middle ("Exploring the Fundamentals"), and end ("Finishing Touches"). Now we move to Step 3 (Buy), where we combine all the pros and cons we've seen and reach a specific buy-or-avoid decision for each stock under consideration. To do that, we have to translate all the facts we collected in Step 2 (Analyze) into an opinion. And take the word "opinion" seriously. There is no single correct answer. We can all look at the same set of facts and come up with different opinions based on our individual investment goals and styles.

The key tools we'll use in Step 3 (Buy) are Analysis Keys and Decision Paths. At first glance, this process may appear extremely simple; it's just a matter of answering three straightforward yes/no questions, and then cataloging the various combinations of answers. But those questions require considerable insight into whether a particular set of data supports, negates, or is neutral toward our investment goals. The good news is that everything needed to form these opinions is clearly laid out. Once you get comfortable working with the content, you ought to be able to breeze through the information in a matter of minutes. But as with many aspects of life, there's a learning curve. You'll probably find it slow going the first time you do it.

To help you get comfortable forming opinions about the data, this chapter presents a "Data Guide" that features a set of questions for each item of content you'll encounter during Step 2 (Analyze). But this isn't a simple checklist. For example, you'll be prompted to consider whether the company's trailing 12-month operating margin is above the average for its industry. You'd say yes if the company margin is 12.3 percent and the industry average is 12.2 percent. You'd also say yes if the company margin is 12.3 percent and the industry average is 4.6 percent. Obviously, one "yes" is more emphatic than another. But even the most vigorous "yes" means little if operating margin comparisons don't have a significant place in your investment philosophy.

There are two response columns for each question. The first asks you to identify the kind of information the question is dealing with. Your choices are P (primary information), S (secondary information), and G (general information). These classifications were discussed in Chapter 10. The second column addresses investment impact. You don't really articulate your answer to the question. Instead, you state whether the answer, whatever it is (vigorous yes, mild yes, mild no, vigorous no, unknown), has a positive (+), neutral (0), or negative (−) impact on an investment case based on your goals.

Let's go back to the operating margin example. If your screen is based on company quality and includes margin tests, you'd answer "P" in the first column, since this constitutes primary information for you. For the second column, it's easy to eliminate a "−" answer since above-average margins are better than below-average margins. If the company's 12.3 percent margin compares to a 4.6 percent industry average, we'd describe the impact as "+" (positive). But suppose the industry average is 12.2 percent, meaning the company beat the benchmark only by the skin of its teeth. You could still answer "+" (positive). If your desire for a truly strong operating margin is emphatic, you might drop your answer to "0" (neutral), or even "−" (negative). It all depends on how aggressive you are regarding this aspect of your investment philosophy.

You might even invent an in-between answer ("+?"). Or you may start with one answer ("0") and come back later and change it based on other data items. You might wind up with enough "+" answers to other quality-oriented questions that you become more willing to live with a barely positive company-to-industry comparison in this particular item. In fact, the other indications may be sufficient to make you perfectly content with a company whose operating margin just comes close to the industry average (e.g., a company margin of 12.3 percent compared to a 12.5 percent industry average). So you'd change your answer from "0" or "+?" to "+."

On the other hand, suppose you're a momentum investor and operating margin isn't a primary focus. Now, you'd answer "S" (secondary information) in the first column, or even "G" (general information) if you are completely oblivious to the topic. For this sort of investment philosophy, an operating margin anywhere close to the industry average might be seen as a bonus warranting a "+" answer in the second column.

It's immaterial whether the question is phrased in such a way as to associate a "yes" answer or a "no" answer with superior investment characteristics. Regardless of how the question is worded, answer "+" if you, based on your individual goals and style, draw favorable investment conclusions from the issue being addressed by the question.

Don't worry about the absence of clear-cut answers. What's most important is to come up with reasonable assumptions about the right questions. That's what the Data Guide and the rest of Step 3 (Buy) are designed to help you accomplish. When all is said and done, no matter how systematic we are, every investment we make is at the mercy of the great unknown—future events. So let's not lose sight of the value of subjective assessment. Subjectivity can get us into trouble if we simply chase stocks we like without basing our positive feelings on a proper set of factual underpinnings. But after having gone through Step 1 (Find) and Step 2 (Analyze), subjective judgment is channeled in such a way that it serves us very effectively.

Don't worry if the Data Guide seems time-consuming. Actually, I hope you will eventually come to see it this way only because you've become comfortable looking at data and can instantly spot relationships that are important to you. That's really the goal. The Data Guide is just a tool to help you move along the learning curve associated with what may, for you, be a new way of analyzing companies and stocks.

Treat the Data Guide like a set of bicycle training wheels. Use it for as long as you feel you need help recognizing what to look for in the data. Eventually you'll find yourself able to look at the Analysis Keys that will be presented in Chapter 13 and confidently answer the questions posed without going line by line to the Data Guide. And by the way, this is not an all-or-nothing proposition. You can always revisit the Data Guide periodically, in detail or through general eyeballing, to refresh yourself (i.e., to make sure you didn't let the heat of battle lull you into omitting something important).

After the Data Guide, we'll discuss the "Guru Shortcut," another aid to helping you make sense of the information you've accumulated. These are Web reports that show you how certain well-known investors might balance pros and cons gleaned from the data. Like the Data Guide, the Guru Shortcut is a tool that helps you get comfortable identifying and prioritizing important information you encountered in Step 2 (Analyze).

DATA GUIDE

Tables 12.1 to 12.8 are organized on the basis of the data review sequence presented in Chapter 11 and the content presented on the MultexInvestor .com web site. You can easily adapt it to any other sequence and/or web site you might use.

TABLE 12.1 Getting Acquainted

	Information P/S/G	Impact +/0/–
First Impressions		
Is the company's business one in which you are willing to consider investing?		
Is the company's market capitalization acceptable in light of your investment goals and style?		
Is the stock's trading volume satisfactory for your purposes?		
Is the stock's float acceptable for your purposes?		
Does your first glance at the chart reveal any trends you find disturbing?		
Does the summary numerical data leave you willing to continue to analyze this company/stock?		
Early Turnoffs		
Have company shares traded publicly for a long enough time to be consistent with your investment goals and style?		
Is the percent share ownership by insiders or other large shareholders acceptable to you?		
If there are multiple classes of common stock, is this acceptable to you?		
Is the capital structure (in terms of convertible securities and/or preferred equity) acceptable to you?		
Is there anything about the history of stock splits or stock dividends you find troubling?		
Are historic comparisons distorted to a degree you deem unacceptable by mergers, divestitures, restructurings, or changes in accounting procedures?		
The Company's Business		
Can you adequately comprehend the nature of the company's business based on your own general understanding?		
Are you able to comprehend the nature of the company's business based on additional content (such as 10-K filings, company annual reports, company web site descriptions, third-party descriptions, or analyst research reports)?		
Is your understanding of the company's business, however derived, satisfactory in light of your investment philosophy?		
Given what you learned about the business beyond the initial first impression, is it one in which you remain willing to consider investing?		
The Stock Price Chart		
Is the stock's recent performance relative to the overall market acceptable to you?		
Is the stock's recent performance, relative to other comparative benchmarks such as the industry average, acceptable to you?		

TABLE 12.1 *(Continued)*

	Information P/S/G	Impact +/0/−
Is the stock's present price in a position, relative to its recent trading range (e.g., relation to 52-week high/low, stochastic oscillator, etc.), consistent with your investment style?		
Is the stock's recent trend (e.g., as reflected in moving averages, MACD, etc.) consistent with your investment style?		
Is your attitude toward the stock impacted, for better or worse, by the presence or absence of any indication that it may be breaking out of an established range?		
Are volume-related issues (e.g., as reflected in on balance volume, accumulation/distribution, visual examination, etc.) consistent with your investment style?		
What's Happening? Are you comfortable continuing to consider this company/stock in light of recent company announcements and/or news events?		

TABLE 12.2 Exploring the Fundamentals—Stock Price Rationale

	Information P/S/G	Impact +/0/−
Are the EPS numbers used to calculate forward-looking P/E ratios more or less normal (i.e., not distorted by temporary developments that cause them to be unsustainably high or low)?		
Is the relationship between the forward-looking P/E ratios and the projected long-term EPS growth rate (the PEG ratio) acceptable to you?		
Are the stock's TTM valuation ratios below peer group averages?		
If you seek income, is the dividend yield acceptable to you?		
If you seek income, is the dividend growth rate above the peer group average?		
If you seek income, is the payout ratio below the peer group average?		

Notes
- The preferred peer group is the industry average. If you believe the company is not comparable to others in its industry, use sector average or S&P 500 average as the peer group.
- TTM means trailing 12 months.
- The TTM valuation ratio questions can be applied to price/earnings, price/sales, price/book value, price/cash flow, price/free cash flow, price/book value, and/or price/tangible book value.

TABLE 12.3   Exploring the Fundamentals—Expectations and Credibility

	Information P/S/G	Impact +/0/−
Is the number of analysts issuing long-term EPS growth projections extremely small?		
Is there wide variation between the highest and lowest long-term EPS growth projections?		
Do the long-term EPS growth projections seem plausible in light of the historic track record and your assessment of where the company stands within its business life cycle?		
Is the number of analysts issuing near-term EPS estimates extremely small?		
Is there wide variation between the highest and lowest near-term EPS estimates?		
If the company reports earnings in line with near-term estimates, would that mark a noteworthy break, for better or worse, from the recent trends in quarterly year-to-year comparisons?		
If there has been or is likely to be a noteworthy break, for better or worse, from the recent trends in quarterly year-to-year comparisons, are the reasons acceptable to you, given your goals?		
If there has been or is likely to be a noteworthy break, for better or worse, from the recent trends in quarterly year-to-year comparisons, are you satisfied regarding the likelihood the company will later return to or maintain an acceptable longer-term trend?		
Do earnings surprise trends, if any, raise red flags that shake your confidence in the extent to which analysts comprehend company business trends?		
Do estimate revision trends, if any, raise red flags that shake your confidence in the extent to which analysts comprehend company business trends?		
Does the trend of estimate revision suggest analysts are chasing reality upward or downward?		
Does the stock appear to be priced correctly in light of the most recent set of earnings estimate revisions?		
Generally speaking, is the analyst recommendation profile bullish, bearish, or neutral?		
In the recent past, has the recommendation profile been turning more bullish or bearish?		

TABLE 12.4 Exploring the Fundamentals—General Sentiment

	Information P/S/G	Impact +/0/–
Has the stock been outperforming the overall stock market?		
Is the industry strong relative to the overall market?		
Has the stock been performing well compared with others in the same industry?		
Is the number of institutions that own shares acceptable to you?		
Is the institutional percentage share ownership acceptable to you?		
Is the comparison between institutional percentage share ownership and the industry average institutional percentage share ownership acceptable to you?		
Is the recent trend of institutional buying or selling acceptable to you?		
Are recent trends in insider buying and/or selling acceptable to you?		
Is there a noticeably high level of short interest?		
Has the short interest been climbing or falling?		
Is the relationship between short interest and trading volume (as reflected in the number of days it would take to clear the short interest) noteworthy?		

Note: The preferred peer group is the industry average. If you believe the company is not comparable to others in its industry, use sector average or S&P 500 average as the peer group.

TABLE 12.5 Exploring the Fundamentals—Footprints of Success

	Information P/S/G	Impact +/0/−
Growth Rates		
Is the company's MRQ growth rate above the peer average?		
Is the company's TTM growth rate above the peer average?		
Is the company's five-year average growth rate above the peer average?		
Is the company's MRQ growth rate above the company's TTM growth rate?		
Is the company's MRQ growth rate above the company's five-year average?		
Is the company's TTM growth rate above the company's five-year average?		
Is the relationship between the company's MRQ and TTM growth rates superior to that of the peer group?		
Is the relationship between the company's MRQ and five-year average growth rates superior to that of the peer group?		
Is the relationship between the company's TTM and five-year average growth rates superior to that of the peer group?		
Is the company's five-year average capital spending growth rate above the peer average?		
Is the company's five-year average capital spending growth rate above the company's five-year rate of sales growth?		
Is the relationship between the company's five-year rates of capital spending and sales growth similar to that of the peer group?		
Margin		
Is the company's TTM margin above the peer average?		
Is the company's five-year average margin above the peer average?		
Is the company's TTM margin above the company's five-year average?		
Is the company's trend in margin (compare TTM to five-year average) superior to that of the peer group?		
Is the company's tax rate in line with the peer group average?		
Is the company's tax rate in line with the company's five-year average?		
Returns on Capital		
Is the company's TTM return above the peer average?		
Is the company's five-year average return above the peer average?		
Is the company's TTM return above the company's five-year average?		

TABLE 12.5 *(Continued)*

	Information P/S/G	Impact +/0/-
Is the company's trend in return (compare TTM to five-year average) superior to that of the peer group?		
Is the company's financial aggressiveness (return on equity divided by return on investment or assets) above that of the peer group?		
Financial Strength		
Is the company's quick ratio better than the peer average?		
Is the company's current ratio better than the peer average?		
Is the company's long-term debt to equity ratio better than the peer average?		
Is the company's total debt to equity ratio better than the peer average?		
Is the company's reliance on short-term debt (compare the total debt to equity ratio with the long-term debt to equity ratio) greater than that of the peer average?		
Is the company's interest coverage ratio better than the peer average?		
Efficiency		
Is there reason to expect the company's labor efficiency data to be generally in line with the peer average?		
Is the company's revenue/employee better than the peer average?		
Is the company's net income/employee better than the peer average?		
Is the company's receivable turnover ratio better than the peer average?		
Is the company's inventory turnover ratio better than the peer average?		
Is the company's asset turnover ratio better than the peer average?		

Notes
- The preferred peer group is the industry average. If you believe the company is not comparable to others in its industry, use sector average or S&P 500 average as the peer group.
- MRQ means to the most recent quarter (e.g., the quarter ending 9/02 compared with the quarter that ended 9/01).
- TTM means trailing 12 months (e.g., the four quarters ending 9/02 compared with the four quarters that ended 9/01).
- The growth rate questions can be applied to sales growth and/or EPS growth.
- The margin questions can be applied to gross margin, operating margin, EBITDA margin, pretax margin, and/or net margin.
- The returns questions can be applied to return on assets, return on investment, and/or return on equity.

TABLE 12.6   Finishing Touches—Analyst Research Reports

	Information P/S/G	Impact +/0/−
Does the tone of the research report make you comfortable regarding near-term earnings trends?		
Does the tone of the research report make you comfortable regarding underlying longer-term prospects?		
Does the research report give reason to expect this company to perform better or worse than it has in the past?		
Does the research report make you comfortable regarding the company's ability to perform better than its peers?		
Does the research report make you comfortable regarding the company's prospects beyond the degree of comfort you get based on the fact that management guidance may be a major source of information?		
Does the research report make you comfortable that the stock's price (i.e., valuation measures) is reasonable in relation to where the company stands in terms of its business life cycle?		
Are the forecasts presented by the analysts based on factors that seem reasonably predictable (as opposed to a situation in which analysts are acting as if they can reliably forecast something that is not even remotely predictable)?		
Does the research report make you comfortable about the extent to which the analyst justified his/her conclusions?		
Are the analyst's reasons for liking/disliking the stock consistent with your investment style and goals?		

TABLE 12.7   Finishing Touches—Financial Statements

	Information P/S/G	Impact +/0/−
Are sequential (consecutive quarter and/or consecutive year) trends in key income statement items unduly volatile?		
Are unusual income/expense items sufficiently conspicuous as to alter conclusions you may otherwise have drawn regarding earnings-related data items?		
Do nonoperating items consistently comprise an unduly large portion of the income statement or balance sheet?		
Are nonoperating items unduly volatile from one period to the next?		
On the statement of cash flows, do miscellaneous categories of inflows or outflows seem unduly and consistently large?		
Does the company have a disturbing propensity to make acquisitions and/or divestitures?		
Is cash generation sufficiently high and return on capital sufficiently low to raise the specter of event risk?		

TABLE 12.8 Finishing Touches—The Executive Suite

	Information P/S/G	Impact +/0/−
Is the company generous in terms of the amount of information it discloses regarding key executives?		
Are you impressed with the credentials (work background, experience) of the key executives?		
Does the monetary compensation given to key executives seem reasonable in light of the need to attract talented individuals without being exorbitant?		
Does the monetary compensation given to key executives seem reasonably balanced between salary and incentive bonuses?		
Do stock options appear to be contributing to the company's efforts to recruit and retain talented individuals?		

GURU SHORTCUT

As you look at pros and cons the data have revealed and start thinking about whether the stock satisfies the criteria most important to you, it's possible you may, especially if you are new to this style of analysis, wonder how Warren Buffett or some other well-known investment guru might react to what you are seeing. If you use Stock Investor Pro, you can simply run the guru-based preset screen and see if your stock makes the list.

Quicken.com's one-click scorecard provides another solution that fits more directly into the Step 3 (Buy) framework. It lets you see, at a glance, how Quicken believes a stock would measure up under analytic criteria set forth by Robert G. Hagstrom Jr. in his book, *The Warren Buffett Way* (John Wiley & Sons, 1994), Geraldine Weiss as per her blue-chip value strategy, Motley Fool's Foolish 8 (small cap) approach, or the growth-stock criteria articulated by the National Association of Investors Corporation (NAIC).

Don't fret if you are not familiar with any of these methods. Quicken.com provides, on its site, an explanation of each investment philosophy, a verbal list of specific tests relating to each philosophy, and computer-generated text and graphic commentary on how a company fares under each test. (Figure 12.1 features the NAIC approach.) It concludes with a statement of whether the stock is of interest under the guru's approach.

These guru reports are helpful in showing you how to extract from Web-based data reports information relevant to a particular philosophy and weigh the pros and cons to determine whether the stock complies with the investment style. That's the kind of determination you will be continually asked to make in Step 3 (Buy) and Step 4 (Sell). Also, this content provides real-life examples of how a stock can be considered at least somewhat attractive even if it doesn't pass every single requirement of one's investment philosophy. That is an important idea that will be addressed time and again in the third and fourth steps. So all in all, these guru reports are great learning tools.

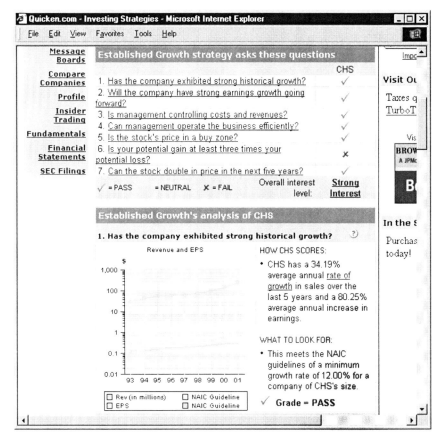

FIGURE 12.1   Quicken.com's One-Click Scorecard.
Source: Quicken.com. Reprinted with permission.

Beyond that, if you personally agree with or wish to adopt the guru philosophy embodied in Quicken's One-Click Scorecard, the answers provided by these reports can jump-start your efforts with the Analysis Keys that will be presented in Chapter 13. Just make sure you really do accept the philosophy. Even if you think you are familiar with the guru's ideas, it's important to study the explanations posted on Quicken.com. It's hard to know to what extent, if any, the guru would actually use the scorecard ostensibly based on his/her ideas. It does appear that the gurus identified on Quicken.com may have had at least some participation in the creation of the content attributed to them. But for your purposes, the only thing that really counts is your willingness to use the specific criteria articulated on the site. If you like an approach, use it without worrying about whether it really and truly is something a particular guru would use.

13

Analysis Keys

We've now come to the main portion of Step 3 (Buy). This is where we translate what we have learned about companies and their stocks into specific here-and-now investment decisions. Chapter 11 discussed what to look for and how to interpret what we see. So it may seem as if the resolution, a decision to buy or not buy, ought to be obvious. That would be so if everything we learned in Step 2 (Analyze) pointed toward the same answer.

Traditional books about investing often proceed under this very assumption. One of my favorite investment books lists 13 elements of a great investment opportunity. The author acknowledges in one clause of one sentence that no company is perfect, but fails to give guidance to how different pass/fail combinations should influence an investment decision. Another book, one of the truly great classics in the field, lists 39 important quantitative measures of company success, but likewise gives no guidance to investors wondering how to reach decisions about real-world companies that will, more often than not, meet some criteria and falter on others.

There's no point in naming the books. They just happened to be the first two I grabbed from my shelf as I was writing this chapter. Chances are you'll find similar things in any investment book you pick up. What's most important is to understand that the process of securities analysis, however you define it, leaves you with some sort of checklist. It can be a formal checklist such as the Data Guide presented in Chapter 12. Or it can be a casual mental checklist. In either case, every item on that list has one answer that is associated with superior investment performance.

There's nothing wrong with these books. They are addressing the topic of investment analysis. And their culminations, the checklists, are exactly what you should expect to have at the end of the analytic process. What makes this market screening method different is that it views analysis as only one part of a four-step process. Chapters 4 to 9 covered important tasks, comprising Step 1 (Find), which should be completed before analysis can begin. Chapters 12 to 16, covering Step 3 (Buy) and Step 4 (Sell), present tasks that are undertaken after the analysis has been completed.

Indeed, we need to do some postanalytic work before we can buy because we'll usually see both positives and negatives in any investment opportunity we consider. This should not come as a surprise. After all, every stock market transaction has a buyer and a seller. You can't necessarily assume that one party is more knowledgeable than the other. Most of the important yes-or-no answers are based on facts that are equally available to and often known by both parties. Investment decisions are typically based on how the "yes" and "no" answers match each party's particular investment philosophy. Many investors base decisions on exorbitant attention to just a few facts (such as the latest quarterly earnings announcement). If you consider that approach misguided, understand that it does not reflect ignorance of analytic facts. Instead, it's an investment philosophy that chooses to ignore many key facts and/or reflects the investor's failure to organize known facts in a way that truly matches his/her investment philosophy. Recognizing the nature of these matchups is the essence of Step 3 (Buy). And we do this in a way that builds upon the work done up until now in Step 1 (Find) and Step 2 (Analyze).

INTRODUCING THE ANALYSIS KEYS

We begin the decision-making process by organizing what we learned about each company that remains on our evaluation lists after Step 2 (Analyze). During that phase, we moved far beyond our original screening endeavors and looked at a wider range of information than could have been accommodated on any single screen. To put it all into a usable context, we now apply three Analysis Keys, each of which is a yes/no question. The questions are simple, but answering them requires us to consider a lot of data. If you feel you need help organizing your thoughts along these lines, use the Chapter 12 Data Guide. Here's a summary of the Analysis Keys.

▦ **Analysis Key 1: Does the situation truly fit the theme you originally chose?** Screening isn't a perfect science; there's plenty of art mixed in. So even the best-constructed screen is likely to pull in some companies that don't quite match what you had in mind when you constructed and ran the screen. If you use the Data Guide, look for a preponderance of positive (+) answers relating to information identified as primary (P).

▓ **Analysis Key 2: Are there factors different from your original theme that you consider positive?** Companies come in many different sizes and shapes. No matter how precise a screen you used, you will always discover new things as you go through Step 2 (Analyze). From an investment standpoint, you'll find some of these things very appealing. If you use the Data Guide, look for a preponderance of positive (+) answers relating to information identified as secondary (S) and to a much lesser degree, general (G).

▓ **Analysis Key 3: Is this investment opportunity free of any factors that you consider negative?** The companies you discover will all have some flaws. Unless you're willing to wait indefinitely for the perfect company, you won't dismiss these companies right way but will instead want to balance imperfections against positive factors. If you use the Data Guide, look for negative (–) answers, regardless of information category. Assume all companies will have some negative answers. When considering Analysis Key 3, look for multiple negative answers clustered around data categories.

It might seem that if we answer "no" for Analysis Key 1 (we decide the stock does not truly fit our original theme) we should discard it. Not so fast! Let's continue. Suppose Analysis Key 2 (additional positive factors) gets a "yes" answer and we answer "yes" for Analysis Key 3 (freedom from negative factors). Even though our analysis tells us this isn't really the kind of company we had in mind when we ran the screen, the stock may still be an attractive candidate for purchase. And it may even turn out to be a better choice than another company that was more consistent with the original idea behind the screen.

The scenario described does not follow the typical investment script. Usually, the process is seen as following a very linear route: These are my goals. These are the companies that seem consistent with my goals. Upon further review, this specific company is or is not a good example of the sort of company I seek. Therefore, I will/will not buy the stock.

The approach presented here borrows a concept from the arts known as the "happy accident." This is especially popular among watercolor artists. If you every try to paint this way, you'll quickly grasp the idea. It's extremely hard to be precise when applying paint with a soaking wet watercolor brush. However careful you are, some color is likely to run to a place where you didn't originally want it to go. You can soak it up with a sponge and start again. But often you'll be content to leave things as they are and incorporate the unplanned effect. Even though the painting doesn't look exactly like what you originally set out to achieve, you often find it looks pretty darned good and that you're perfectly happy to keep it as it is.

Investors, too, can benefit from the happy accident. This is why, during Step 2 (Analyze), we paid so much attention to secondary information. The idea was to give ourselves opportunities to see attractive ideas we didn't expect to encounter. We shouldn't be the least bit shy about borrowing a concept from a field that seems as far removed as one can get from disciplined stock selection methods. By the time we reach Step 3 (Buy), we've articulated our goals, translated them into a series of screening tests, eliminated companies we quickly recognized as being clearly unsuitable for us, and studied a lot of information about all the others. We have been through a process that is far more disciplined than anything most investors do. Having accomplished that and narrowed our potential choices from thousands to a mere handful, we have earned the right to relax and buy any among the remaining stocks that fares well under Step 3 (Buy), even if we do find ourselves wondering how it found its way onto the screen in the first place.

Next we'll discuss each of the Analysis Keys in more detail. Then, in Chapter 14, we'll introduce a series of Decision Paths that translate the three-way yes/no combinations into final buy or avoid decisions.

ANALYSIS KEY 1: DOES THE SITUATION TRULY FIT THE THEME YOU ORIGINALLY CHOSE?

There are two sets of reasons why the above question needs to be explicitly addressed at this stage of the process. First, no matter how effectively constructed your screen is, you'll probably find there were loopholes that allowed companies to get through even though they aren't really what you had in mind. Second, there are just so many tests you can put into any one screen, so companies on your list might not have made the cut had the screen had room for additional tests consistent with your overall theme.

Through the Loopholes

Screening is limited to objective variables. Anytime qualitative factors are omitted, we become vulnerable to the possibility something will slip through the cracks. For example, if you are a growth investor, you probably want companies that are growing because of expanding demand for existing products, new product lines, market share gains, territorial expansion, and so on. You probably don't really want companies with mature product lines, no new opportunities, and stagnant sales trends that are managing to increase profits only by cutting costs. If your screen didn't include sales growth tests, the latter type of company might well find its way onto your growth list.

The most blatantly nonconforming companies may have been dropped from consideration during Step 2 (Analyze). But issues like this are often subtle. For example, you may start out with the theme of accelerating EPS growth and wind up seeing a company with a growth ratio comparison table that looks something like Table 13.1.

Strictly speaking, the company delivers everything you sought. The rate of EPS growth has, indeed, been accelerating, this being a condition that was necessary for the company to pass the screen. And for added measure, the company outperformed its industry average in each time period. But look at how the pattern of company acceleration compares to that of the industry. It looks as if the company was ahead of its peers in the past, but that the period of relative acceleration may be winding down. I'd still like the company as a basic growth story. But based on this data, I'm not impressed with it as an example of the acceleration theme. I'll answer "no" to Analysis Key 1, unless other data shows that recent company growth rates are being restrained by some factor that will not persist into the future.

Remember, screening is a computerized number-crunching exercise. Use Analysis Key 1 as an opportunity to say, "Strictly speaking, this company passed my screen, but. . . ." Don't be shy about doing this. It doesn't mean you're dropping it from consideration. We have two other Analysis Keys, and this hypothetical company's basic growth qualities may cause it to garner a "yes" under Key 2. By taking the trouble to use the Analysis Keys to articulate relationships between each situation's pros and cons and the goals we started with, we will be better able to prioritize among the dozen or so stocks still under consideration.

TABLE 13.1　Growth Ratio Comparison Table

	Company	Industry
TTM EPS Growth	25%	24%
3 Year Average EPS Growth	24%	20%
5 Year Average EPS Growth	21%	15%

Note: TTM means trailing 12 months.

Omitted Screening Tests

Sticking with the example involving an accelerating EPS growth theme, chances are if you want to invest this way, you'd also want to see a pattern of accelerating sales growth. And you probably are inclined toward the momentum style of investing, so you'd want to see increasing share-price relative strength. Recognizing the ever-present risk that something in the future may soon cause growth to stop dead in its tracks, you might want to add some behavioral tests relating to upward revisions in analyst estimates and recommendations (reasoning that analysts wouldn't be doing this if they saw something bad on the horizon). As I wrote this, I paused to create a screen with all the tests mentioned. As you might expect, the number of passing companies was zero. I have no doubt you, too, could easily drive your result total down to zero if you try to build tests based on every possible idea consistent with your overall theme.

As discussed earlier, the solution is to pick a few favorites among all the possible tests you can conceive and build those into the screen. The remaining criteria are addressed in Step 2 (Analyze). This, as you recall from Chapter 10, is primary information, which stretches beyond the actual screening data to include information very similar to that which you included in the screen.

Look at this full body of what could be called extended primary information, and see if, on balance, it is consistent with the theme of your screen. Rather than approaching this in a hard-and-fast way, we're looking for the flavor of the data. We'll answer "yes" to Analysis Key 1 if the preponderance of what we see is consistent with our theme, even if there are some data relationships that don't strictly make the grade.

Table 13.2 is a different example of what we might learn in Step 2 (Analyze) from an accelerating EPS growth screen.

The sales and EPS trends clearly measure up to what we had in mind. We see clear patterns of acceleration, and there are no troublesome disparities between sales and EPS. And in both instances, the company's trends look good relative to industry averages. But had we continued on to include all the possible acceleration-related tests suggested earlier, we see the company would not have passed the screen. The four-week share price change is above the industry average, but that wasn't the case over the 13-week span. And analyst estimates and recommendations haven't risen. They stayed the same.

Still, I'm going to give a "yes" answer to Analysis Key 1. The imperfections are very modest. They do not negate the basic accelerating EPS growth theme. Even in areas where the company underperformed its in-

TABLE 13.2 Accelerating EPS Growth Screen

	Company	Industry
TTM Sales Growth	27%	20%
3 Year Average Sales Growth	20%	18%
5 Year Average Sales Growth	15%	15%
TTM EPS Growth	26%	23%
3 Year Average EPS Growth	20%	20%
5 Year Average EPS Growth	12%	15%
4 Week % Share Price Change	8%	6%
13 Week % Share Price Change	12%	15%
Analyst Estimates or Recommendations Past 13 Weeks	No change	—

dustry average, it at least stayed close. I'm encouraged to see that relative share price strength improved in the most recent interval. And even though rising analyst expectations are usually seen as more bullish, the stability I see here is sufficient to tell me what I most need to know: that analysts aren't seeing clouds on the horizon that spell the end of the company's pattern of acceleration.

Table 13.3 illustrates a variation that would cause me to say "no" in Analysis Key 1. I would have been willing to tolerate modest share price underperformance over the 13-week span. But the extent of the shortfall and the relative strength deterioration in the more recent period raises some concern. It may not be the end of the world. Analysts haven't lowered expectations. And the stock may, ultimately, be a terrific investment. Perhaps some segments of the investment community have interpreted some issue in an overly pessimistic way. But the acceleration theme is related to momentum, and stocks whose relative strength deteriorates that way are not suitable for this broad category of investments. So if I wind up buying this stock, it would have to be due to Analysis Keys 2 and 3.

TABLE 13.3 Price Comparison Variation

	Company	Industry
4 Week % Share Price Change	−10%	6%
13 Week % Share Price Change	12%	15%

ANALYSIS KEY 2: ARE THERE FACTORS DIFFERENT FROM YOUR ORIGINAL THEME THAT YOU CONSIDER POSITIVE?

This is where happy accidents and secondary information (data relationships that have investment significance but are unrelated to the theme of your screen) take center stage, a situation that carries over into Analysis Key 3. The job of Analysis Key 2 is to give you an opportunity to use what you learned during your analysis to provide a basis for purchasing attractive stocks that don't fulfill the spirit of your screen as cleanly as you might have wished. We throw open the door to any positive investment qualities we see, of whatever kind and from whatever source.

Let's go back to the first example discussed in Analysis Key 1, a company that never quite measured up to our full idea of how an accelerating growth company should look because it seemed to be running out of gas. The data we started with can be found in Table 13.4. Now, let's add some additional facts. (See Table 13.5.)

We have already acknowledged that we aren't looking at a good acceleration-based investment candidate. Hence we answered "no" to Analysis Key 1. But the secondary information we saw in Step 2 (Analyze) is very interesting. It shows considerable strength from a company quality standpoint. Also, valuation metrics and analyst sentiment are both favorable. We weren't originally screening based on these other things. But we don't want to brush aside this company; clearly, something good is happening here. (By the way, if you think the good qualities of the hypothetical company in the example have been overly exaggerated to make a point, just wait till you start screening! Companies like that really do exist, and Chapters 5 to 9 showed you exactly how to find them.)

We don't know for sure that we're going to buy this stock. We still have to look at Analysis Key 3. And all our answers to all three Analysis Keys will be compared using the Decision Paths that will be discussed in Chapter 14. But this stock remains very much in the running. And don't

TABLE 13.4 Starting Data

	Company	Industry
TTM EPS Growth	25%	24%
3 Year Average EPS Growth	24%	20%
5 Year Average EPS Growth	21%	15%

TABLE 13.5 Additional Information

	Company	Industry
Price/Earnings TTM	22.7	28.4
Price/Sales TTM	1.4	2.6
Quick Ratio	2.10	1.67
Current Ratio	3.42	2.75
Long-Term Debt Ratio	0.00	0.27
Total Debt Ratio	0.00	0.85
Operating Margin TTM	11.7%	6.4%
Operating Margin 5 Year Average	9.9%	6.8%
Pretax Margin TTM	10.3%	3.1%
Pretax Margin 5 Year Average	9.0%	3.5%
Return on Assets TTM	10.4%	4.3%
Return on Assets 5 Year Average	10.0%	4.6%
Return on Investment TTM	15.6%	7.6%
Return on Investment 5 Year Average	14.1%	8.4%
Return on Equity TTM	15.6%	9.8%
Return on Equity 5 Year Average	14.1%	10.0%

	Now	4 Weeks Ago
Consensus Current Year EPS Estimate	1.30	1.24
Consensus Next Year EPS Estimate	1.64	1.33
# Strong Buy Ratings	5	3
# Buy Ratings	1	2
# Hold Ratings	0	1
# Underperform Ratings	0	0
# Sell Ratings	0	0

worry that we might wind up hopping about erratically from one investment philosophy to another. The Decision Paths will help us maintain appropriate discipline.

Note that our inquiry in this key is not completely balanced. We aren't looking for negatives. All we seek are noteworthy positive features. A neutral reaction to non-screen-related data is all it takes to trigger a "no" answer to Analysis Key 2. We'll deal with negatives separately in Analysis Key 3.

ANALYSIS KEY 3: IS THIS INVESTMENT OPPORTUNITY FREE OF ANY FACTORS THAT YOU CONSIDER NEGATIVE?

The first thing you may notice about this key is the less-than-straightforward way it is phrased. It would have been more direct to simply ask: "Are there any factors you consider negative?" But it's worth a little bit of grammatical juggling in order to produce answers that will be most usable when we move to the Decision Paths. In Analysis Keys 1 and 2, "yes" answers were those that supported investment in the stock, while factors pushing you away from the stock caused you to say "no." We want to maintain that style in Analysis Key 3. We want a "yes" answer to encourage you toward purchase and a "no" answer to steer you away.

This may not seem like a big deal now. But trust me—you'll appreciate it later, when you're actually working with the Decision Paths. It's a lot easier to recognize at a glance that a set of answers reading "yes-yes-yes" is very bullish. If the keys were phrased such as to have the most bullish pattern expressed as "yes-yes-no," you'd constantly find yourself stopping to review the strict phrasing of the keys. I think you'll agree you have better things to do with your time than to constantly backtrack to take another look at these definitions.

When we talk about negatives here, we aren't merely referring to a failure on the part of the company to measure up to the theme of your screen. Situations like that garnered their "no" answers in Analysis Key 1. We're talking about negatives relating to issues beyond those that were built into the screen. This includes all the negatives you found in Step 2 (Analyze) after having completed the Get Acquainted phase.

By now, it should be clear why I asked you to refrain from continuing to drop companies as you progressed all the way to the end of the analytic process. The worst of the negatives are those that jumped out at you during the Get Acquainted stage. Those companies are gone. At this point, the negatives that remain will cause you to answer "no" to Analysis Key 3. You may still wind up avoiding the stock. Or you may buy it. The outcome will depend on how Analysis Key 3 combines with the other two keys (as per the Decision Paths), and what sort of patterns we see for the other stocks still under consideration.

What constitutes enough of a negative to cause you to answer this key "no" depends on your individual investment style. That doesn't necessarily match the situation we dealt with in Analysis Key 2. Take another look at Tables 13.4 and 13.5. Chances are most investors, possibly even all investors, would regard those factors as positives. Whether you're a value investor, a momentum investor, a growth investor, a long-term investor, a short-term trader, or even an income seeker, you probably will agree that high margins are better than low margins, that high returns on capital are better than low returns on capital, and that improving analyst sentiment is better than deteriorating analyst sentiment.

The following example shows how personal investment philosophy enters into Analysis Key 3. Table 13.6 gets us off to a good start. We see that the company measured up to our vision of a true accelerating growth story. We give a "yes" answer for Analysis Key 1. Moving on to the secondary information in Table 13.7, we see that this is a generally high-quality com-

TABLE 13.6   Starting Data

	Company	Industry
TTM Sales Growth	27%	20%
3 Year Average Sales Growth	20%	18%
5 Year Average Sales Growth	15%	15%
TTM EPS Growth	26%	23%
3 Year Average EPS Growth	20%	20%
5 Year Average EPS Growth	12%	15%

TABLE 13.7   Additional Information

	Company	Industry
Quick Ratio	2.10	1.67
Current Ratio	3.42	2.75
Long-Term Debt Ratio	0.00	0.27
Total Debt Ratio	0.00	0.85
Operating Margin TTM	11.7%	6.4%
Operating Margin 5 Year Average	9.9%	6.8%
Pretax Margin TTM	10.3%	3.1%
Pretax Margin 5 Year Average	9.0%	3.5%
Return on Assets TTM	10.4%	4.3%
Return on Assets 5 Year Average	10.0%	4.6%
Return on Investment TTM	15.6%	7.6%
Return on Investment 5 Year Average	14.1%	8.4%
Return on Equity TTM	15.6%	9.8%
Return on Equity 5 Year Average	14.1%	10.0%

pany. We give a "yes" answer for Analysis Key 2. But the last group of data (Table 13.8) shows the company has hit a major bump in the road. In the latest quarter, it reported surprisingly weak EPS. Analysts reduced estimates and downgraded their ratings, and the stock got hammered.

What impact does Table 13.8 have on your answer to Analysis Key 3? This data would cause many investors to answer "no." That's easy to understand. All you need do is look at analyst reaction and stock price movements to see how bearish many people believe this scenario to be. But I don't necessarily agree. Some of the best investment decisions I ever made were purchases of stocks that had just plunged because of bad earnings. I am willing to own such stocks as long as I am satisfied that the company is (and remains) a high-quality company and that the problem that caused the earnings shortfall is likely to prove temporary.

This isn't the only example. Some investors would say "no" to Key 3 if they see high stock valuation metrics. Others are attracted to the momentum qualities of such stocks. Some see rising short interest as a negative. Others envision a short squeeze and are, hence, bullish. Some see lackluster returns on capital as reason to say "no" to Key 3. Few investors would actually be attracted to such stocks. But many couldn't care less one way or another about return on capital. Since this key seeks only negatives, neutrality is enough to justify saying "yes" in response to Analysis Key 3.

TABLE 13.8   Reduced Estimates

	Company	Industry
4 Week % Share Price Change	−21%	6%
13 Week % Share Price Change	12%	15%
	Reported	**Estimate**
Latest Quarter EPS	0.15	0.37
	Now	**4 Weeks Ago**
Consensus Current Year EPS Estimate	1.43	1.76
Consensus Next Year EPS Estimate	1.55	2.50
# Strong Buy Ratings	0	5
# Buy Ratings	1	4
# Hold Ratings	9	0
# Underperform Ratings	0	0
# Sell Ratings	0	0

MOVING ON

By now, each stock has a three-part evaluation key. The best is a "yes-yes-yes" combination. The worst is "no-no-no." You don't really need to go any further to know how to treat stocks at each of the extremes. Common sense alone will tell you to avoid the triple-no stocks, and that triple-yes issues represent your best buying opportunities. The last remaining task is to prioritize among the six other potential combinations. Chapter 14 will assign each to a Decision Path and rank all the paths from best to worst.

Decision Paths

The Analysis Keys described in Chapter 13 provide you with a three-way combination of yes-or-no answers to important questions. The Decision Paths help you match each three-way combination with a final buy-or-avoid decision. At the end of the preceding chapter we acknowledged the obvious. A "yes-yes-yes" set of answers is the best combination, and these stocks are the most buyable. A "no-no-no" set of answers is the worst combination, and these stocks should be avoided. The more interesting part of the exercise is dealing with the six combinations in between these two extremes.

Suppose we answered "no" for Analysis Key 1. In other words, we say the stock isn't really what we had in mind when we screened. It seems tempting to discard it right away. But suppose we answer "yes" in response to the other keys. That means the stock has clear investment merit based on criteria other than those that formed the basis for our screen, and that there are no factors that we consider negative based on our investment philosophy. Such a stock might be an attractive candidate for purchase. That might be especially so if none of the other stocks under review pass Analysis Key 1.

Notice how I didn't come right out and describe this "no-yes-yes" combination as a buy. Whether or not it achieves that status depends on what Analysis Key combinations exist for other stocks still under consideration. There may be seven stocks on the list, four of which seem at least somewhat buyable. We'll need to prioritize them, since you may not have enough cash to buy all of them. The Decision Paths can help.

Suppose Smith Company and Jones Company both earn "yes" answers for Analysis Key 1 (consistency with the screening theme). But with Analysis Key 2 (additional positive factors), Smith Company gets a "yes" answer while Jones Company gets a "no." In terms of priority, Smith Company just pulled ahead because it goes beyond the screen and adds other positive qualities. But before buying, let's consider Analysis Key 3 (freedom from negative factors). Assume that here Smith Company gets a "no" while Jones Company gets a "yes."

Now, the various "yes" and "no" answers may be starting to give you a headache. And we're only comparing two stocks. Imagine if we had a dozen. Once you get comfortable with the logic of the Decision Paths, you'll need only a few minutes to balance all the "yes" and "no" answers for all the companies that remain under consideration.

Let's take a quick preview right now. In Table 14.1 you will find the eight possible Decision Paths ranked from best (A) to worst (H). For Smith Company, the Analysis Keys came out "yes-yes-no." That corresponds to Decision Path D. For Jones Company, the Analysis Keys came out "yes-no-yes." That corresponds to Decision Path B.

Now it's easy. Jones Company is on the higher Decision Path and accordingly gets a higher priority. If you're going to buy only one stock, Jones is the winner. Both exemplify what we had in mind when we screened. Briefly, it looked like Smith might be the better choice because it also has positive qualities beyond the screen. But Smith also forces us to accept some baggage that is contrary to our investment goals. With Jones, we got what we were looking for. We didn't get more, but we aren't forced to accept qualities we find distasteful. Hence Jones is more compatible with our investment philosophy.

TABLE 14.1 Decision Paths

Decision Path	Analysis Key 1 (Screening Theme)	Analysis Key 2 (Additional Positives)	Analysis Key 3 (Absence of Negatives)
A	Yes	Yes	Yes
B	Yes	No	Yes
C	No	Yes	Yes
D	Yes	Yes	No
The Neutral Zone			
E	No	No	Yes
F	Yes	No	No
G	No	Yes	No
H	No	No	No

Let's now take a closer look at each Decision Path.

DECISION PATH A: YES-YES-YES

Here are the qualities a stock must exhibit to be on Decision Path A.

> **Analysis Key 1—Yes:** The situation measures up to what we were seeking when we created and ran the screen.
> **Analysis Key 2—Yes:** The situation offers attractive investment features apart from those used as the basis for the screen.
> **Analysis Key 3—Yes:** The situation is free from factors that are regarded by our investment philosophies as negatives.

The stock offers everything we hoped to get, and more. The extra positives reflected in Analysis Key 2 make it likely the stock will appear on other kinds of screens created by other investors with philosophies that differ from ours. For example, we may say "yes" to Key 1 because the stock measured up to our growth criteria, and we say "yes" to Key 2 because the data suggests the stock has appeal based on value. Hence the stock will appeal to two different kinds of investors.

The more investment philosophies a stock satisfies, the more likely it is that demand for shares will exceed supply. That, of course, is the basis for above-average share price performance. The presence of other negative factors could be a fly in the ointment. But the "yes" answer to Key 3 tells us this is not a factor here.

This does not guarantee the stock will be a winner. It's possible the screen may have been based primarily on a theme that is about to hit a cold spell. An example would be a growth theme that falters as the economy slides into a downturn. We must also remember that Analysis Key 3 depends heavily on our subjective sense of what makes for a good or bad investment. But the market may be entering into a period in which its ideas about good and bad differ from ours.

Over time, different investment styles move into and out of favor. Eventually, all reasonable philosophies have their day in the sun. (Note the word *reasonable*: If you seek high area code–to–zip code ratios, don't be surprised if centuries pass without this style ever leading to good performance.) What Decision Path A can guarantee is that the stock represents the strongest application of your individual investment philosophy. Absent psychic powers that allow you to look up future stock prices, this is as good as it gets.

DECISION PATH B: YES-NO-YES

Here are the qualities a stock must exhibit to be on Decision Path B.

> **Analysis Key 1—Yes:** The situation measures up to what we were seeking when we created and ran the screen.
>
> **Analysis Key 2—No:** The situation does not offer attractive investment features other than those used as the basis for the screen.
>
> **Analysis Key 3—Yes:** The situation is free from factors that are regarded by our investment philosophies as negatives.

Readers who skipped earlier chapters might assume these stocks represent the best-case scenario. Unless you read the material dealing with the role of secondary information in Step 2 (Analyze), it might not occur to you to focus so intently on the presence or absence of positive qualities outside those we incorporated into the screen.

If you aren't actively looking for additional positives, you'd have to be impressed by what Path B stocks offer: They give us everything we hoped to find when we created and ran our screen, and they do not require us to cope with anything we see as negative baggage. It's easy to like such stocks. The only reason you might not purchase a stock from this path is because you find one on Decision Path A that offers the same qualities as these but also adds extra qualities that give rise to a "yes" answer to Analysis Key 2.

DECISION PATH C: NO-YES-YES

Here are the qualities a stock must exhibit to be on Decision Path C.

> **Analysis Key 1—No:** The situation does not really measure up to what we were seeking when we created and ran the screen.
>
> **Analysis Key 2—Yes:** The situation offers attractive investment features apart from those used as the basis for the screen.
>
> **Analysis Key 3—Yes:** The situation is free from factors that are regarded by our investment philosophies as negatives.

This is the path of the "happy accident" as discussed in Chapter 13. This stock is not what we had in mind when we were screening, and we wouldn't feel crushed if it never came to light. But based on luck, coincidence, synchronicity, or whatever else you want to call it, the stock did come to our attention and stayed around long enough to pass the Get Acquainted phase of Step 2 (Analyze) and go through the rest of the analytic process. As it turns out, even though it wasn't what we had in mind, this interloper stock actually winds up looking pretty good, and it carries no negative baggage.

The "no" answer to Analysis Key 1 tells us it didn't match our preferred theme. But the "yes" answer to Key 2 tells us it does still have something going for it, and probably would wind up on screens created by other investors with other investment philosophies. Because it met their screening themes, they'll put the stock on Path B. The only reason we drop it down a notch to Path C is because we have different goals, not because the company is inherently inferior to those we placed on Path B.

When reading about the "happy accident" in Chapter 13, you may have wondered whether it was wise to suggest that you might want to buy a stock that does not meet your original theme (those for which Key 1 gets a "no" answer). After all, successful investors don't flit about from style to style. Indeed, we would not consider buying a Path C stock if there are any available from Path A or B.

The real question is how we should react when there are no Path A or B stocks. It means there are no truly good candidates consistent with the original theme. I would not argue with a choice to refrain from making new investments if we can't find any that meet our screening goals. The main debate is how we react to Key 3. The paths are ordered in such a way as to push stocks that garner "no" answers to Key 3 downward. That's because the key addresses factors that are deemed negative based on our individual investment goals. Given the prevalence of loss aversion among investors, most of us will sleep better at night owning shares of great companies we didn't initially expect to uncover, as opposed to other stocks that conform to our goals that also include factors we know are distasteful to us.

Finally, let's remember that none of the keys or paths are carved in stone. If you prefer to switch Paths C and D (or any others), you obviously can do so. What's most important is that you approach such issues in a thoughtful way. If, after such consideration, you decide you wish to be more tolerant of stocks that fail Key 3, that's fine and well within the scope of this method.

DECISION PATH D: YES-YES-NO

Here are the qualities a stock must exhibit to be on Decision Path D.

> **Analysis Key 1—Yes:** The situation measures up to what we were seeking when we created and ran the screen.

Analysis Key 2—Yes: The situation offers attractive investment features apart from those used as the basis for the screen.

Analysis Key 3—No: The situation is not free from factors that are regarded by our investment philosophies as negatives.

This is the flip side of the "happy accident" debate from Key C. There, we favored great companies with no baggage that did not measure up to our initial screening goals. Here, we are considering a stock that offers what we expected when we built and ran our screens, as well as the added bonus of being attractive to others who create other kinds of screens. But there's baggage. The nature of the baggage depends on our individual philosophies. To some of us, it may be a set of unduly high valuation metrics. To others, it may be negative earnings and/or share price momentum. Another group of investors may wish to avoid below-average financial strength ratios. Others may be turned off by skimpy analyst coverage.

As discussed earlier, some readers may prefer to accentuate the positives (the fact that the stock meets our screening theme and other themes articulated by other investors) and deemphasize the presence of baggage. They would switch Paths C and D. Others may intermingle these two paths and decide case by case based on the intensity behind the answers to Keys 1 and 2 on the one hand and Key 3 on the other hand.

THE NEUTRAL ZONE

As we've seen, Paths A and B describe stocks that clearly represent excellent investment opportunities. The ideas that can be found on Paths C and D are not quite as powerful and there's lots of room for debate as to whether C is really better than D or vice versa. But for the most part, the stocks that are on Paths C and D are acceptable. A market screening journey that brings you to either of those paths still constitutes a solidly thoughtful process that leaves you knowing why you're buying what you buy, how you found it, and how it meshes with your investment philosophy (the Buy Zone). That's a lot more than many investors can claim.

The same cannot be said of the remaining paths. Path E, the best of the rest, features stocks that offer nothing positive but also carry no negatives. That's hardly a glowing recommendation for purchase. If you feel tempted to buy a stock on this path, it means your efforts in Step 1 (Find) and Step 2 (Analyze) did not produce as many purchase candidates as you need in order to invest as much money as you need to invest right now. If you find yourself in that position, you probably would be better off creating a new screen, rather than dropping down to the lower paths. You need not abandon your original goals. As we saw in Chapter 6, there are far more potential screening tests available for each goal than can fit into any single screen. If your first effort didn't produce enough ideas, create another screen using some of the tests that didn't make it into your first screen.

Paths E, F, G, and H (the Avoid Zone) are more relevant to Step 4 (Sell). Chapter 16 will describe a selling discipline based on the same principles as applied thus far. The process will culminate in three Update Keys that function similarly to the three Analysis Keys, and eight Reconsideration Paths that are analogous to the eight Decision Paths being discussed here. The two path hierarchies are summarized in Table 14.2.

Accordingly, we'll introduce Paths E through H in a general sense here. We won't focus closely upon them since they are less attractive for purchase. These lesser key combinations are more relevant to the Reconsideration Paths that will be covered in connection with Step 4 (Sell).

DECISION PATH E: NO-NO-YES

Here are the qualities a stock must exhibit to be on Decision Path E.

> Analysis Key 1—No: The situation does not really measure up to what we were seeking when we created and ran the screen.
> Analysis Key 2—No: The situation does not offer attractive investment features other than those used as the basis for the screen.
> Analysis Key 3—Yes: The situation is free from factors that are regarded by our investment philosophies as negatives.

The best thing you can say about the stocks on Decision Path E is that they aren't bad. Analysis Key 3 tells us that there's nothing here we see as

TABLE 14.2 Decision Paths in Context

Decision Paths		Reconsideration Paths	
A			A
B	Buy Zone	Hold Zone	B
C			C
D			D
E			E
F	Avoid Zone	Sell Zone	F
G			G
H			H

being negative. The problem is that there's nothing really good about these stocks. They didn't fit our screening criteria and they offer no particular benefits outside the context of our screen.

DECISION PATH F: YES-NO-NO

Here are the qualities a stock must exhibit to be on Decision Path F.

> **Analysis Key 1—Yes:** The situation measures up to what we were seeking when we created and ran the screen.
>
> **Analysis Key 2—No:** The situation does not offer attractive investment features other than those used as the basis for the screen.
>
> **Analysis Key 3—No:** The situation is not free from factors that are regarded by our investment philosophies as negatives.

We have seen that investors could plausibly differ as to whether they agree that the key combination in Path C really should be placed ahead of the Path D combination. A similar debate can occur with Paths E and F. Path F meets our screening goal, but comes with other qualities we deem distasteful. The sequence chosen here assumes that the absence of negatives is more desirable than the presence of positives.

Some might wonder why this path isn't placed in the buying zone. It is similar to Path D, where we got what we wanted when we screened but had to accept some negatives. The difference is that in Path D, the basic positives came with some extra oomph—a "yes" answer to Key 2 (indicating that there were additional positives above and beyond the scope of the screen). Considering the personal nature of Key 3 (things that aren't generically negative, but are seen as such based specifically on our individual investment philosophies), it's hard to make a case for this path, given that it does not get any sort of boost from Key 2.

DECISION PATH G: NO-YES-NO

Here are the qualities a stock must exhibit to be on Decision Path G.

> **Analysis Key 1—No:** The situation does not really measure up to what we were seeking when we created and ran the screen.
>
> **Analysis Key 2—Yes:** The situation offers attractive investment features apart from those used as the basis for the screen.
>
> **Analysis Key 3—No:** The situation is not free from factors that are regarded by our investment philosophies as negatives.

We're moving down the food chain. As was the case with Key F, we have some positives and some negatives. The problem is that the positives are unrelated to our original screening goal. We were willing to live with only unrelated positives in Key C, the "happy accident," because there were no negatives. But here, with Key 3 having turned to "no," we have a less happy accident.

DECISION PATH H: NO-NO-NO

Here are the qualities a stock must exhibit to be on Decision Path H.

Analysis Key 1—No: The situation does not really measure up to what we were seeking when we created and ran the screen.
Analysis Key 2—No: The situation does not offer attractive investment features other than those used as the basis for the screen.
Analysis Key 3—No: The situation is not free from factors that are regarded by our investment philosophies as negatives.

These stocks offer the worst of all possible worlds. There are qualities we regard as distasteful, and they are not balanced by any significant positives of any kind from any source. There is no rational reason to consider purchasing any of these stocks.

four

Sell . . . Stocks That, after Review, No Longer Seem Suitable

The Hard Part

The three steps we used to reach our buy decisions covered a lot of ground. So, too, do other books on stock selection, most of which view the stock purchase as a happy ending. But we all know it's not nearly this easy. There will be many occasions calling for a decision whether to continue holding or to sell. Mistakes here can frustrate investment performance at least as badly as poor buying decisions.

It's often said that selling is harder than buying. Such assertions are typically accompanied by pop psychology explaining how hard it is to admit mistakes or part with much-beloved stocks that served us so well. I agree that the sell decision is hard, but I don't believe psychological issues are nearly as troublesome as many claim. Instead, I believe selling is difficult because the topic rarely is treated in anywhere near as logical a way as is the buy-oriented analytic process. Too often, reason goes out the window and is replaced by folklore.

TUNING OUT TROUBLESOME FOLKLORE

But before focusing on the specifics of Step 4 (Sell), we'll have to discuss some of the most prevalent and potentially troublesome elements of sell-related folklore. It's important that we address these issues openly, because you're going to be hearing about them day in, day out from the media, from your friends, and from other sources, and you'll need all the fortitude you can muster to tune it all out.

Cutting Losses/Taking Profits

I can't count how often I hear the following dialogue when I listen to call-in investment programs:

CALLER: I own XYZ shares. Do you think it's still a good investment?
HOST: What did you pay for them?
ME (*wanting to smash the radio*): Who cares what the caller paid?

One of the most distracting aspects of sell-related discussions is the notion that we should care about the price paid when the stock was purchased. The only possible justification would relate to tax planning, which will be discussed in the next section. And much media hullabaloo about cutting losses and taking profits is way out of proportion to bona fide tax considerations.

Here's a simple example that shows how flawed this approach to selling really is. Assume Jones buys XYZ at a price of 40. Later on, the company announces that the next quarter's earnings will be lower than what analysts had previously been anticipating. The stock quickly drops to 28. Jones decides to hold, believing the problems are not representative of what can be expected from the company over the long term. Smith, who hadn't previously owned XYZ, notices the company on a contrarian screen and, reaching the same conclusion as Jones, buys near the low, at, say, 29. A few weeks later, the stock is at 33.

What should Jones and Smith do now? According to the conventional cut losses/ride profits wisdom, Jones should sell and cut his loss at 17.5 percent (the percent decline from 40 to 33). In fact, Jones really should have cut his loss as quickly as possible. That would have meant taking a 30 percent loss, when the stock first dropped to 28, which, given the way today's markets work, was probably the first price Jones could have gotten after the bad news came out. Meanwhile, conventional wisdom would tell Smith to let her profit (which currently stands at about 14 percent based on the move from 29 to 33) ride. So she should hold.

This is unacceptable. (To really nail this down, let's assume Smith and Jones both own the shares in individual retirement accounts (IRAs), so taxes are irrelevant.) We're giving diametrically opposed recommendations regarding the same stock at the same time to two different investors based on facts that have absolutely nothing to do with what is likely to happen to XYZ in the future. It's a 100 percent certainty that one of these investors is going to get bad advice. If XYZ recovers to 40, Jones will have been hurt by advice to cut his loss. If XYZ turns out to have really experienced fundamental deterioration and the stock slides again, Smith will have been burned by having been advised to hold at 33 (as opposed to booking a quick, and probably lucky, profit).

This is not to say there is only one answer for everybody. It would be legitimate to give different advice to Smith and Jones if they have differing investment goals. We were already told that Smith is a contrarian. Hence it is probably proper for her to continue to hold. We can assume she evaluated the fundamental risks and potential rewards. But we never considered Jones' goals. Conventional wisdom tells him to sell simply because he has a loss. Suppose Jones is also a contrarian. Perhaps he bought at 40 believing this to be a good entry point for a stock that had already fallen from a 52-week high of 65. That purchase decision was proven wrong. But he ought not be encouraged to follow mistake number one (buying too high) with mistake number two (selling too low). What Jones really needs to do is reevaluate the fundamentals and let those conclusions guide his next decision. (Suppose, however, Jones is a momentum investor. In that case, it would be more appropriate for him to sell because, contrarian opportunities notwithstanding, he'd rather shift the proceeds tied up in XYZ to an alternative momentum situation.)

Taxes

Taxes constitute the one legitimate aspect of the losses/profits basis for decision making. We all know that long-term capital gains are taxed more favorably. But if we really think about it, we have to admit it's better to take a short-term gain and pay the higher tax than to hold too long and wind up with a big loss. In deciding when to take a profit, you've got no shortage of things to think about and decisions that might go wrong. You don't help yourself adding to your list of concerns the possibility you may get hammered on a stock you knew should have been sold at a much higher price but held because you wanted to trim your tax bill. I know there are also opportunities to share losses with Uncle Sam, but frankly I'd rather share gains.

Perhaps the most logical time to consider taxes is toward the end of the year. The wash sale rule allows you to sell a losing position and deduct the loss if you stay out of the stock for 30 days. The idea is that you benefit from the tax loss and get to buy the stock back after 30 days, assuming it's one you want to continue to own. The risk you assume is that the stock might move higher before the 30-day period expires. Bear in mind, however, that tax strategies are at the fringe of the process. And if you're investing in a tax-deferred account such as an IRA, you need not consider these issues at all.

Difficulty in Recouping Losses

Proponents of the cut-your-losses approach tend to offer some simple mathematics in support of their views. They say, suppose you buy a stock at 40 and it falls to 20. That's a 50 percent loss. But a recovery from 20 to 40 will require a 100 percent gain, and it's harder to get a 100 percent move than a 50 percent move. The arithmetic may be correct, but it bears no relation to what happens in the real world. When stock prices move, they don't care where they are going in terms of percentage relationship to some prior price. They just go. Pick your favorite financial web site and start looking at price charts, one after another. It won't be long before it becomes obvious that such recoveries happen often, and within very reasonable time frames.

The Rearview Mirror

Let's suppose an academician constructs a study that counts the number of times that fallen stocks recover to prior highs and finds that it happens much more rarely than I just suggested. My response would be: "Who cares?" In truth, the whole topic is irrelevant. We can see this by going back to the same example we used in the preceding section.

Suppose you buy a stock at 40 and it falls to 20. You're very depressed because so many market pundits, backed now by (hypothetical) academicians, are telling you how hard it will be for the stock to climb back to 40. Let's accept this gloomy assessment. Suppose the best the stock is likely to do in the coming year would be to reach 24. That would be a 20 percent gain above the present price. Before you give in to the doomsayers and sell, you ought to think carefully about your investment alternatives. A one-year 20 percent gain is pretty good. It isn't as exciting as what day traders got accustomed to for a brief period in the late 1990s. But investors who are familiar with the stock market's long-term performance know full well how good it is to get 20 percent in a year.

This is a very real scenario. A couple of weeks before writing this chapter, I had planned to make this sort of point on a scheduled television interview at CNNfn using Cisco Systems as an example. It seemed like a good idea because pundits were then saying it would take years, if ever, before Cisco went back above 60. The last time I looked at Cisco the stock was a little below 12, so it really did face a long recovery voyage. I advocated a different decision-making framework. My plan was to mention that even if it took a year to reach 15, a 25 percent gain (from 12 to 15), that would still be more attractive than what one could achieve in many alternative investments. But I had to shift gears. By the time I went on the air, just a few days later, Cisco had already moved above 16.

So forget the rearview mirror. Look forward. Even if you have owned the stock for years, treat the situation as if you were considering a new purchase at today's price. This means viewing the stock through the eyes of investors who would be buying your shares if you choose to sell. Don't deprive yourself an opportunity to achieve a strong gain because you're frustrated about a prior bad decision that cannot be undone.

Bad News

Perhaps the single most pervasive idea about selling is that you have to do it whenever bad news comes out, especially if the bad news is related to earnings. There's nothing inherently wrong with this notion. Selling would be appropriate if the news is such as to make the stock unacceptable in light of your investment philosophy. The problem is that many investors are quick to assume just this: that bad news makes the stock unsuitable. Slow down. Make sure that's really the case.

Recall our example in which XYZ announces that earnings for the upcoming quarter will come in below expectations and its stock plummets from 40 to 28. We see incidents like this frequently nowadays, as investors automatically assume that bad earnings reports mean the stock must be sold. Such attitudes derive from traditional growth/momentum-oriented investment philosophies that favor shares of companies whose earnings are growing faster than benchmarks (usually industry or market averages).

But such investment methods took hold when stocks were much less volatile than they are today. Traditionally, it was assumed that shares of companies with relatively good earnings would outperform the market, and that shares of companies with relatively weak earnings would underperform the market. Times have changed. Now we might say shares of companies with relatively good earnings would outperform the market to a massive degree, and shares of companies with relatively weak earnings would underperform the market to an extent that is grotesquely out of proportion to the extent of the bottom-line challenges.

Consider the following experiences for Procter & Gamble stock.

■ During the three-calendar-year period covering 1990–1992, Procter & Gamble's worst one-day price performance was –5.47 percent (and its best single-day performance was +5.66 percent). This was a generally bad period characterized by a recession and a war in the Middle East.

▧ During the three-calendar-year period covering 1998–2000, Procter & Gamble's worst one-day stock price performance was –31.38 percent (and its best single-day performance was +9.52 percent). This was a generally good period characterized by a booming economy, a bull market, and reasonable stability on the general world scene (at least as much stability as in any other modern three-year period).

Why did Procter & Gamble experience a much more traumatic one-day decline in the latter good period? The answer: The company issued a disappointing earnings announcement one day in March 2000. Aside from that, the company hadn't changed dramatically. Admittedly, it didn't stay exactly the same, but the changes were evolutionary within the context of its business (acquisitions, management changes, etc.). After all, this isn't a maker of exotic high-tech products that may be overtaken by competition. Procter & Gamble was a large household products company in 1990–1992, and it was still a large household products company in 1998–2000. The difference is that in 1990–1992 investors didn't react as aggressively to earnings announcements as has been the case in recent years.

I wonder whether investors who took the one-day 31.38 percent Procter & Gamble loss in March 2000 thought about how much the market had changed in barely a decade. A sell-on-bad-news strategy in 1998–2000 had very different implications than it did in 1990–1992. If your investment goals are such that you really want to ignore the valuation implications of a modern sell-on-bad-news strategy and choose to follow that strategy, so be it. My only concern is that your decision be a thoughtful one based on all relevant facts. Unfortunately, judging from the way the media reports bad-news stories, I suspect many investors completely ignore the relationship between share price movements and news, and continue to invest as if the market is still behaving the way it did years ago.

THE NEXT STEP

Step 4 (Sell) is a folklore-free zone. I believe you'll find this step easy to understand and implement because it draws so heavily on the material that has already been covered. It adapts the Find-Analyze-Buy steps we already learned to a sell-oriented three-step process that identifies sale candidates, analyzes them based on updated facts, and balances the pros and cons in a review process that leads to a specific hold-or-sell decision. These sell-oriented steps are called Alert-Update-Reconsider. Let's now go to Chapter 16 and take a close look at each of them.

16

Encore

I t should come as no surprise to see that Step 4 (Sell) is pretty much an en-
core for everything that was done in connection with the decision to buy.
Once we strip the folklore away from the selling process, as we did in
Chapter 15, we can see there is very little difference between buying and
selling. In both cases, a stock has come to our attention and we are called
upon to assess the relationship between current company fundamentals
and the current stock price, culminating in a decision based on how we expect the stock to perform in the future. In a sense, we're doing everything
we did before, but this time around we're trying to imagine how other investors, the ones who are considering whether to buy the shares we'd be
selling, would view the situation. If it looks as if the other guys ought to
like what they are seeing and be eager to buy, that generally means we
ought not to be selling.

So the selling process is really a reprise of our previously established
Find-Analyze-Buy discipline. You'll see that selling requires two basic
adaptations. The first is the way we decide which stocks we'll examine. In
contrast to Step 1 (Find), we start with a much more manageable-sized list
of possibilities. So rather than seeking techniques to narrow a massive
database, we seek ways to tell us we need to give special attention to stocks
we already know about. The other is based on the passage of time. Obviously, facts change. So, too, do our goals. So even if we do exactly the
same things we did in Step 2 (Analyze) and Step 3 (Buy), we will often
wind up with a different set of answers.

We manage the selling process by breaking it down into three phases
that are equivalent to the three steps we already covered. Sell Phase A,
called Alert, is an adaptation of what we did in Step 1 (Find). Sell Phase B,
known as Update, is similar to Step 2 (Analyze). And Sell Phase C, Reconsider, parallels Step 3 (Buy). We reconsider by balancing the most up-to-

date set of pros and cons using three Update Keys (similar to the Analysis Keys discussed in Chapter 13) and Reconsideration Paths (similar to the Decision Paths discussed in Chapter 14).

SELL PHASE A: ALERT . . . CALLING ATTENTION TO THE NEED FOR REVIEW

Nobody has time to study every stock that's out there. Step 1 (Find) addressed that by providing a method for identifying a reasonable-size group of stocks that were worthy of close attention. A similar situation exists with regard to stocks you already own. Few investors are able to review every stock every day. Sell Phase A (Alert) tells you which of your holdings require attention right now.

This process helps you use your time most efficiently, focusing your attention where it is most needed when it is most needed. But no set of procedures can offset a basic truth. The more stocks you own, the more often you will be called upon to devote some time to your portfolio. This should influence how you react to the ever-present controversy regarding the number of stocks one ought to own. Some investors like to hold many positions. Others prefer focused portfolios that concentrate funds in just a few stocks, one's so-called best ideas. Speaking for myself, rather than describe a particular company in such terms, I tend to see this screening method as my single best idea. So in theory, I'm willing to hold dozens, or even hundreds, of positions as long as they are based on an idea (the market screening method) about which I have strong conviction. The only reason I don't actually own so many stocks is because it would be impractical for me to review too large a number in a timely manner.

Viewed this way, the diversification question becomes easy to resolve. The number of stocks you hold should be based on the number you can manage under Step 4 (Sell). If you aren't sure how many that is, you will learn very soon after putting the Alert process into action. I suggest starting with a fairly traditional number, somewhere in the 10 to 20 range, and gradually increasing it to the extent that you are able to keep pace with all the alerts you get.

There are three different ways you can be alerted to the need to review a position: in response to specific events, based on a preset routine, and based on sell-oriented screens. Let's look separately at each situation.

Events

I doubt there are many investors who need to be persuaded to review an existing holding in response to a significant event impacting the company. Earnings-related announcements are the most frequent example. And these may well have the biggest impact in determining how many stocks can comfortably be included in your portfolio. That's because these announcements tend to cluster just before the end of a quarter (when preannouncements are issued to help analysts update their forecasts) and just after the start of the next period (when earnings for the most recent quarter are formally announced). Realistically, you can often stop short of a full-blown review in response to earnings announcements. You may instead compare the news to the latest set of analyst expectations and accept that all is well if you see that things are progressing as expected. Time management considerations suggest you devote most of your attention to situations involving the greatest variation between reality and prior expectation. But even with this proviso, if you are monitoring too many stocks you'll still get overwhelmed during "earnings season."

There are other kinds of events that should trigger an update. Any sort of news having a major bearing on the company's strategic direction (mergers, divestitures, new products, restructurings, etc.) would qualify. So, too, would utterances of analysts or journalists if they have an impact on the stock price. You need not agree with what is being said. But you should at least refresh your understanding of the situation. Indeed, if you disagree with an opinion that has sparked a major share price decline, that can create an interesting opportunity to purchase more stock. Conversely, if you think an exaggerated bullish article or report sent the stock too high, that can trigger a sell decision.

Sometimes, you'll see a sharp share price movement that appears to have no explanation. My experience is such that the absence of explanation will almost always be a mirage. It will rarely take more than a few days for some explanation to become visible. Hence any unusually large share price movements ought to be seen as events that alert you to the need for further review.

Routine

Financial information has a finite shelf life. Companies are required to report results every three months (except for certain situations wherein non-U.S. companies have longer reporting intervals). So even if nothing else happened, you at least get a set of updated financial statements, as well as updates to all ratios based, in any way, on those numbers. Therefore, it's wise to set a personal policy to the effect that every stock you own will be reviewed as a potential sale candidate if three months have passed since the last such review.

When determining whether the company has been reviewed in the past three months, don't count event-driven glances comparing company earnings announcements to analyst expectations if they did not progress beyond a quick look. Try, to the extent practical given your time constraints, to follow up these situations with complete reviews as soon as possible after the first earnings season glance. What we're aiming for, here, is a habit of putting each stock through the entire review process (all the way through the Update Keys and Reconsideration Paths described later in this chapter) at least once every three months.

I suggest doing this even if you consider yourself a long-term investor. A preference for a long or short time horizon should relate to how long you are willing to wait for a situation to come to fruition. Contrarian and value investors are usually willing to hold on quite a bit longer than, say, momentum investors. But that doesn't mean the former should lock the stock in a drawer. Even if, at the outset, you expected the situation to take a year or two to pan out, you should still refresh your views at least once every three months, to make sure the scenario you originally envisioned remains plausible, or, if not, that you are willing to accept whatever modifications are dictated by events. Look at it this way: A two-year investor is equivalent to a three-month investor who came up with the same answer eight times in a row.

Sell-Oriented Screens

The first two alert categories, specific events and a preset routine, are generally passive. You wait until a reason for review jumps out at you through either specific news events or the passage of time. Sell-oriented screens are different. Here, you actively search for selling opportunities.

The strictest approach to sell-oriented screening is to simply take note of companies that fall off the screen you originally used. But that alone is likely to produce an intolerable work burden. Those screens were designed to call attention to stocks worthy of further analysis. They were never intended to articulate ironclad investment rules. That's why we went through Step 2 (Analyze) and Step 3 (Buy), which expanded our inquiry beyond the narrow confines of the screen. Now, in Step 4 (Sell), there's no point getting rid of a stock simply because it no longer meets one or more of the original tests that, at the end of the day, may not have had much impact on the ultimate buying decision.

If possible, create one or more screens that are specifically designed to spotlight sell opportunities. Ideally, you should use screeners that accept user-defined portfolios so you can substitute the 20 or so stocks you own for the complete 9,000-plus stock database. Multex's premium application accepts user portfolios and can, therefore, easily accommodate sell screens. So, too, can the moderately priced Stock Investor Pro application (you'll want to be especially vigilant about downloading and installing the weekly updates from the AAII.com web site, so you have the most up-to-date data possible).

If you run a sell-oriented screen through the full database, the resulting list will be very clogged with stocks you don't own. That's not a fatal flaw. You can often use search functions to determine whether the stocks you own are among those that show up in the screen. But your sell-screening efforts will be hampered if the application you use limits the number of companies that can make a screen. If that's the case, you cannot feel completely safe just because a particular company doesn't appear. For all you know, one of your holdings might rank 151st and therefore stay invisible because the application cannot show more than 150 companies.

If you find yourself in this situation, you have two options. One is to simply accept the limitations and if your companies don't show, to assume you can still spot problems through event- or routine-based alert methods. This is tolerable, albeit not ideal. The other approach involves what I refer to as shadow screens. This procedure is designed for use with applications that can't accommodate user-defined portfolios. It can also be used with the free application available on the MultexInvestor.com web site. The latter does allow you to set up user portfolios. But the available variables tend to be simple and, hence, unable to accommodate the sort of sell-oriented tests discussed in this chapter.

Let's now move on to the sell-oriented tests. Generally, these are similar to the behavioral tests discussed in Chapter 7. They examine the actions of market participants and call our attention to stocks toward which they seem to have grown cool. Then, we'll look at how shadow screens can help if you are using less sophisticated applications. Even if you use one of the latter, at least stay aware of the more aggressive possibilities. Screening product lines are still evolving for the better. So it's possible you may soon find yourself using a screener that will allow for more sophisticated sell-oriented screening.

Relative Share Price Performance   Poor relative performance may be one of the best alert signals. Since stock price movement reflects the aggregate of all opinions formed by all investors who look at a stock, bad showings tell us the opinion has turned unfavorable. If we narrow our focus to bad relative performance, it's more likely the negative aggregate opinion is based on company-specific, rather than general market, factors.

If your application uses relative strength, consider a cross-sectional test like this.

> Relative Strength Last 4 Weeks < (Industry Average Relative Strength Last 4 Weeks) * .65

Here's a time-series variation.

> Relative Strength Last 4 Weeks < (Relative Strength Last 13 Weeks) * .65

If you can't use relative strength, try this alternative.

> Price Change Last 4 Weeks < (Industry Average Price Change Last 4 Weeks) * .65

Note the use of multiplication factors. These are important in helping you avoid clutter. By definition, approximately half of all stocks in a database are below average. And over the normal ebb and flow of time, different stocks gain and lose relative strength even without significant changes in fundamentals. For purposes of an alert screen, it's more efficient to look for stocks whose performances were not just weak, but very weak.

Here's an interesting, albeit more complex, approach. (In Stock Investor Pro you'll need to create separate components as custom fields.)

> (Price Change Last 4 Weeks – Industry Average Price Change Last 4 Weeks) < (Price Change Last 13 Weeks – Industry Average Price Change Last 13 Weeks) * .65

This test searches for instances where the relationship between the stock's performance and that of its industry has deteriorated. The example seeks situations where the four-week relationship is less favorable than the 13-week relationship. Use of the multiplication factor means we want the relationship to have deteriorated to a significant degree.

Look closely at the way we define the relationship. You might have expected us to divide the stock performance by the industry performance to compute a ratio or percent. If the stock rises 5 percent but the industry average is 4 percent, the relationship is 1.2 (5 percent divided by 4 percent); in other words, the stock's performance was 20 percent better than that of the industry average. But suppose the stock rose 4 percent and the industry declined 2 percent. Now, dividing the stock by the industry gives a ratio of –2. If, over the 13 weeks, the stock performed exactly in line with the industry (the stock's performance divided by the industry average performance equals 1), our alert would be triggered because it seems that the relationship deteriorated badly (–2 is significantly lower than 1). That's not the kind of answer we want.

We solve the problem by using subtraction to define the relationship. Going back to the example, the four-week relationship is 6 (the stock's 4 percent change minus the industry's –2 percent change gives a result of 6), which is much greater than the zero we would have computed for the 13-week period. Hence we will not get a sell alert.

Admittedly, division gives a more mathematically pure answer than subtraction. But this isn't a math quiz. We're looking for sell alerts, and the mathematical nature of division (the answer being negative if either of the numbers has a minus sign) hampers our task.

This test (and similar ones you can create using relative strength) is, definitely, cumbersome. But it has an important virtue that can make it worth the extra effort. It gives a very early alert signal that will be triggered even if the stock is still leading the industry, if the margin of victory narrows significantly. Consider Table 16.1.

The stock rose 5 percent over the past 13 weeks and 2 percent over the past four weeks. The industry average was –2 percent over the past 13 weeks and +1 percent over the past four weeks. This triggers an alert. The stock's four-week margin of victory over the industry average is +1. The 13-week margin is +7. The stock is still outperforming its peers, but it's clearly falling back toward the pack. A value investor may not want to bother about this sort of thing. But if you're a growth or momentum in-

TABLE 16.1   Test for Sell Alerts

	Share Price Performance	
	Last 4 Weeks	Last 13 Weeks
Stock	+2%	+5%
Industry average	+1%	–2%
Stock's margin of victory	+1%	+7%

vestor, it may be well worth your time to check these early warnings. Many will be false alarms. But even a few real hits per year can make a noticeable difference in your portfolio's performance.

Volume   A recent and substantial increase in trading volume might signal problems. But it could parallel an increase in volume throughout the market. Or it might signal a company-specific increase in attention due to bullish considerations. So if you use a volume test, make sure it's done in conjunction with (i.e., in support of) other tests that point more clearly in a bearish direction. And if you're using a Multex screener or Stock Investor Pro, remember to adjust the three-month and 10-day volume data points so the numbers are equivalent, as we did in Chapter 6.

Analyst Actions   There are several ways to approach this topic. One is to focus on the recommendations. Here are some examples.

Mean Rating > (Mean Rating 4 Weeks Ago) * 1.25

Remember, from Chapter 6, the definition of mean rating: higher numbers are more bearish than lower numbers. The example includes a multiplication factor that confines the results only to situations where there has been a large deterioration in analyst opinion. Note, though, that in the workaday world, big changes in analyst rating profiles don't occur often. So it would be perfectly reasonable, here, to drop the multiplication factor and simply screen for any increase in the mean rating.

You could also create tests aimed directly at each rating category. Normally, most analysts issue ratings within the top three (strong buy, buy, or hold). Hence a lower rating would be unusual and would signal the need for review.

\# Underperform Ratings > 0
\# Sell Ratings > 0

You need not wait for both conditions to be satisfied. An alert could be triggered if there's an increase in either one of those bearish rating categories. So make sure your program is using the "OR" logic. Also, the above example assumes there was no pending underperform or sell rating when you bought the stock. If you were willing to buy stocks rated that way, here's an alternative pair of tests you may find more usable (again, make sure they are joined via the "OR" logic).

\# Underperform Ratings > \# Underperform Ratings 4 Weeks Ago
\# Sell Ratings > \# Sell Ratings 4 Weeks Ago

Similar tests could be built to search for noteworthy declines in the number of strong buy or buy ratings. Here's an example.

\# Strong Buy Ratings 4 Weeks Ago – \# Strong Buy Ratings Now >= 3

You might also want to screen for a noteworthy decrease in the number of analysts covering a stock. The practical implication, the diminished availability of research, is one issue. Another factor is that at times analysts discontinue coverage because they no longer find the stock worthy of attention. (This may be one reason why there are so few sell recommendations. Rather than continue covering and recommending sale, analysts often drop coverage altogether and devote their efforts to stocks they deem more attractive.) Cynics could say reduced coverage reflects a diminution in the likelihood a company will need investment banking services in the foreseeable future (and hence be of less interest to analysts who hope positive coverage will attract such business to their firms). No matter. The decrease in so-called sponsorship still merits our attention. (Remember, we're not automatically selling. All we're doing is deciding which companies we're going to review more closely.)

Another approach is to look at analyst estimates. You could create tests based on unfavorable earnings surprises, downward estimate revisions, or declines in consensus estimates compared with prior periods. Here are some examples.

Latest Quarter Earnings Surprise < 0

\# Downward Estimate Revisions Last 4 Weeks > 0

Consensus Estimate Now < Consensus Estimate 4 Weeks Ago

Sentiment Criteria   Reporting lags prevent sentiment data from competing, in terms of speed, with other indicators. But this category can still be interesting. Suppose there are no event-based alerts and that screening tests based on price, volume, and analyst data turn out benign. Yet you see marked increase in institutional selling or short interest.

Such occurrences may not have meaning. Things may have changed for the better before new institutional or short interest data finds its way into the screening databases. But it can still be worthwhile to pursue these alerts. Even if sentiment tests alone don't cause you to go all the way through the rest of Step 4 (Sell), at least take a quick glance at the situation. At worst, you'll waste only a modest amount of time, given that you'll check only the stocks you already own. But at best, you can get an early warning in situations where short sellers or a few institutions are quicker to see problems than are analysts or the full roster of market participants.

Here are some sample sentiment tests.

Institutional Shareholders < (# Institutional Shareholders 4 Weeks Ago) * .85

Institutional Net Shares Purchased < 0

Short Interest Now > Short Interest 4 Weeks Ago

Short Interest Now/Short Interest 4 Weeks Ago > 1.5

Note the absence of tests relating to insider selling. As discussed in Chapter 6, insider sales are not as reliable as a basis for bearishness as we might like.

Shadow Screening   Unless you're using an especially powerful screener like the premium Multex screener or Stock Investor Pro, you are likely to be stymied by the unavailability of the variables you need to create these tests and/or by your inability to create user-defined portfolios. Shadow screens provide a useful alternative. These are generally similar to the screens you used for buying, but the tests are now more relaxed. In this procedure, we reverse our behavior. Up till now, an alert was triggered by a stock's presence on a sell-oriented screen. With shadow screening, the alert is triggered by a stock's absence from the screen. In other words, if your stock appears on the shadow screen, it need not be reviewed now. If it is missing from the shadow screen, that's an alert signaling the need for closer inquiry.

I'm going to warn you up front that shadow screening is a bit cumbersome and acknowledge that I do not use it. The first choice is to create sell-oriented screens using the kinds of tests just discussed. Shadow screening is offered only as a second choice to those who want screen-based alerts but don't have access to applications that let them create good, clean, sell-oriented screens. As to the quality applications, I'm obviously partial to the premium Multex offering. But I'm not trying to overwhelm you with a hard-core sales pitch. You can also create good sell-oriented screens with the lower-priced Stock Investor Pro and Smart-MoneySelect.com offerings.

Moving on to the shadow screening procedure, our starting point is the notion that in theory the stocks that make your regular screens will also make your shadow screens. In reality, that won't always be so. For one thing, you may not want to bother always using one-for-one shadow-to-regular screen matchups.

Another issue is the nature of the variables. A regular screen might seek a trailing 12-month return on investment (TTM ROI) above the industry average. Ideally, a shadow screen might relax this test to seek companies whose TTM ROI is no worse than 85 percent of the industry average TTM ROI. But in the real world, if you're using shadow screens in the first place, your screener probably can't create the latter test (which involves use of a multiplication factor). It's even possible your shadow screener may be unable to handle cross-sectional ROI comparisons. (That could occur if you bought based on more sophisticated tests because you used preset screens created with a premium application.) So a more realistic shadow test might seek a TTM ROI above a modest numeric threshold, say 8 percent. Now, suppose the TTM ROI for XYZ Company is 6 percent and its industry average is 4 percent. It will make the regular screen but fail the supposedly easier shadow screen.

There's an easy solution: Make shadow screening a two-step procedure. First, we check to see if the stock remains on the regular screen. If so, case closed: We won't bother to look at a shadow screen. We'll just say that no screen-based alert has occurred. We look at the shadow screen only in connection with stocks that have fallen off the regular screen.

One way you can use this procedure is to create shadow screens that closely match your regular screens. The other option is to use a general shadow screen to back up several regular screens. Here's an example showing how you can closely match a shadow screen to the MSN .Money preset screen named GARP Go-getters. Here's the regular GARP Go-getters screen.

Market Capitalization <= 1,000,000,000
Income per Employee >= Industry Average Income per Employee
Inventory Turnover >= Industry Average Inventory Turnover
Debt to Equity <= 0.5
5 Year Revenue Growth >= 20
EPS Growth Next Year High as Possible
P/E Ratio Current <= EPS Growth Next 5 Years

Here's a shadow screen I created. It follows the same theme, but is much less stringent than the original.

Debt to Equity <= 0.75
5 Year Revenue Growth >= 20
EPS Growth Next Year >= 1
P/E Ratio Current <= EPS Growth Next 5 Years

In the shadow screen, I stop trying to find the highest possible year-ahead EPS growth projections. Now, I'll accept almost any positive rate of growth. I also relax the balance sheet requirement and eliminate the tests relating to market capitalization, income per employee, and inventory turnover. If the stock is on the shadow screen, I need not do anything even though it dropped off the regular version. But if the stock fails to make either the regular screen or the shadow screen, I'll consider myself alerted to the need for review.

Now let's look at an example of how we can use more generalized shadow screens. Here's one I created, using the free Multex application, based on a broad shadow value theme.

Forward-looking P/E Ratio < 20
Forward-looking P/E Ratio/Projected Growth Rate <= 1.75
Most Recent Quarter EPS Growth >= 5
TTM EPS Growth >= 10

This is much less stringent than the value screens I usually use. If I'm seeking to buy based on the growth at a reasonable price (GARP) approach, I usually set the target PEG ratio closer to 1.00, rather than at 1.75, as seen in the shadow screen. My regular value screens tend to include growth tests (in an effort to bar stocks whose P/E ratios are low because the companies are doing poorly). But there, I prefer cross-sectional and/or time-series growth tests. And even as numeric tests go, the ones you see here are fairly lenient. When I don't use GARP, my alternative value approach involves looking at a variety of ratios in terms of industry comparison, rather than the single numeric test you see in the shadow screen. Regardless of which value approach I used for buying, if a stock I own fails to make the original screen and fails to make the shadow value screen, I would review it.

It is entirely possible a still-good company will fail to make the shadow value screen. A stock with a P/E of 25 combined with a company growth rate of 40 percent would seem attractive, but it would fail the shadow test because the P/E is above 20. But remember, I'm only looking at the shadow screen because the company already dropped off my regular screen. Even then, I'm not necessarily going to sell. All we seek, at this juncture, are alerts telling us which of our existing holdings warrant a closer review—a review that could just as easily lead to a hold decision.

Here's another example of a shadow screen, this one based on company quality.

Tax Rate >= 40
TTM Operating Margin >= 8
TTM Operating Margin >= (5 Year Average Operating Margin) * .9
TTM ROI >= 12
TTM ROE >= 15

This is much simpler than the regular quality screens I use, which depend heavily on cross-sectional comparison and make greater use of time-series testing than we see here. But again, I'll use the shadow screen only in connection with companies that drop off the regular screen.

Finally, you can create more generalized shadow screens that can be used in conjunction with any kind of buy-oriented screen. Here's an example using tests from Multex's free screener.

Stock Price % Change Last 4 Weeks >= −5
Mean Analyst Rating <= 2.5
EPS Surprise Latest Quarter >= 0
EPS % Growth Latest Quarter >= 3
Short Interest Ratio Now <= (Short Interest Ratio 1 Month Ago) * 1.1
Institutional Net Shares Purchased (millions of shares) >= −1

Needless to say, you can, and should, modify this screen based on changing market conditions. For example, at the time I created this screen I perceived the market to be experiencing a bear market rally. Had I believed the market to be in a more normal bullish phase, I would not, even in a shadow screen, have used a stock price change base as low as −5 percent. But even with modifications, you would still aim to have the shadow screen remain fairly lenient, too lenient for use in Step 1 (Find).

The day I created this screen, 198 companies (out of a data universe consisting of 9,466 companies) passed all the tests. If you want more companies to pass, you could relax the criteria even more. (Since our alert signals are triggered by the company's absence from the screen, we would seek a larger result set if we want less frequent alert signals.) Or you could split the screen. Here is one way to do that.

Version A

Mean Analyst Rating <= 2.5
EPS Surprise Latest Quarter >= 0
EPS % Growth Latest Quarter >= 3

Version B

Stock Price % Change Last 4 Weeks >= −5
Short Interest Ratio Now <= (Short Interest Ratio 1 Month Ago) * 1.1
Institutional Net Shares Purchased >= −1

The day the screens were created, 702 companies passed Version A and 1,996 passed Version B. Hence we now have 2,698 names, only 198 of which met both sets of criteria (we know this because the original version, which used all six tests at once, produced 198 names).

As you can see, there are many ways you can use the shadow screening procedure, based on how tightly you want to stick to the investment theory embodied in your original screen and how frequently you want to receive screen-generated alerts. Regardless of the choices you make along these lines, if a stock that is reviewed based on shadow screening winds up as a hold by the time you finish Step 4 (Sell), it probably will not be fruitful to continue to look at it again and again every time it fails the shadow test. From this point on, you can wait and allow the next review to be prompted by an event or routine (i.e., the passage of time).

SELL PHASE B: UPDATE . . .
THE SITUATION IN LIGHT OF NEW INFORMATION

This part of Step 4 (Sell) is very familiar and, hence, needs little discussion. We go back to the same sources (data reports, news items, etc.) we consulted in Step 2 (Analyze) and pretty much repeat what we did back then.

Don't be disappointed by the absence of an elaborate new evaluation procedure. This is an occasion where the simple answer is also the most powerful. As noted at the beginning of this chapter, we're putting ourselves in a position to see the stock through the eyes of other anonymous investors who might simultaneously be working toward a decision whether to buy any shares we choose to sell. This perspective will lead to far more sensible hold-or-sell decisions than any folklore-based strategy.

The real key to Sell Phase B (Update) is to be found in the name. The data tables will be the same type, but often the information has changed. Be especially attentive to the stock price. One aspect of folklore calls for selling shares of a still-beloved company if the stock has "gotten ahead of itself." At first glance, that sounds reasonable. The hard part is defining what it means for a stock to be "ahead of itself." That phrase means different things to different investors. We address the issue by treating the stock price as just another item of updated information. Naturally, we do likewise for the related data discussed in Chapter 11 (information bearing on the rationale for the stock price, the credibility of expectations, and sentiment). Looking at this data with fresh eyes, we'll easily recognize whether the stock has gotten ahead of itself based on however we choose to define that concept. If we believe the stock is an attractive investment at the current price, we'll hold even if the stock has already tripled or quadrupled since it was purchased. If not, we'll take our profit or loss, regardless of how big or small it may be.

One notable difference between Step 2 (Analyze) and Step 4 (Sell) is that now it's no longer necessary to learn about the company's business. We did that the first time around. If there are major changes, we'll catch those when we review recent developments. But even if there were no changes, it can sometimes be worthwhile to refresh our understanding of the firm by taking another look at the business. That is especially so if the company was unfamiliar the first time around and several months have passed since we last looked at it.

SELL PHASE C: RECONSIDER . . . WHETHER YOU SHOULD STILL HOLD THE STOCK

After updating our analysis, we reach the familiar position of having to balance a set of pros and cons. Back in Step 2 (Analyze), when we were trying to narrow down a large collection of potential investments, we weren't sure all the stocks we looked at would make it to Step 3 (Buy). To keep the process manageable, we had to make some strategic decisions about the circumstances that would cause us to drop a stock before Step 3 (Buy).

Step 4 (Sell) is different. Every stock that goes through Sell Phase B (Update) will also go through Sell Phase C (Reconsider). That means we are continually subjecting each stock we own to three Update Keys that are modeled on the Analysis Keys described in Chapter 13.

Update Keys

Update Key 1: Is Your Original Reason for Buying the Stock Still Valid?   In this context, the phrase "original reason" will sometimes relate to your original screen, but that won't always be the case. We are dealing here with what you did in Step 3 (Buy). As you recall from Chapters 13 and 14, your purchase decision may have resulted from a mixture of the original screen and additional positive factors that came to light during Step 2 (Analyze), plus a willingness to tolerate some negatives that surfaced during the course of the analysis. Update Key 1 is asking if the situation remains consistent with the sum total of all that was done in Step 3 (Buy).

Suppose the stock originally came to our attention on a growth screen, but the things we did in Step 2 (Analyze) and Step 3 (Buy) caused us to invest because we were attracted to the company's tendency to generate lots of excess cash flow and a low price/earnings-to-growth (PEG) ratio (a "happy accident" scenario). When we apply Update Key 1, we are not thinking of the original growth screen since it was not what motivated the purchase decision. (So if you are using shadow screens to generate alerts, a general or value-oriented screen would be appropriate for this situation, rather than one based on a shadow growth theme.) Now we're asking whether this investment can still be considered as a reasonably valued play on excess cash flow. If the stock jumped 150 percent in six months and now has a very high PEG ratio, it's no longer a good value. Hence we would answer "no" to this key even if cash generation remained substantial.

Update Key 2   Are There Any New Factors You Regard as Positive?   We're now asking whether the passage of time has brought forth new factors that we consider to be positive. A classic example would be a company that displays better-than-expected EPS growth. The more challenging situations are those that invite us to consider alternative investment philosophies.

Let's go back to the discussion in Chapter 15. Folklore tells investors to sell in response to bad news. Suppose a company issues an unfavorable earnings report. We can easily see that Update Key 1 should be answered "no" if quarterly earnings momentum motivated the purchase. But Update Key 2 is more interesting. Suppose the bad news causes the stock to immediately drop from 40 to 25. Even one who usually favors momentum might find it hard to ignore the new value story and might be very tempted to answer "yes."

Update Key 2 works best when we are liberal in saying "yes" whenever we can bring ourselves to do so. This helps us open our eyes to new possibilities. Don't worry about being bludgeoned into flip-flopping. Those who are truly inclined to stick to their guns (their original investment goals) will find all the intellectual ammunition they need in Update Key 3, which we'll look at next.

Update Key 3: Is the Situation Free of New Factors You Regard as Negative?

This is the flip side of Update Key 2. Now we're asking if the passage of time has brought forth new factors we consider negative. (More specifically, we're asking if, after the passage of time, the situation remains free from additional negative factors. As we did with Analysis Key 3, we phrase the question such that "no" answers are associated with negative investment implications.) Since we're dealing not only with facts about the company or its stock but also with individual investment styles, different investors will give different answers to Update Key 3.

If we are averse to owning shares of companies that experience earnings disappointments, we will answer "no" to Update Key 3. Continuing with the example of an earnings disappointment, even if we acknowledge the attractive value angle, we'll still wind up having answered the three Update Keys "no," "yes," and "no," respectively. As we'll see in our discussion of Reconsideration Paths, this pattern is akin to a strong sell.

It is not the function of the Update Keys to push us into changing our views. Instead, they are designed to help us clearly articulate what our views really are and see how they impact hold-or-sell decisions. The end result in the example, selling in response to an earnings disappointment, seems commonplace. What's unique here is the fact that we truly considered all aspects of the situation and made a thoughtful decision to allow a bad earnings report to override the a new and strong value angle. There's a big difference between thoughtfully weighing these alternatives versus never considering the value angle at all. The Update Keys are designed to prevent the latter.

Reconsideration Paths

As was the case with the buy decision, the factual aspects of the sell decision are there for all to see. And often they are easy to understand. The key to a sound selling strategy is achieving a proper match between facts and investment goals. The Update Keys were an important first step in that they caused us to ask the right questions and get a clear view of the pros and cons. The Reconsideration Paths, which function much the way the Decision Paths did in Step 3 (Buy), help us put it all together and reach specific decisions.

Table 16.2 ranks the possible yes/no Update Key combinations from best to worst. The stocks on Reconsideration Path A are the ones that most clearly ought to remain in the portfolio. Any stock on Reconsideration Path H should be sold immediately. The other paths represent the various in-between scenarios.

TABLE 16.2 Reconsideration Paths

Reconsideration Path	Update Key 1 (Original Reason for Buying)	Update Key 2 (New Positive Factors)	Update Key 3 (Absence of New Negative Factors)
A	Yes	Yes	Yes
B	Yes	No	Yes
C	No	Yes	Yes
D	Yes	Yes	No
The Neutral Zone			
E	No	No	Yes
F	Yes	No	No
G	No	Yes	No
H	No	No	No

Reconsideration Path A (Yes-Yes-Yes) Here are the qualities a stock must exhibit to be on Reconsideration Path A.

> Update Key 1—Yes: The situation remains consistent with what we expected when we originally bought the stock.
>
> Update Key 2—Yes: Since the original purchase or the most recent review, additional positive factors (according to our investment philosophies) have emerged.
>
> Update Key 3—Yes: The situation is free from negative factors (according to our investment philosophies) that emerged since the time of the purchase or the most recent review.

This stock offers the best of all possible worlds, and we hope we can have as many of these as possible in our portfolios. They continue to match our original investment goals, new positives have merged over time, and no negatives have surfaced.

This is not to say that you would never sell a Reconsideration Path A stock. Selling decisions are based on market and company-specific factors. Bigger picture considerations may cause you to anticipate a widespread bear market and cause you to liquidate or reduce your portfolio. In such a case, you might sell all or part of a Path A position. The only other reason you might sell such a stock is that you need to raise cash and Path A stocks are the only ones you have. There's just so far you can go with any system, so you'll have to use your own judgment to decide which Path A stock should go first. But don't expect much sympathy if you fret to colleagues about how hard it is to choose. Most investors would love to be saddled with a problem like that!

Reconsideration Path B (Yes-No-Yes)   Here are the qualities a stock must exhibit to be on Reconsideration Path B.

> Update Key 1—Yes: The situation remains consistent with what we expected when we originally bought the stock.
>
> Update Key 2—No: Since the original purchase or the most recent review, no additional positive factors (according to our investment philosophies) have emerged.
>
> Update Key 3—Yes: The situation is free from negative factors (according to our investment philosophies) that emerged since the time of the purchase or the most recent review.

This is not the best of all possible worlds, but most investors would be delighted if the worst thing about their portfolios was that all stocks were on Reconsideration Path B. These stocks continue to offer everything we wanted when we bought them, and since then, no negative factors have emerged to taint the picture. No additional positive qualities have surfaced (this being the difference between these stocks and those on Path A). But we can live with that. Many investors, when reviewing their portfolios, aren't even on the lookout for additional positives. Market factors aside, the only reason a Path B stock should be sold is if we need to raise cash and the only other kinds of stocks we own are on Path A.

Reconsideration Path C (No-Yes-Yes)   Here are the qualities a stock must exhibit to be on Reconsideration Path C.

> Update Key 1—No: The situation is no longer consistent with what we expected when we originally bought the stock.
>
> Update Key 2—Yes: Since the original purchase or the most recent review, additional positive factors (according to our investment philosophies) have emerged.
>
> Update Key 3—Yes: The situation is free from negative factors (according to our investment philosophies) that emerged since the time of the purchase or the most recent review.

Stocks on this path are still quite attractive, but we have slipped below slam dunk territory. They require a bit more soul-searching than those on Paths A and B. Not too much, just a bit. No negative factors have surfaced. But the investment goal that originally motivated the purchase has ceased to be valid. The good news is that the stock now satisfies an alternative investment goal that is compatible with some aspect of one's individual investment philosophy.

Reconsideration Path D (Yes-Yes-No) Here are the qualities a stock must exhibit to be on Reconsideration Path D.

> Update Key 1—Yes: The situation remains consistent with what we expected when we originally bought the stock.
> Update Key 2—Yes: Since the original purchase or the most recent review, additional positive factors (according to our investment philosophies) have emerged.
> Update Key 3—No: The situation is not free from negative factors (according to our investment philosophies) that emerged since the time of the purchase or the most recent review.

When we first discussed the paths in the context of buying decisions, we saw that it wasn't easy to determine the priority ordering between Paths C and D, since different investors might take different views regarding the relative desirability/undesirability of a "no" answer regarding our original goals versus a "yes" when it comes to freedom from negative factors. To some extent, a similar debate can occur here. Stocks on Reconsideration Paths C and D are both flawed, but not so much so as to make them high-priority sale candidates.

I laid out the paths in such a way as to favor (via the better path designation) a stock that requires us to switch goals but avoids negative baggage. Stocks on Path D adhere to our original goals but force us to accept some traits that we, based on our individual styles, deem negative.

As was the case with the Decision Paths used in Step 3 (Buy), you might want to switch Reconsideration Paths C and D if you have a different view of the trade-off between new baggage and adherence to the original goal. But in this context, you may want to be a bit more hesitant about doing so. When in Step 3 (Buy), we were looking at stocks we didn't own. The worst that could happen with an erroneous decision would be an opportunity loss—a failure to participate in what turns out to have been a lucrative situation. But no existing funds were lost. Moreover, the screening method is such that there's a respectable probability that an alternative stock you purchased (from the same screen following the same analytic process) could be just as attractive as the one you bypassed.

Now, the setting is different. We own the stocks. The prospect of an opportunity loss (selling prematurely) is no longer the worst-case scenario. There is now exposure to a direct loss. This makes "no" answers to Key 3 (dealing with negative factors) harder to tolerate.

The Neutral Zone   Reconsideration Path D does raise an eyebrow, given the presence of negative factors. But even with these stocks, there are still enough positives (as evidenced by "yes" answers for Keys 1 and 2) that we could reasonably decide to hold. We can feel even more comfortable with stocks on higher paths. Hence Reconsideration Paths A through D can be referred to are the Hold Zone, with differentiation serving to identify selling priorities in case we need to raise cash. This situation parallels our experience in Step 3 (Buy), when we designated Decision Paths A through D as the Buy Zone based on the tendencies of those paths to point us toward purchasing.

The same parallels apply in the lower portion of the hierarchy. In Step 3 (Buy), Decision Paths E through H were dubbed the Avoid Zone. We indicated there was little reason to buy any of those shares. Here, in Step 4 (Sell), Reconsideration Paths E through H make up the Sell Zone. The relationship between the two sets of paths is again summarized in Table 16.3.

The stocks in the Sell Zone are not equally undesirable. The sequence from E through H is based on a bad-to-worst hierarchy. But logically, it's hard to make a case for holding any stock falling on one of the lower paths. Still, it would be unrealistic to imagine that emotion can ever be

TABLE 16.3   Reconsideration Paths in Context

Reconsideration Paths		Decision Paths	
A			A
B	Hold Zone	Buy Zone	B
C			C
D			D
E			E
F	Sell Zone	Avoid Zone	F
G			G
H			H

completely banished from the investment process. Everybody occasionally feels reluctant to pull the trigger on a stock that, viewed objectively, really should be sold, simply because they "really like" the company. The hierarchy among the lower paths indicates how hard you should try to have logic prevail over emotion.

Reconsideration Path E (No-No-Yes)   Here are the qualities a stock must exhibit to be on Reconsideration Path E.

> Update Key 1—No: The situation is no longer consistent with what we expected when we originally bought the stock.
>
> Update Key 2—No: Since the original purchase or the most recent review, no additional positive factors (according to our investment philosophies) have emerged.
>
> Update Key 3—Yes: The situation is free from negative factors (according to our investment philosophies) that emerged since the time of the purchase or the most recent review.

These are the inertia stocks. They aren't really horrible. No negative factors have emerged, and many investors would be perfectly content to continue to hold them indefinitely. But if you are applying the market screening method diligently, it's hard to imagine that you won't be finding better opportunities as you refresh your screens. There is no longer any discernible connection between these stocks and your investment goals. The only bona fide reason to hold a Path E stock is a significant tax consideration necessitating deferral of gain.

Reconsideration Path F (Yes-No-No)   Here are the qualities a stock must exhibit to be on Reconsideration Path F.

> Update Key 1—Yes: The situation remains consistent with what we expected when we originally bought the stock.
>
> Update Key 2—No: Since the original purchase or the most recent review, no additional positive factors (according to our investment philosophies) have emerged.
>
> Update Key 3—No: The situation is not free from negative factors (according to our investment philosophies) that emerged since the time of the purchase or the most recent review.

We couldn't be accused of inertia if we wanted to hold these stocks. They do remain consistent with our original goals. But something new occurred that we deem negative. This path is the one that contains the classic profit-taking opportunities. Suppose we buy a stock because we like the company's growth opportunities. Over time, the company performs pretty much as we expect. But the market notices and the stock skyrockets. Valuation may not have been much of a factor in our decision to buy. But by now the stock has moved so high as to make us believe it's overvalued. Hence we're now willing to cite it as a negative factor. The fact that this path is in the Sell Zone tells us to take our profits.

Reconsideration Path G (No-Yes-No)   Here are the qualities a stock must exhibit to be on Reconsideration Path G.

> **Update Key 1—No:** The situation is no longer consistent with what we expected when we originally bought the stock.
> **Update Key 2—Yes:** Since the original purchase or the most recent review, additional positive factors (according to our investment philosophies) have emerged.
> **Update Key 3—No:** The situation is not free from negative factors (according to our investment philosophies) that emerged since the time of the purchase or the most recent review.

These stocks are similar to those on Path F in that they do satisfy some investment goals but carry some negative baggage. The reason they are positioned lower is because the goals they satisfy, although acceptable to us, aren't among our first choices (the ones we had in mind when we purchased).

Reconsideration Path H (No-No-No)   Here are the qualities a stock must exhibit to be on Reconsideration Path H.

> **Update Key 1—No:** The situation is no longer consistent with what we expected when we originally bought the stock.
> **Update Key 2—No:** Since the original purchase or the most recent review, no additional positive factors (according to our investment philosophies) have emerged.
> **Update Key 3—No:** The situation is not free from negative factors (according to our investment philosophies) that emerged since the time of the purchase or the most recent review.

Sell any stock having these qualities. You're looking for trouble if you allow inertia, emotion, or even tax considerations to cause you to continue to hold.

SUMMARY

Let's review how Sell Phase C (Reconsider) works by focusing on a sample selling scenario that we touched on before and that gets a lot of attention nowadays, the earnings disappointment. Assume Smith and Jones both buy XYZ shares because they both have favorable views of the company's near-term earnings prospects. After the company issues an unfavorable earnings announcement, the stock immediately drops from 40 to 28. Smith and Jones would both answer "no" to Update Key 1, since the here-and-now growth story is no longer valid. Both parties do the same arithmetic and see the same compelling valuation case for the stock. So both answer "yes" to Update Key 2.

Update Key 3 will play the decisive role in determining whether the stock is held or sold. Smith does not want to own shares of companies that experience earnings disappointments. Hence she will say "no" in response to Update Key 3. That leaves her with a "no-yes-no" combination. This equates to Path G, which is deep within the Sell Zone. She will therefore bail out of the stock even though many would argue that the price has dropped so far, the shares now seem bargain priced even in light of the recent bad news.

One of those who makes the valuation argument is Jones. Given his druthers, he'd prefer to stick with companies whose growth trends are intact. But he is willing to tolerate an earnings problem if he believes the present situation is not representative of the company's underlying fundamental condition. His work in Sell Phase B (Update) causes him to reach that conclusion regarding XYZ. He answers "yes" for Update Key 3. That means his key combination is "no-yes-yes." That equates to Reconsideration Path C, which is comfortably within the Hold Zone.

Speaking for myself, my approach is similar to that of Jones. I'm willing to tolerate earnings disappointments that I don't believe will be long-term in nature. But I still have to respect the position taken by an investor like Smith. She saw the same facts and gave thoughtful consideration to the same questions. She reached a different conclusion because her goals are different. That's her prerogative.

Suppose the stock doesn't drop far enough to create an attractive value opportunity. In this case, Jones answers "no" to Update Key 2. Now he has a "no-no-yes" combination that drops the stock down to Path E, the inertia path. It's the highest level of the Sell Zone, but a sell nonetheless.

As you can see, there's no magic here. The process is built entirely on the basis of thoughtful answers given to commonsense questions. Compare this to the folklore we reviewed in Chapter 15. Investors who follow this process will, at times, make the same decisions as those who follow folklore. The difference is that those who utilize Step 4 (Sell) know exactly why they are doing what they are doing in every situation. They know the difference between fact and opinion, and they understand the boundaries between broad investment principles and individual goals. And even when they let emotion enter the picture, they at least recognize and admit this is what they are doing. All this increases the probability that successful hold-versus-sell decisions are based on more than luck, and can therefore be repeated, more often than not, in the future.

Conclusion

## CHAPTER 17

Benefits of the Four-Step
Market Screening Method

There are many different approaches to investing. Most work well some of the time, and falter at other times. Hence this four-step market screening method should be viewed as one alternative among many. But I will go one step further and say I believe it's a very desirable alternative for the following reasons.

THE METHOD IS WIDE-RANGING

Running a screen against a large database puts you in a position where you are always able to identify any worthwhile (based on your criteria) stock. It doesn't matter how obscure it is. It doesn't matter what headlines you read or what gossip you hear. The only thing that matters is that the stock demonstrates some objective showing of merit based on your investment goals. If it's good under that criterion, you can find it.

THE METHOD IS NONJUDGMENTAL

Unfortunately for my ego, this book is not likely to ever lead to creation of a Gerstein guru stock screen. That's because the market screening method does not hand you a recipe and tell you this is what you need to do. Instead, it accepts any method you favor and shows you how you can implement it more effectively.

If you are a value investor, screen based on value. If you prefer growth stocks, then screen for them. If you like technical analysis, you can use screening to help you decide which companies have stock price charts worth looking at. If you want blue-chip stocks, use a screen seeking the best opportunities in that category. And so on and so forth. Rather than preaching a Gerstein recipe, the book taught you how to create your own.

THE METHOD IS ACCESSIBLE

If you can truly learn all the intricacies of what makes a company tick, go for it. But that's no small task. Philip A. Fisher, in his investment classic *Common Stocks and Uncommon Profits* (John Wiley & Sons, 1996), suggests investors ought to examine such issues as whether the company has an above-average sales force, outstanding executive relations, management depth, and so on. Those are great questions. But is a method like that truly accessible to most investors? When it comes to uncovering such information, Mr. Fisher comes straight out and advises investors to rely on scuttlebutt, or the business grapevine.

If you have access to reliable scuttlebutt, by all means use it. The operative word, of course, is "reliable." The sprouting of Internet message boards produces an avalanche of scuttlebutt every day. But little if any of this anonymous content is reliable. I doubt the message boards bear any resemblance to what Fisher had in mind.

Most investors, even professional investors, cannot expect to rely on scuttlebutt on a consistent basis, if ever. (There's more data available than ever before. But as time passes, it's getting harder, not easier, as our contemporary legal environment more tightly controls the flow of information.) Fisher is rare in that he openly steers investors toward the grapevine. Other authors pose similar questions but aren't clear as to how you should go about finding answers.

This market screening method is unique in that you are perfectly capable of answering every question it suggests. You can see that simply by going back to the Data Guide presented in Chapter 12. It poses many questions, more than most other methods. But each fact it references can be learned in a matter of minutes. The effort comes in deciding how you choose to react to the answers. The method calls for you to weigh and balance the facts in terms of your individual risk-reward tolerances. You might give great emphasis to something that you'd have been better off dismissing, or dismiss something you should have considered more carefully. So this method is not a simple connect-the-dots type of exercise. It takes effort. But at least you have full access to all the facts you need to make it work. It does not guarantee success. But it does guarantee a full and fair opportunity to succeed, regardless of whether you are one of today's fortunate few with access to reliable scuttlebutt.

This accessibility point holds true even if you lack the background to understand as much as you think you should about the qualitative aspects of a company's business. Remember the wide-ranging nature of the method. If you look at a company and find that you really don't get it, the solution is simple. Skip the company and move on to something else. There are thousands of excellent opportunities out there every day. Most investors have been conditioned to believe that if they bypass XYZ Company because they don't understand the situation and miss out on a doubling of the stock price, they have failed. I reject that notion. If you bypass XYZ because you don't understand the situation, you're being sensible. If, instead of dealing with XYZ, you understand and buy ABC and it, too, doubles, there's no reason to second-guess your aversion to XYZ. There are many fish in the sea and many stocks in the market. There are more than enough opportunities, and this screening method helps you find them. The bottom line: No matter who you are and what your background is, what you know, and what you understand, you have a full and fair opportunity to invest successfully.

THE METHOD IS PURPOSEFUL

It's easy to get lulled into believing investing is easy if only you can uncover the necessary facts. But as discussed in the preceding section, fact gathering is actually the easy part. The real key is how you interpret the facts. And as you can see by observing the marketplace on a day-to-day basis, there is no single correct answer.

Sometimes a buyer or a seller fails to do his/her homework properly and really is wrong. But it would be naive to assume one of the parties is always going to be proven wrong. If you really look closely at what motivates each party, you'll usually find that each is contemplating the same set of facts but interpreting them in light of different investment goals.

Success often depends not so much on knowing more facts, but on doing a better job of using the facts to determine which stocks really match your goals. Purposeful investors are more likely to have done a better job identifying the right stocks to own during times when their methods are in favor. And purposeful investors whose goals and portfolios are properly aligned have the patience to hold firm during bad times or make well-reasoned decisions to shift gears if a goal seems likely to remain unsuccessful for a prolonged period.

An important strength of this market screening method is the diligence it promotes. It continually asks you to understand your goals and determine how well a particular stock matches up. Goal orientation is necessary to create screens in Step 1 (Find), to assess the importance of information learned in Step 2 (Analyze), and to use the Analysis Keys in Step 3 (Buy) and the Update Keys in Step 4 (Sell).

THE METHOD IS SYSTEMATIC

Investors are human, and humans have emotions. Nothing can change that. But because the four-step market screening method is so systematic, we can always recognize when our inclinations are based on emotion and when they are based on fact.

If you aren't convinced, wait until one of your stocks plunges in response to bad news and everybody who talks about the situation seems gripped with panic. You, too, will feel fear, or at least unhappiness. That's okay. You're human and humans do that. But if you're using the method, you can immediately call upon Step 4 (Sell) and review the situation. You may still wind up bailing out. But unlike many others, you will know exactly why you are doing what you are doing. You won't always be right. Nobody is. But if you think about your reasons for acting, over time your good decisions will far outnumber your bad ones.

The same holds true on the upside. When the market is euphoric and driving certain fad stocks higher and higher, check your screens. This doesn't mean you have to invest like a plodding turtle. If you like excitement, use momentum screens. Don't be shy. But you'll see that not every hot stock is worthwhile, even from a momentum-oriented risk taker's point of view. If you can avoid just one bursting bubble per year, you'll have, in effect, earned back the price of this book (and any screener you use) so many times over, you won't even bother counting.

If you still want to speculate, go for it. As long as you know what you're doing, taking a plunge with money you can afford to lose, you can really have fun. Knowing this is what you're doing (instead of fooling yourself into believing you're making a sound investment) will allow you to sleep comfortably at night, no matter how much hysteria ensues if you get caught after a bubble bursts. You will know you were taking a plunge, more for entertainment than for serious investing. And you will have kept your exposure to loss appropriately small.

THE METHOD IS FLEXIBLE

If you want the four-step market screening method to be simple, then make it simple. Just pick out some preset screens (if you have trouble selecting, pick a guru screen in Stock Investor Pro), check it at regular intervals, and look at the stocks that appear on those lists. And if Analysis/Update Keys and Decision/Reconsideration Paths seem too formal for you, a casual eye-balling of the key questions will still leave you better positioned than many others who don't take the trouble to articulate why they do what they do.

But if you want to dive all the way in, purchase access to a top-of-the-line screener and create your own screens, including perhaps use of the lay-ered technique. Develop your own sequence for reviewing data under Step 2 (Analyze), explicitly identify each Analysis Key and Decision Path for Step 3 (Buy), and meticulously pursue Step 4 (Sell), including use of sell-oriented alert screens, at least once per week.

There are also countless in-between solutions. If you seek a middle-of-the-road approach, I recommend that you use preset screens and focus your heaviest effort on Step 2 (Analyze). There are many fine preset screens. And you can easily modify any test that strikes you as not being quite right. If you aren't sure how to modify tests, review my pet peeves from Chapter 9. The reason I suggest that middle-of-the-road investors lighten up in Step 1 (Find) and try to go as full-out as possible with Step 2 (Analyze) is that it's hard to find a good substitute for the comprehensive data presentation de-scribed in Chapters 10 and 11. If you go all through that, you'll gain in-sights you didn't realize you could get based on data review.

Ultimately, it's all up to you. Simply going through the process of thinking about how simple or complex you want your efforts to be (what kinds of screens you want to use and what kinds of reports you'll consult in the analysis phase) already amounts to more self-examination than most investors ever undergo. Since so much of the success of the method de-pends on matching stocks to goals, simply asking yourself who you are and what you want to do places you well on your way.

Printed in the United States
117772LV00004B/58/P